❁ T H E ❁
MEXICAN
CORRIDO

The Virgin of Guadalupe

❂ THE ❂

MEXICAN
CORRIDO

A Feminist Analysis

MARÍA HERRERA-SOBEK

INDIANA UNIVERSITY PRESS
Bloomington and Indianapolis

The paper used in this publication meets the minimum requirements of American
National Standard for Information Sciences—Permanence of Paper for Printed
Library Materials, ANSI Z39.48-1984.

Manufactured in the United States of America

Library of Congress Cataloging-in-Publication Data

Herrera-Sobek, María.
  The Mexican corrido : a feminist analysis / María Herrera-Sobek
    p.   cm.
  Includes bibliographical references (p.).
  ISBN 0-253-32739-3 (alk. paper)
  1. Corridos—History and criticism.   2. Folk-songs, Spanish—
Mexico—History and criticism.   3. Women in literature.   I. Title.
PQ7180.H4   1990
782.42′1626872—dc20   89-45568
                                                            CIP

1 2 3 4 5   94 93 92 91 90

To my grandmother
Susana Escamilla de Tarango
(1896–1985)
Rancho de la Soledad
Valparaiso, Zacatecas

CONTENTS

Illustrations are on pages 77–83

Preface

The monochromatic and stereotypical images of the *Mexicana* predominating in recent decades in the mass media and in literature prompted me to study these feminine images in a unique source: the *corrido,* Mexico's folk ballad. The genre proved to be a fruitful medium by which I could explore the portrayal of women's social roles. The present study examines the archetypal representation of women in a specific genre for a specific culture complex: Mexican and Chicano. It defines four female archetypes from a feminist perspective and with reference to the influences of the Western literary tradition, patriarchal ideology, social class structure, and the historical context in which the songs appeared.

I examined more than three thousand corridos for this study; the texts came from numerous sources. Details about the major corrido collections I consulted are at the end of the book as part A of Works Cited and Consulted, which also provides lists of references and other secondary sources I found useful. Here I would like to highlight four important sources for the corridos. In 1979, as I began fieldwork in Mexico City, I was pleased to find a significant collection of *hojas sueltas* (broadsides) in the Eduardo Guerrero Collection housed in the Archive Section of the Biblioteca Nacional. This collection provided extensive primary data. The Biblioteca del Museo de Antropología e Historia and the Biblioteca de México also had large collections of corridos that were indispensable for this study. A second valuable source of corrido texts in addition to the libraries was found in the small printing house editions of *cancioneros.* Cheaply made and inexpensive, they contain hundreds of texts; bibliographic citations for these editions are included in the list of collections consulted. I found most of these materials in the small bookstores and bookstalls, the *mercados* and flea markets of Mexico City, which I diligently canvassed through the summer of 1979.

A third important source of ballads is the recording industry. Corridos are particularly popular in the southwestern United States, where Latin *discotecas* (record stores) provide an excellent supply of recorded versions of these songs. With the spread of industrialization and urbanization, the recorded radio performance has been a major factor in keeping these musical traditions alive. The corrido song style is thriving not only in Mexico, particularly in rural areas, but also in such large urban centers in the United States as Los Angeles, Detroit, and Chicago. Some insightful studies of the radio and record industry's role in the dissemination of corridos are in print: Stanley Robe's "A Border *Cancionero:* A Regional View of Folksong" in the *New Scholar,* volume 6 (1977); Dan William Dickey's *The Kennedy Corridos: A Study of the Ballads of a Mexican American Hero* (1978); Guillermo Hernández's *Canciones de la Raza: Songs of the Chicano Experience* (1978); and Chris Strachwitz's "The 'Golden-Age' of the

Recorded Corrido" in *Texas-Mexican Border Music*, volume 2, linear notes (Folkloric LP 9004, 1975). More recently, Manuel Peña's *The Texas-Mexican Conjunto: History of a Working-Class Music* (1985) describes the significant contribution radio and record promoters have made to the evolution of *conjunto* music. I have included a selected discography as part D of Works Cited and Consulted.

I also gained valuable insights from conversations with individual corrido singers, mariachi groups, duets, and trios whose repertoires included many traditional songs. Research and collecting was done mainly in Arizona, Mexico City, northern Mexico, the San Luis Río Colorado area of Sonora, Baja California, and southern California.

I began collecting corridos in 1975 while working on my first book, *The Bracero Experience: Elitelore versus Folklore* (1979a). As my corrido collection increased to include more than three thousand texts (many of which are variants, of course) of both corridos and *canciones* (songs), I became keenly aware of the role of women in the genre and saw the possibilities of undertaking extensive research on the topic. My first seed article—which bears in part the title of this book, "Mothers, Lovers, and Soldiers: Images of Women in the Mexican Corrido" (Herrera-Sobek, 1979c)—briefly explored various representations of Mexicanas in the ballad. A second article, "La Mujer Traidora: The Treacherous Woman Archetype in the Corrido" (Herrera-Sobek, 1981), leaned toward the application of archetypal criticism to the Mexican ballad. Chapter 4 includes portions of this article. Both articles were well received. The second was published in both the United States and Mexico. The initial success of my incursions into exploring the representation of women in the lyrics of the corrido encouraged me to undertake a more sustained analysis.

The corridos are written in Spanish. I have translated all the corridos I cite in the study. Other translations in the text are also mine unless otherwise noted.

I sincerely hope that this study will inspire an appreciation for this marvelous genre and expand the sometimes narrow perception many persons have of Mexican and Chicano women. The Mexican ballad has much to offer, both as a literary text and as a social document. The pages that follow are my contribution to the genre and to women's studies. I hope I have done justice to the creative men and women who lustily sang and continue to sing about both the sublimely heroic and the tragically absurd—which, after all, encompass the gamut of the human condition.

It is with a deep sense of gratitude that I acknowledge the people and institutions who aided me in the production of this book. I thank the Research and Travel Committee of the University of California, Irvine, for providing the seed money necessary to finance the fieldwork undertaken for this project; the university's School of Humanities Research and Travel Committee for the various grants allocated; and the Southern Fellowships Fund for its generous grant, which, together with an Affirmative Action Junior Faculty Development Award, enabled me to devote one full year to writing this book. My deepest appreciation goes to Jaime Rodríguez, Director of the Focus Research Program on Mexico/Chicano Studies, for the many generous grants I received, to Eloy Rodríguez, Director of the International Chicano Studies Program, and to Juliet MacCannel, Director of the Women's Studies Program, for the financial assistance granted to defray expenses incurred in typing and researching the various facets of my study.

I thank Professor Anne Cruz of the University of California, Irvine, for her moral support and encouragement.

Since research does not appear out of a vacuum, I also want to acknowledge the insights I gained from the work of Estella Lauter and Carol Schreier Rupprecht in their seminal study, *Feminist Archetypal Theory: Interdisciplinary Re-Visions of Jungian Thought* (1985), and the scholars included in that anthology. I found much affinity between their work and mine, and their study helped me clarify various points related to feminist archetypal theory.

The completion of a manuscript implies the work of several persons. It is my pleasure to acknowledge the many students who helped me type the various drafts of this study in addition to assisting me with many hours of library research: Cynthia Norte, Bertha Lemus, Sonia Ibarra, Juan Bernal, David Becerra, Jennifer Windburn, Noé Chávez, María González, Esther Soto, and Julie Foraker. A note of appreciation is due Geneva López, Tina Metevier, Selene Beckman, Doris Earnshaw, and Anthony Parrino. I also thank my brother José Luis Herrera for his help in securing corrido texts in Arizona and northern Mexico.

I am very grateful to Eleazar López Zamora, Director of the Fototeca of the Instituto Nacional de Antropología e Historia (the Photograph Section of the National Institute of Anthropology and History), located in the Ex-Convento de San Francisco in Pachuca, Hidalgo, México, for providing me with the photographs from the Agustín Casasola Collection included in this book. I thank Dover Publications for use of the José Guadalupe Posada drawing of the Revolutionary Calavera. I also thank Marie and Isabelle Pérez, present owners of De Guadalupe Publications (P.O. Box 370107, El Paso, Texas 79937), for permission to use the Virgin of Guadalupe photograph as the frontispiece.

Most appreciatively I thank my son, Erik Jason, and my husband, Joseph, for their patience and understanding during the long hours the work required.

Canto el corrido que canto
porque es verdad lo que cuenta. . . .

—¡Ay, muchacho, tú no sabes
que el corrido cuando cantas,
tiene voces de llovizna
y sabor de madrugada! . . .

—El corrido canta y canta,
y aunque al cantarlo nos duele,
es voz que cantan los niños,
los hombres y las mujeres. . . .

I sing this ballad
Because its verses are true. . . .

"Oh, young man, you don't know
That the ballad you are singing
Has the sound of rainfall
And an early morning aftertaste!" . . .

"The ballad sings and sings
And even though it pains us to hear it
It's the voice sung by children
By men and women." . . .

—El corrido que yo canto
me lo enseñaron mis padres,
y si afinas tu guitarra
te enseñaré a que lo cantes.

"Corrido de Gabriel Leyva:
   Por Siete Caminos de Sangre"
      (Campos, 1962, vol. 2: 214–219)

"The ballad that I sing
My parents sang to me
And if you tune your guitar
I will teach you how to sing it."

"The Ballad of Gabriel Leyva:
Through Seven Blood-filled Roads"

Introduction

In such a theory [feminist archetypal theory] the archetype cannot be defined as an image whose content is frozen but must be thought of as a process, a tendency to form and re-form images in relation to certain kinds of repeated experiences.

—Lauter and Rupprecht (1985:16)

The corrido, a musical form popular among the folk of Mexico, encompasses three genres: epic, lyric, and narrative. In its epic character the corrido is similar to the *canción de gesta*. Both forms extol the exploits of protagonists, who are usually male. Women generally play secondary roles in the narratives. Mexican heroes, such as Pancho Villa, Benjamín Argumedo, Felipe Angeles, Emiliano Zapata, and Francisco I. Madero, are apotheosized and their deeds immortalized. And famous battles, such as *La toma de Zacatecas* and *Los combates de Celaya*, are the subject matter of a vast number of heroic gests. As for the corrido's lyrical nature, it derives from the affective overtones found throughout the songs. The corrido also generally recounts a story in either the first or the third person; hence its narrative character.[1]

Mexicans apply a variety of descriptive terms to the corrido: *romance, historia, narración, ejemplo, tragedia, mañanitas, recuerdos, versos, coplas.* The *corridista* may insert any of these terms into the lyrics of the song to identify it, often at the beginning or end, though these terms may appear anywhere in the composition.[2]

Corrido scholars Merle E. Simmons, Vicente T. Mendoza, Américo Paredes, and others have focused mainly on the genre's evolution and its importance as a social and historical literary document.[3] As far as I know, no one has attempted to apply archetypal criticism in studying corridos. I will apply feminist archetypal theory to the representation of women in these ballads. I define feminist archetypal criticism as a type of analysis that views archetypes as recurrent patterns in art, literature, film, songs, and other artistic endeavors depending on historical, political, and social forces for their formation. This theoretical construct views the archetypal images as malleable entities and not as solidified images encased in the psyche at birth. Feminist archetypal criticism views the vectors of gender and patriarchal ideology as of paramount importance in archetypal image construction.

A major goal of this work is to demonstrate the validity of my thesis concerning the creation and surfacing of an archetype in a particular culture (Mexico) and a specific genre (the corrido). It is my position that the crystallization of an archetype in a society is the result of a historical process. Theoretically, an infinite number of archetypal images are possible in our mental universe. That is to say, human beings inherit the capacity to form images as they inherit the capacity to speak a language. And just as the language an individual speaks depends on the social context in which he or she is raised, the archetypal images an individual structures depend on his or her historical circumstances. Human beings have the innate capacity to form an infinite number of images as they have an innate capacity to speak (see Hall, 1977). Repeated or recurrent images that surface in our imaging universe we denote as archetypal. The fact that one particular culture privileges one specific archetypal construct as opposed to another is a function of its historical process. I have isolated four components which I consider of paramount importance in the structuring of the archetypal images found in the Mexican ballad: patriarchal ideology, social class of the corridista and the corrido audience, Mexican history, and Western literary tradition.

Once having grasped the cultural vectors converging to form and infuse life into an image, we can proceed to accept or reject the image on rational grounds. The choice thereafter will be ours and ours alone to make.

The multiple meanings associated with the term *archetype* suggest the complexity and attendant danger in using an initially psychological term in a literary study. Nonetheless, the pervasiveness of archetypal images in Mexican folk songs and their strong kinship to mythic figures of antiquity make evasion of the term, even with its concomitant problems, difficult if not impossible. The etymological root of *archetype* comprises *arche* ("beginning") and *typos* ("stamps" or "pattern"). It is conceived to be an original pattern, idea, or model from which copies are made, a prototype.

Complications arise in applying the term *archetype* to the psychological component of the human mind. Jolande Jacobi, a student of the foremost investigator of archetypes, Carl G. Jung, candidly confronted the problem of definition in her study *Complex/Archetype/Symbol in the Psychology of C. G. Jung* (1959), asserting: "It is impossible to give an exact definition of the archetype, and the best we can hope to do is to suggest its general implications by 'talking around' it. For the archetype represents a profound riddle surpassing our rational comprehension" (31).

Jung introduced the term in 1919 and provided a definition in "A Psychological Approach to the Dogma of the Trinity" (1956b):

> Archetypes are, by definition, factors and motifs that arrange the psychic elements into certain images, characterized as archetypal, but in such a way that they can be recognized only from the effects they produce. They exist preconsciously, and presumably they form the structural dominants of the psyche in general. . . . As a priori conditioning factors they represent a special psychological instance of the biological "pattern of behavior," which gives all things their specific qualities. Just as the manifestations of this biological ground plan may change in the course of development so also can the archetype. Empirically considered, however, the archetype did not ever come into existence as a phenomenon of organic life, but entered into the picture with life itself.

Jung viewed the archetype as part of the psychic structure of the individual not yet concretely formed. A stimulus of some kind is required to surface and become noticeable. Archetypal manifestations, or images, are often seen in works of art and literature. The artistic sensibility is often stimulated to produce in its creative work archetypal representations, or "recurrent images." In fact, it is through the surfacing of these images that we can assume the existence of the archetype as a structural entity invisible to the eye but present within the psyche.

Revisionist feminists find Jung's flexible conceptualization of the archetype useful in the analysis of literature. Particularly acceptable to feminists is his statement that we derive the concept of the archetype from observable phenomena, such as myths, fairy tales, and literary works, and from the recurrent images cropping up in individuals' fantasies, dreams, and delusions. Also acceptable is his proposition that the archetype is an "irrepresentable, unconscious, pre-existent form that seems to be part of the inherited structure of the psyche and can therefore manifest itself spontaneously anywhere, at any time," as long as we concede that its manifestations are conditioned by the context in which they appear.[4]

The main quarrel feminists have with the theories of Jung (and some of his followers) involves his polar extremes of animus and anima, logos and eros, which may lead to stereotyping men as thinkers and women as nurturers (see Lauter and Rupprecht, 1985:3–22). Furthermore, what some see as Jung's rather ambiguous position vis-à-vis the archetype and his blurring of the concepts "archetype" (a structure of the psyche that has a tendency to form recurrent images) and "archetypal image" (the actual manifestation of such an image) has produced a reaction in some feminists against incorporating the archetypal approach into their studies of art and literature (ibid.). The tendency of some Jungians to lump women into frozen archetypal categories proved unacceptable to many feminists. As Demaris S. Wehr stated:

> The central problem is this: Jung ontologizes what is more accurately and more usefully seen as socially constructed reality. Even though Jung and Jungians at times describe the archetype as simply a propensity or a predisposition to act or image in a certain way, the category of archetype is often used as a category of Being itself. Thus Jungian theory can function as quasi-religious or scientific legitimation of the status quo in society, reinforcing social roles, constricting growth, and limiting opportunities for women. (Wehr, 1985:23)

Indeed, if we viewed the archetype as a static, transcendental entity, the result would be detrimental not only to women but also to the search for knowledge and understanding of the human psyche. Many scholars who use feminist archetypal theory therefore lean toward a reconceptualization, or "revisioning," of the concept described by Jung. Naomi Goldenberg, an acerbic critic of Jung's formulations, proposed that

> feminist scholars must examine the very idea of archetype in Jungian thought if sexism is ever to be confronted at its base. Indeed, if feminists do not change

the assumptions of archetype or redefine the concept, there are only two options: either (1) to accept the patriarchal ideas of the feminine as ultimate and unchanging and work within those or (2) to indulge in a rival search to find female archetypes, one which can support feminist conclusions. (Goldenberg, 1976:448; also in Lauter and Rupprecht, 1985:9)

Estella Lauter and Carol Schreier Rupprecht, in the introduction to their seminal study *Feminist Archetypal Theory*, question the usefulness of archetypal theory in a feminist context:

> Why does [the concept of the archetype] remain useful? Even more to the point here, why might it remain useful to feminist theory? Presumably the concept survives because of our sense that it refers to something real in our experience—whether we describe that reality as a seemingly infinite variety of related forms, as images that are "unfathomable" and "necessary," as nodal points in an energy field that determine the flow of libido, or as the identifying mark of a transaction that is never fully resolved. The concept survives in these forms because it has real explanatory power.
>
> In the case of feminist theory, if we regard the archetype not as an image whose content is frozen but . . . as a tendency to form and reform images in relation to certain kinds of repeated experiences, then the concept could serve to clarify distinctively female concerns that have persisted throughout human history. Applied to a broad range of materials from women, it could expose a set of reference points that would serve as an expendable framework for defining female experience, and ultimately the "muted" culture females have created. (13–14)

And Lauter further underscores the need for feminists to study the archetype in her article "Visual Images by Women":

> To refuse to see these images together as an archetypal pattern, one of many yet to be seen or described, would be to insist on the integrity of the individual's expression at the expense of collective vision. Yet to take one pattern or one image as ideal, or even as normal, would be to confuse the image with the tendency to form it. Thus the concept of the archetype could, in feminist hands, function as a force against the reification of any one cultural construct of reality. It is the never-to-be exhausted tendency to imagine that is the ultimate justification of cultural pluralism. (Lauter, 1985:62)

With a large corpus of literature already employing the concept of the archetype and with a worldwide group of psychologists and therapists adhering to the Jungian school of thought, it is imperative that feminists not turn a blind eye. We must engage in its study, either to refute it or to add feminist conceptualizations. The archetype exists as a theoretical construct both in literature and in psychology. Feminists need to research it, examine it, confront it, accept it, reject it, or change it. The feminist scholarly community needs to deal with it head on, or others will continue to misuse it. Therapists and mainstream scholars, who are mostly male and who may subscribe to a pa-

triarchal ideology, will continue to put their own stamp—often otherworldly—
on the concept. If feminists do not provide an alternative perspective, this
imprint may well continue to be tinged with a sexist ideology. Feminists need to
plant the concept firmly in the context of the historical, political, and economic
systems in which it arises.

Appropriating a malleable view of the archetype can make it a positive tool in
literary and art criticism, opening new vistas toward a fuller comprehension of
the unconscious, with its tendency to structure social reality and experience in
systematic recurrent patterns. This also will allow us to conceptualize the
archetype in terms of a socially constructed reality.

I include myself among those who perceive that much of our culture's artistic
work reflects a series of patterns to which we can profitably apply the term
archetypal images. I have found most useful the reformulations of the concept of
archetype by certain eminent scholars in the fields of literary criticism and
depth psychology. Erich Neumann, though not a feminist, articulates a definition acceptable to most feminists and congruent with a flexible view of the
archetype. In *Art and the Creative Unconscious* he asserts:

> The archetypes of the collective unconscious are intrinsically formless psychic
> structures which become visible in art. The archetypes are varied by the media
> through which they pass—that is, their form changes according to the time,
> the place, and the psychological constellation of the individual in whom they
> are manifested. Thus, for example, the mother archetype, as a dynamic entity
> in the psychic substratum, always retains its identity, but it takes on different
> *styles*—different aspects or emotional color—depending on whether it is man-
> ifested in Egypt, Mexico, or Spain, or in ancient, medieval, or modern times.
> The paradoxical multiplicity of its eternal presence, which makes possible an
> infinite variety of forms of expression, is crystallized in its realization by man in
> time; its archetypal eternity enters into a unique synthesis with a specific
> historical situation. (Neumann, 1974a:42)[5]

James Hall also views the archetype as flexible:

> There is no fixed number of archetypes, since any recurrent human experience
> can be archetypally represented. It is perhaps more nearly correct to speak of
> an archetypal field, with the observable archetypal images indicating nodal
> points in which the field is particularly dense. Archetypes are not inherited
> images; they are part of the tendency to structure experiences in certain ways.
> (Hall, 1977:116; also in Lauter and Rupprecht, 1984:11)

Other scholars basically in accord with these two include James Hillman (*Re-
Visioning Psychology*, 1975), Eric Gould (*Mythic Intentions in Modern Literature*, 1982), and Northrop Frye, who defines *archetype* as "a typical recurring
image" and adds:

> Archetypes are associative clusters, and differ from signs in being complex
> variables. Within the complex is often a large number of specific learned

associations which are communicable because a large number of people in a given culture happen to be familiar with them. (Frye, 1973:99–102)

Re-visioning of the archetype into a more malleable format makes possible its profitable use as an investigative tool to analyze the representation of women in the corrido. Certainly the concept and its visible manifestations are useful in the study of recurrent patterns in the arts in general. But archetypal images must not be confused with stereotypes. Unlike the archetypal image, which depends on a specific context for its realization and its peculiar traits, the stereotype is a solidified image with no specificity or individuality. It is often a caricaturized, almost unrecognizable version of the original, whereas the archetypal image is complex, varying from culture to culture and even from individual to individual (see Pratt, 1981:4–12).

Mexican ballads are generally written by males. Most of the corridos in the Eduardo Guerrero Collection that exhibit a signature identify a male author. And these male authors have incorporated mostly masculine-oriented themes and a strongly patriarchal ideology. Nevertheless, there is nothing inherently male in the corrido or its structure, which can and does feature female protagonists. It is only a fact of history, not of necessity, that the majority of corridos have been written by males. I categorize the corrido not as a male genre, although many view it as such, but as a male-dominated genre. Women are quite capable of writing corridos; we know, for example, that Graciela de Olmos penned the famous "Siete Leguas." Women may well have written a substantial number of these compositions, but we cannot be certain, for most corridos are by unknown authors. Even so, the representation of women in these songs tends to be from a patriarchal perspective.

It is perfectly feasible that in the future women will appropriate the genre and dominate it with female-oriented themes. The structure of the ballad lends itself to either a male or a female protagonist. The singing of corridos is done by both male and female interpreters, often by mixed-gender duets. Many women in Mexico and the United States have become world-famous corrido singers, including Lydia Mendoza from Texas, Lola Beltrán and Irma Serrano from Mexico, and Linda Ronstadt from Arizona.

My analysis of numerous corridos identified four main types of recurrent images, or patterns, in which women appear: the Good and the Terrible Mother, the Mother Goddess, the Lover, and the Soldier. These categories correspond respectively to four archetypal images posited by Toni Wolff in *Structural Forms of the Feminine Psyche* (1956) and elaborated by Nor Hall in *The Moon and the Virgin: Reflections on the Archetypal Feminine* (1980): mother, medium (or mediator), hetaira, and amazon. After identifying these archetypes in representative corridos, I undertake an analysis of the texts in light of the literary tradition associated with specific archetypes. I further show that while the patriarchal system informs and structures the archetypal images, it is class—the rural, campesino class in this instance—that tempers their specific representation in Mexican society. The campesino world view, the patriarchal system, the historical specificity of a nation, and the nation's literary tradition are the four significant vectors of the archetypal images appearing in these folk songs.

The four archetypal images examined in this book are of course not the only ones present in corridos. I selected these four because they are the ones most frequently found in heroic ballads. The archetypal figures of the Good and the Terrible Mother, the Mother Goddess, the Lover, and the Soldier appear with regularity—though not necessarily simultaneously—in corridos exhibiting the classic formal structure defined by Armand Duvalier. Duvalier, an early corrido scholar, delineated the thematic structure of the genre, identifying six primary formulas: (1) an initial call from the corridista to his or her public; (2) the place, date, and name of the protagonist; (3) a formula preceding the protagonist's arguments; (4) the message; (5) the protagonist's farewell; and (6) the corridista's farewell.[6] But in the literally thousands of corridos in existence women can be found in various roles and guises. Two archetypal representations of women not included in this study are the Immigrant and the Outlaw. The Immigrant type, so far as I know, is not common in Western literature, although migrating tribes and families certainly are. Of the Greek goddesses I can only think of Dido as having migrated and taken her people to a new residence (Monaghan, 1981:84–85). This type, like the Soldier, has its own circumstances: the proximity of the Mexican nation to a wealthy country—the United States—the point of destination of migrating women.

While space and time limit my coverage to the four major archetypes, these representations are only the beginning of what can be a fruitful field of investigation. Other archetypal figures that come readily to mind are the Daughter, the Wife, the Virginal Sweetheart, the Sister, the Mother-in-Law, the Acculturated Woman, and the Independent Woman.[7] All of them appear in the corrido and deserve study.

❂ THE ❂
MEXICAN
CORRIDO

❖ 1 ❖

THE GOOD MOTHER
ARCHETYPE

The portrayal of women in Mexican corridos has been influenced by the portrayal of women in the Spanish epics and romances from which these folk songs ultimately derive. The Spanish epic is concerned primarily with the actions of *guerreros* (warriors), the females being cast mainly in supporting roles as wives, mothers, and daughters. As Menéndez Pidal observed,

> La recia voz que cantaba las conquistas, hazañas, bandas y venganzas de ricos hombres e infanzones so sabía reprimirse para susurrar las delicadas intimidades del amor. Los cantares de gesta eran poesía señorial, de guerra y vida pública; el amor se quedaba para la poesía cortés y burguesa. (The powerful voice that sings about the conquests, deeds, troops, and the vengeance of wealthy men and royalty only knows how to repress itself when whispering the delicate intimacies of love. The epic songs were mainly poetic expressions of war and public life; love themes were reserved for bourgeois and courtly love poetry.) (Menéndez Pidal, 1959:107)

Many corridos exhibit an attitude similar to that of the epic in their depiction of female characters.

In the Iberian ballad the family unit and the heroes' preoccupation with upholding their honor is of the utmost importance. Women in early epics and romances were not generally viewed as love objects in the stereotypical manner of the French troubadours. Portrayal of women in courtly love poetry tended to concentrate on the physical and spiritual attributes of women who were cast in the unvarying mold of pearly white teeth, milk-white skin, and golden hair; this stereotype is mostly absent in the Spanish epic and totally absent in heroic corridos, where women typically appear in a family context (see Sponsler, 1975).

The Mexican ballad is unique, in addition, in the importance accorded the mother. Analysis of corridos yields numerous songs making use of the Great Mother archetype. Appearing in hundreds of folk songs, this archetype has at least three dimensions: good, bad, and divine. The passive Good Mother archetype often assumes a weak, weeping personality; she is a helpless and desolate figure tossed about in the turbulent waters of unceasing tears. The

1

active Terrible Mother archetype assumes a negative function. But whether conceived as positive or negative, the Great Mother is associated with a vital dramatic episode in the corrido: the death of the hero. In this chapter I focus on the Good Mother's multiple functions in the structure of the corrido in her most common representation: *mater dolorosa,* the weeping mother. Later chapters highlight the Great Mother as Terrible Mother and Mother Goddess.

MATER DOLOROSA

The Mother Goddess cults in Mesopotamia and Egypt afford us our first encounter with a written prototype of the mater dolorosa, an image that reverberates through the artistic and religious works of later Western culture and becomes embedded in the lyrics of Mexican corridos. It is in the Mesopotamian cult that the significance of the male in the generative, creative process is first conceptualized and takes expression in the plastic arts. At this juncture the life-producing Mother is assigned a spouse or partner. This partner remains in a subordinate position, either as servant or son.

Abstracting from the vegetative processes of death and regeneration and ritually recreating them in the Mother–Son dyad, people began to conceptualize and recreate the eternal cycle of seasonal change. Mythification of natural phenomena transformed the seasonal changes into Innanna, the Mother Goddess, whose marriage to Dumuzi

> gave expression to the vegetation cycle. As the faithful son of the waters that came forth from the earth, he was essentially the youthful suffering god who was dependent upon spouse-mother, the Goddess Innanna-Istar. Annually, he died in the normal rotation of the seasons and passed into the land of darkness and death. (James, 1959:48–49)

A pictorial representation of this budding religious motif is found in a Late Minoan signet from Mycenea:

> the Goddess is represented in a flounced skirt, apparently as the *mater dolorosa* bowed in grief engaged in lamentation over a kind of miniature temenos within which stands a little beatylic pilar with a small Minoan shield hanging beside it. . . . Therefore, it may be a Minoan version of the Suffering Goddess found in Western Asia in relation to the vegetation cycle: the coming of spring being expressed in the budding leaves and ripening fruits. (135)

Egypt, originator of many of Western civilization's beliefs and ideas, also had a mater dolorosa cult, which was inherited by the Greco-Roman world. The cult there centered on the figure of Isis, who, with her son and spouse Osiris, held sway over much of the population. The Isis-Osiris myth informs us that

> Osiris is killed, and Isis, keening for her lost love, wanders the world in search of his body [and] when she finds it, the Goddess threw herself upon the coffin

with . . . dreadful wailing. . . . Then, when she was quite by herself, she opened the chest and laid her face upon the face within it and caressed it and wept. (Warner, 1976:208)

The Mother Goddess–Son motif was not limited to the Old World. Like the theological practices of Paleolithic, Neolithic, and Chalcolithic peoples, Aztec theology encompassed the figure of the Mother Goddess. The pre-Conquest pantheon comprised the primal creator gods, the progenitors of the human race as male and female: Ometecutli and Omeciuatl, father and mother. The names signify Lords of Duality and Lords of the Two Sexes. This ontological pair was also known as Toactecutli and Tonacaciuatl (Lord and Lady of Our Flesh and Subsistence).

The myth of the Great Mother and her sacrificed son who is both her lover and fecundator is repeated in Aztec mythology. According to Neumann (1974:192), "As goddess of death, the Great Mother bears the obsidian knife; the youthful moon god Xipe-totec which the obsidian knife masks is associated with her and enters into her ritual, in which the youthful son is dismembered or castrated. This is the typical self-sacrifice of the moon, leading to its rebirth."

A direct line of artistic and theological kinship can be mapped between the mater dolorosa of archaic cultures and the imagery that arose in Renaissance Europe associated with the Virgin Mary. I am not positing here the theory that the Mother Goddess of antiquity and the Christian Mary were one and the same. Theological scholars are careful not to postulate a one-to-one connection. Nevertheless, the resemblance between the two mater dolorosa themes is too close to be purely coincidental. As Marina Warner writes in her book on the cult of the Virgin Mary:

Under her aspect the Mater Dolorosa, Mary most resembles the fertility goddesses of antiquity. For she receives the broken body of her son in her arms and gazes upon his features with such avidity not only because she mourns his loss—for she knows, as theology states most clearly, that he will rise from the dead—but also because she is propitiating those same forces of sterility and death that the sacrifice of her son is attempting to appease. . . . He is the blood offering, she the principle of the abiding earth. The tears she sheds are charged with the magic of her precious, incorruptible, undying body and have power to give life and make whole. (Warner, 1976:221)

Warner cites an example of the liturgy sung in ancient Sumer around 3000 B.C.:

Into his face she stares, seeing
what she has lost—his mother
who has lost him to death's kingdom
O the agony she bears,
shuddering in the wilderness,
she is the mother suffering so much. (206)

This is the Goddess Innanna weeping for her dead son, Dumuzi, but she closely resembles the mater dolorosa of Catholic ritual and Mexican corrido. The connection between the ancient fertility rites of spring and the Christian liturgy relating to the crucifixion of Christ has not been lost on scholars (208). Frazer, in fact, asserts that Christian atonement is the last version of the ancient sacrifice of the fertility god (1975:308–330). Inheritance of the psychological affinity for the suffering mother is credited to Abraham, who, coming from the land of the Goddess Innanna, the Sumero-Akkadian empire (2170–2062 B.C.), preached the admonitions of Jehovah against women mourners (Warner, 1976:208).

Middle Eastern cultures favored emotionally charged scenes, such as the one depicted by the weeping mother–dead son motif. During the Crusades, the cult of the mater dolorosa began making definite inroads in Western Christendom. By the fourteenth century, the cult of the suffering mother had a solid hold in Italy, France, England, the Netherlands, and Spain. The dramatic teaching of Franciscan priests popularized the sufferings of Mary and implanted them in the imagination of the people. The dramatization of the stations of the cross during Easter season, for instance, was instrumental in fueling the faithfuls' fervor and spreading the use of iconography depicting the sorrowful scenes which a stoic Mary had to endure (211).

Catastrophic events in Europe such as the Black Plague, which ravaged one-fifth of the European population, helped predispose people to accept the cult. Christians projected their pain on the suffering Madonna and readily sympathized with her travails. Statues of the Virgin were carried to the different villages in hopes of banishing the dreaded plague from the countryside (214–215).

Not long afterward, the Spaniards Christianized the native Americans using the techniques that had been effective in Europe. Many of the early friars were Franciscans, and dramatic reenactments of key passages from the Bible proved quite successful. The Indian populations were enthralled with the sacramentals (sacred plays) and vied for the privilege of participating in them (see Sten, 1982, and Arróniz, 1979). The mournful figure of the mother was as touching to the native Americans as it had been to the Europeans.

FORMULAIC FUNCTION

Analysis of the suffering-mother motif in the corrido points to a formulaic function. The mater dolorosa motif is specifically instrumental in organizing and developing the theme, form, closure, and emotional core of numerous Mexican ballads.

McDowell (1972) pointed to the formulaic character of the corrido. Carefully basing his work on the Parry-Lord oral-formulaic theory, McDowell successfully applied its tenets to the study of these Mexican folk songs.[1] He established three important considerations in the application of the Parry-Lord theory: the shift in genre, the precise nature of a formula, and the definition of the corpus.

The first point does not present a major problem, since, although the corrido is far shorter than the Serbo-Croatian epics from which the theories emanated, the Mexican ballad does approximate the formulaic nature of the epic.

With respect to the second point—the precise nature of a formula—Parry's definition of the formula as "a group of words which is regularly employed under the same metrical conditions to express a given essential idea" (Parry, 1930) and McDowell's application of formulaic theory to the corrido—"Formula in corridos always encompasses at least one entire line containing several words. The formula is a metric entity in the corrido. The line is (oftentimes) octosyllabic, and the musical phrases establish a consistent stress pattern maintained throughout" (1972:206)—together help to establish the meaning and nature of formula in these songs.

With respect to the third point—definition of corpus—we confront the same problem McDowell points out, since there is great difficulty in obtaining collections of oral corridos. Most of the collections intersperse both oral and literary specimens. It is therefore difficult to differentiate between the two. In the present study, however, the large number of corridos examined, both from southern and northern Mexico and from the southwestern United States, provide enough material to gain insight into the nature of the formulaic character of these songs.

To understand the formulaic use of the mater dolorosa motif, it is important to examine the nature of the formula within a stanza. Owing to the nature of the rhyme scheme, which frequently is ABCB, the corridista generally expresses thoughts in two-line units. The last word in each two-line thought thus is important in the rhyme scheme and must be easily manipulated by the corridista. Formulas are readily inserted to conform to the exigencies of rhyme. Here are examples from several corridos of binary structuring in the mater dolorosa motif:

Su pobre madre lloraba	A	His poor mother cried	
lloraba muy afligida	B	She cried very sadly	
¿Quién ha sido ese malvado	C	Who's been the evil one	
que te ha quitado la vida?	B	Who's taken your life away?	
Su esposa lloraba mucho	A	His wife cried a lot	
su madre con más razón;	B	His mother with greater reason;	
de ver a Miguel tendido	C	Upon seeing Miguel laid out	
que murió sin confesión.	B	Who had died without confession.	
Su pobre madre lloraba	A	His poor mother cried	
debajo de unos jarales:	B	Under some reeds:	
—Hijo, ¿cómo te levantas,	C	"Son, how can you get up?	
si son heridas mortales?	B	These are fatal wounds."	
Su madre lloraba	A	His mother cried	
con un dolor muy profundo	B	With profound grief	
porque su hijo querido	C	Because her beloved son	
ya había partido del mundo.	B	Had parted from this world.	

Su pobre madre lloraba	A	His poor mother cried
debajo de los nogales	B	Under the walnut trees
—¿cómo quieres levantarte	C	"How can you get up?
si son heridas mortales?	B	These are fatal wounds."
Si su mujer lo lloraba	A	If his wife cried for him
su madre con más razón	B	His mother with greater reason
de ver el cuerpo de su hijo	C	Upon seeing her son's body
que lo echaron al panteón.	B	Buried at the cemetery.
Si su mujer lo lloraba	A	If his wife cried for him
su madre con más ternura	B	His mother cried more tenderly
de ver el cuerpo de su hijo	C	Upon seeing her son's body
al pie de la sepultura.	B	At the foot of the sepulchre.
Su pobre padre lloraba	A	His poor father cried for him
su madre con más razón,	B	His mother with greater reason
de ver a su hijo querido	C	Upon seeing her beloved son
que lo echaron al cajón.	B	Being placed in the coffin.
La madre cuando lo supo	A	His mother when she found out
sus ojos eran cristales	B	Her eyes turned to crystal
de ver a su hijo querido	C	Upon seeing her beloved son
con tres heridas mortales.	B	With three mortal wounds.
Sus hermanas le lloraban	A	His sisters cried for him
su madre con más razón	B	His mother with greater reason
de ver a su hijo querido	C	Upon seeing her beloved son
traspasado el corazón.	B	With his heart wounded.
Su pobre madre lloraba	A	His poor mother cried
lloraba sin compasión	B	Cried without stopping
y pedía no lo mataran	C	And begged them not to kill him
y menos sin confesión.	B	Not to do it without his confession.
Lloraba su pobre madre	A	His poor mother would cry
cuando le llegó el aviso	B	When she heard the news
que ese don Jesús Aceves	C	That Mr. Jesús Aceves
le había fusilado a su hijo.	B	Had shot her son.
La madre de esta Martina	A	The mother of this Martina
lloraba sin compasión	B	Cried without stopping
de ver a su hija querida	C	Upon seeing her beloved daughter
herida del corazón.	B	Wounded in the heart.

It is evident that the corridista creatively integrates the mater dolorosa motif from the formula pool extant in the oral tradition. The basic imagery is that of the weeping mother at the death scene of her son (in one case a daughter). The most repeated formula is "su pobre madre lloraba." The lines here are all octosyllabic with a rhyme scheme of ABCB. An extension of this one-line formula is

Si su mujer lo lloraba	If his wife weeped for him
su madre con más razón	His mother [wept] with greater reason.

In three of our examples, speech acts follow the formulas and are, therefore, of a preparatory nature, setting the dramatic stage for the scene that is described by the disconsolate mother. In this particular formula the mater dolorosa motif is integrated in the mythic structure of the corrido.

The narrative nature of these ballads requires a beginning, middle, and end. The mater dolorosa motif in its "pieta" variant generally appears a few degrees below the middle, between point 4 (the message) and point 5 (the protagonist's farewell) of Duvalier's structure (see Introduction). The "farewell to poor mother" motif generally occurs toward the close of the song.

The balladeer does not limit himself to one structure of the mater dolorosa motif. Another formula relating to the mother figure is found in the following stanzas from various corridos:

Ya te doy mi despedida	I bid you farewell
madre, de mi corazón	Mother of my heart
desde el cielo donde estás	From heaven where you are
mándame tu bendición.	Send me your blessings.
Adios mi papá y mi mamá	Good-bye my mother and father
ya me voy	I am leaving
y a mis hermanitos	And my little brothers
los voy a dejar.	I shall leave behind.
Como a la una del día	At about one in the morning
partió ese ferrocarril;	That train did leave
Adios, mi madre querida	Good-bye my beloved mother
yo ya me voy a sufrir.	I go away to suffer.
Adios, padre y madre	Good-bye Mother and Father
adios hermanitos	Good-bye little brothers
aquí se purgaron	Here I pay
todos mis delitos.	For all my crimes.
Decía Leandro Rivera	Leandro Rivera did say
—¿Qué me quedrá suceder?	"What will happen to me?
¡Adios, mi padre y mi madre	Good-bye my mother and father
mi familia y mi mujer!	My family and my wife!"
Adios, mi señora madre	Good-bye my dear mother
adios, todos mis chamacos	Good-bye all my sons
adios, todos mis amigos	Good-bye all my friends
les encargo a mis muchachos.	Take care of my boys.

The mater dolorosa image serves as the point of departure from this life. If the death of the hero is perceived as a return to the womb of the earth from whence he sprouted, the imagery of the mother holding her dying son in her lap is most apt; the tripartite connection is logically made—Mother: Earth: Death. The mother figure, even in her beneficent aspect as mater dolorosa, has overtones of death.

THEMATIC STRUCTURE

The mater dolorosa motif serves as an integrating element in the overall thematic structure of the corrido. Since a principal theme of heroic corridos is the protagonist's sacrificing of his life for a belief or his unrelenting search for freedom and justice for his people, the hero is perceived by the people as a Christ figure who has been sacrificed in the interest of a higher good, an ideal. The mater dolorosa motif strengthens the cohesiveness and integrity of the theme by providing a ready-made figure that brings to mind the parallel lives and goals of the corrido hero and Christ. The suffering mother recalls the mother of Christ at the foot of the cross weeping for her dead son. The mater dolorosa motif poetically connects the two figures to emphasize the significance of the beliefs and ideals for which the Mexican hero dies.

With the stroke of a pen and a two-line verse the bard creates a visual image that resonates not only with biblical echoes but also with the plastic arts tradition of Western civilization. The words bombard the receptive mind with memories of Medieval, Renaissance, Baroque, and Neoclassical paintings and sculptures, such as Michelangelo's *Pieta*, depicting the Virgin Mary with her dead son in her arms. This verbal *cuadro* or *retablo* is a superb example of the dexterity and creativity of the corridista. For this pictorial representation in words heightens emotions and tensions, providing a dramatic locus from which to proceed to the close of the ballad.

That corridistas made a conscious selection of the mater dolorosa motif may be deduced by a priori reasoning. Because the authors of these compositions had several possible alternatives to the mother image, including father, brother, sister, wife, girlfriend, friend, son, and daughter, they must consciously have selected the figure of the mother for the literary and artistic possibilities inherent in her motif throughout history.

CLOSURE

Barbara Herrnstein Smith, in *Poetic Closure: A Study of How Poems End* (1968), highlights four basic functions associated with the end of a poem:

> Closure occurs when the concluding portion of a poem creates in the reader a sense of appropriate cessation. It announces and justifies the absence of further development; it reinforces the feeling of finality, completion, and composure which we value in all works of art; and it gives ultimate unity and coherence to the reader's experience of the poem by providing a point from which all the

proceeding elements may be viewed comprehensively and their relations grasped as part of a significant design. (36)

Smith adds that "closure is the final brush stroke . . . which integrates, clarifies, and completes all the disparate lines and colors of the (work) and reveals the ultimate principle and cause of their existence." Since the mater dolorosa motif often occurs toward the end of the ballads, usually after the protagonist dies, it is clear that this motif plays an important role in the formal structure of the corrido. The death of the hero in a song signals that closure is imminent. The weeping mother element further reinforces and adds closural force to the stanzas that terminate the ballad.

CULTURAL VECTORS

As we have seen, the archetypal image of the mater dolorosa is a passive figure, normally represented as weeping for her dead or dying son. Such archetypes ultimately derive from the collective unconscious. Sociological, historical, and geographical factors are instrumental in the formation and acceptance of archetypal images. Thus an examination of the sociopolitical and cultural characteristics of Mexican society vis-à-vis women in their maternal roles will help explicate the relationship between the figure of the mother as she is formulated in the corrido and the society that was instrumental in sculpturing this image.

It is almost a tautology to state that the mother is the most important person in the Mexican family structure. The corrido reflects her central position by granting the mother figure a high degree of affectivity within its lyrics. This is particularly true in the case of the mater dolorosa motif. The corridista is relying in part on Western European and Middle Eastern traditions, inserting the mother figure as a dramatic prop to enhance emotionally charged scenes. But the insistence on this particular prop, its constant reiteration throughout these songs, reflects a specifically Mexican preoccupation with the mother. As early as the 1930s, sociological studies of the Mexican family reflected on the centrality of the mother. Octavio Paz's *Labyrinth of Solitude* (1961), Samuel Ramos's *Profile of Man and Culture in Mexico* (1975; originally published in 1934), Rogelio Díaz-Guerrero's *Psychology of the Mexican* (1967), and Santiago Ramírez's *El mexicano, psicología de sus motivaciones* (1977) all point to the mother as a figure of paramount importance in the Mexican psyche.[2]

These studies, focusing mainly on the characteristics of the Mexican personality, also provide provocative theories on the dynamics of the mother–son relationship. In the past two decades these theories have become extremely controversial and have been rigorously questioned by revisionist scholars in the United States. These early studies invariably portray the Mexican as psychologically sick, suffering from an inferiority complex whose cause goes back to the

Conquest and women's role in the Conquest. Ramos attributes this sense of inferiority to the discrepancy between what the young Mexican nation wanted to do and what it was able in reality to achieve. It was then, he believes, "that the conflict broke out between ambition and the limits of natural capacity" (10). Other tenets of this theory include the idea that the Mexican's sense of inferiority derives from feelings of impotence and outrage at being subjugated and conquered by the Spanish soldier, who was at once father and conqueror to the mestizo population born immediately after the Conquest of New Spain. Furthermore, these scholars claim that since the mestizo offspring was frequently the product of an illicit union between Spaniard and Indian, the bastard child hated his father (who often abandoned the mother) and despised his mother for having submitted to the Spaniard. These negative feelings toward the mother were repressed and sublimated, however, and the idealized figure of the mother emerged.

The psychiatrist Díaz-Guerrero comments:

> a dramatic interpersonal interaction lies at the historical roots of the Mexican socioculture. . . . Its whole historical background is based upon the union of a conqueror—the powerful, the male, the Spaniard—and the conquered—the female, the subjugated, the Indian. . . .
>
> Sometime, somehow, consciously or unconsciously, this relationship crystallized into a decision that seems to hold the key to most dealings both within the Mexican family and within the Mexican socioculture. The decision was that all power was to be in the hands of the male. Ever since, it appears, the male obtains the love of the female through a mythical mixture of power and love; any power the female acquires is by her loving behavior. (Díaz-Guerrero, 1967: xv–xvi)

In discussing the family structure as it evolved in Mexico, Díaz-Guerrero posits that it is characterized by a neurosis attributable to the pattern that crystallized at the onset of the Conquest. He offers two fundamental propositions upon which the Mexican family rests: the unquestionable and absolute supremacy of the father and the necessary and absolute self-sacrifice of the mother (3–4). To substantiate his theories Díaz-Guerrero conducted a poll among Mexicans residing in Mexico City. Included in the questions administered to 516 informants (of whom 294 answered the questionnaire) was: "Is the mother the dearest person in existence?" Ninety-five percent of the male and eighty-six percent of the female respondents answered in the affirmative. Díaz-Guerrero concluded that most Mexican males suffered from "a syndrome for which the common denominator is guilt" and that

> the extreme separation between the "female set" of values and the "male set," plus the fact that it is the female who teaches and develops the personality of the child, often provokes in the male guilt regarding deviations from the female pattern. Actually, in order to be at ease with the male pattern, he must constantly break with the female one. Perhaps it is not an accident that the

main religious symbol is a woman: The Virgin of Guadalupe. From their behavior it appears that the males are caught in a compulsive asking for forgiveness from the same symbol they must betray if they are to be masculine. (12)

The political scientist Evelyn P. Stevens takes a different approach to the study of the mother figure and woman's position in general, both in Mexico and in other Latin American countries. Stevens (1977) focuses on the phenomenon of Marianismo, or the cult of "la superioridad espiritual femenina, que enseña que las mujeres son semidivinas, superiores moralment y más fuertes espiritualmente que los hombres" ("the spiritual superiority of women that teaches women are semidivine, morally superior, and spiritually stronger than men"). She perceives *Marianismo* as intimately related to *machismo*, which she defines as "el culto de la virilidad. Las características principales de este culto son agresividad e intransigencia exagerada en las relaciones de hombre a hombre, y arrogancia y agresión sexual en las relaciones de hombre a mujer" ("the cult of virility. The principal characteristics of this cult are exaggerated aggressiveness and intransigence in the social relations between males and arrogance and sexual aggression in the social relations between male and female").

Machismo and Marianismo are thus seen as a kind of yin and yang of Mexican social intersexual relationships, existing side by side in a more or less symbiotic relationship. The Mexican woman derives power, prestige, and status from her femininity and her position as mother and wife. She commands respect and love and exercises power within the confines of the home as long as she nourishes and sustains the machismo of her male counterpart and other male members of the family. Marianismo is closely associated with and in part derives from the cult of the Virgin Mary, the idealization of Mary in her position as mother of God. In time this idealization was transferred to women in general.

As Stevens writes (128):

Entre las características de este ideal están la semidivinidad, la superioridad moral y la fuerza espiritual. Esta fuerza espiritual engendra abnegación, es decir, una capacidad infinita para la humildad y el sacrificio. Ninguna auto-negación es demasiado grande para la mujer latinoamericana, no puede ser adivinado ningún límite a su vasto caudal de paciencia con los hombres de su mundo; aunque puede ser rígida con sus hijos, y aún cruel con sus nueras, es y debe ser complaciente con su madre y su suegra, pues también ellas son reencarnación de la gran madre, también as sumisa hacia las exigencias de los hombres: esposos, hijos, padres, hermanos. (Among the characteristics of this ideal are the belief in semidivinity, the moral superiority and spiritual strength [of women]. This spiritual strength provides the mother with abnegation, that is to say, an infinite capacity for humility and sacrifice. No self-sacrifice is too much for the Latin American woman; one cannot guess the extent of reserves of her patience with the males of the world; even though she may be inflexible with her children and even cruel with her daughters-in-law, she is complacent with her mother and her mother-in-law for they too are a reincarnation of the Great Mother. She is also submissive toward the exigencies of men: husbands, sons, fathers, brothers.)

At times women in Latin America use Marianismo as a lever. It can serve to the Latina's advantage as a socially acceptable mechanism in dealing with the demands of society. For example, if her family is ill, she has a legitimate excuse to be absent from work. The cult of Marianismo stipulates that the family's welfare comes first, Stevens points out, and Mexican employers obey this precept.[3]

Investigators subscribing to the inferiority complex theory and focusing on negative aspects of machismo have been caustically criticized by Chicano sociologists such as Alfredo Mirandé, Evangelina Enríquez, Maxine Baca Zinn, Miguel Montiel, and others for the facile explanations they offer and the "pop psychology" tenor of their analyses. (This issue is discussed further in chapter 2.) Citing poor methodological techniques, inappropriate conceptual approaches, and a lack of solid empirical studies to substantiate the supposed machismo and inferiority complex mystique, revisionist social scientists are challenging the old theories. Modern sociologists, particularly Chicanos, are reevaluating the Mexican family structure and seeking new answers to old problems. These scholars are discovering that the mother is not as passive or stereotypical as depicted in earlier sociological works. The Mexican mother is found to play a significant and dynamic role in family affairs, at least in the United States. Extensive studies of this kind are not readily available on the family in Mexico. But two works, Allen Griswold Johnson's doctoral dissertation, "Modernization and Social Change: Attitudes toward Women's Roles in Mexico City" (1972), and Silvia Marina Arrom's *Women of Mexico City, 1790–1857* (1985), provide significant new information to challenge earlier views on Mexicanas' status and role in Mexican society.

Corridos exhibit several profiles of the mother figure. They support some of Díaz-Guerrero's contentions regarding the Mexican mother, particularly in her mater dolorosa role. At the same time they balance this representation with that of more forceful and dynamic mother figures (see chapter 2).

Analysis demonstrates that the corrido genre offers a more dynamic view of the mother than other sources. For example, the Mexican canción, particularly the canción ranchera, a composition closely related to the corrido in its rural and campesino heritage, presents a unidimensional view of the mother: she is the mater dolorosa.[4] A heavy emphasis on the wickedness of the son or daughter who is singing the song is evident, and this wickedness is contrasted with the purity of the mother. These songs portray the wayward offspring in a repentant frame of mind, asking forgiveness for having caused pain, anguish, and suffering to their saintly mother. These popular lyrical compositions, which are heard frequently on Spanish-speaking radio stations, evidence a binary structure. A listing will illustrate the general structure of the canción's mother themes (for recordings, see the discography, part D in Works Cited and Consulted).

"Adiós Madre querida" ("Good-bye Beloved Mother")	Mother dead: Son suffers
"La Madre abandonada" ("The Abandoned Mother")	Mother dying: Wicked daughter
"Amor de Madre" ("Mother Love")	Mother dead: Son prays
"No sufras Madre" ("Do Not Suffer, Mother")	Mother suffers: Son dying
"El Hijo ingrato" ("The Ungrateful Son")	Mother dead: Son suffers
"Cariño sin condición" ("Unconditional Love")	Mother only true love: Son worships her
"Por el amor a mi Madre" ("For My Mother's Love")	Mother suffers: Son transformed
"Ni por mil puñados de oro" ("Not for a Thousand Handfuls of Gold")	Mother dead: Son suffers
"Consejos de una madre" ("A Mother's Advice")	Mother suffers: Wicked son dies
"Perdón Madrecita" ("Forgive Me, Mother")	Mother suffers: Wicked son transformed
"Con la tinta de mi sangre" ("Written with my Blood")	Mother dead: Son in jail mourning
"El rebozo de mi Madre" ("My Mother's Shawl")	Mother dead: Son mourns
"Hija mía" ("My Daughter")	Mother dead: Mother offers advice
"Madre mía" ("Mother of Mine")	Mother dead: Son worships her
"Madrecita" ("Beloved Mother")	Loving Mother: Son suffers from unrequited love
"Me lo dijo mi madre" ("My Mother Warned Me")	Mother advises son against love: son suffers
"Mi Madre anoche lloró" ("My Mother Cried Last Night")	Mother suffers: Son suffers from unrequited love
"Segunda Madre" ("Second Mother")	Mother dead: Son sees wife as second mother
"Por mi Madre ausente" ("In My Mother's Memory")	Mother dead: Son mourns

The corrido, by contrast, features not just the mater dolorosa but the Great Mother, the Magnus Mater. Corridos arise from the peasant class of workers; they have a strong agricultural element, as befits a genre of tillers of the soil. There is an almost mystical closeness to the *tierra*, the *terruño*, and the individual. Depth psychologists such as Neumann and Jung and scholars of myth such as Eliade and Campbell point to the predominance of the vegetative cycles and seasonal changes incorporated into the myths, rites, and religions of agricultural people. A strong connection between Magnus Mater and Mother Earth is frequently observed. The dual nature of Mother Earth is inevitably felt: the Good Mother who provides food and sustenance to her children and the Terrible Mother who devours her children and who, upon the demise of human beings, claims them back into her bowels. The corridista, with deep campesino roots, incorporates in his folk songs these two archetypal images.

The campesino social class to which corridistas and the corrido audience generally belong proved to be an important factor in the conceptualization of women in the ballad. The corridos portray women in a less stereotypical mode than do artistic forms emanating from the ruling classes, which have more at stake in reinforcing ideological concerns. The corrido is the artistic form of expression of peasants or newly transplanted campesinos living in the city; they are the ones who compose, buy, hear, and sing corridos. The campesinos and poor urban dwellers have a realistic view of women's roles in society, since they see them working and struggling. Women are not necessarily perceived as weaklings or unable to do "men's work" because reality contradicts the stereotype: Women work in the fields plowing, planting, hoeing; they rise at dawn to engage in all manner of farm chores. Poor working-class city dwllers see their women family members struggling for survival as maids, factory workers, clerks. For the poor, women are not pampered dolls but hard-working partners in the common battle for daily survival.

Nevertheless, Mexican culture as a whole (and even more broadly speaking, Latin American and North American culture) is dominated by a traditional patriarchal ideology. Hence the ambiguous image of the mother figure. For while fieldworkers such as those who canvassed for Díaz-Guerrero may find respondents answering that the mother is the dearest being in their life, popular culture demonstrates a profound devaluation of the mother in common street expressions, such as "Chinga tu madre" ("Fuck your mother"), "Vale pinche madre" ("It's worth a fucking mother"), "Dale en la madre" ("Hit him in the mother"), "Puta madre" ("Whoring mother").

The Mexican psychiatrist Santiago Ramírez (1977) analyzed this phenomenon, applying Freudian theories to what he called *importamadrismo*. Ramírez postulated three basic components of the Mexican psyche derived from childhood: an intense relationship between mother and infant, a weak father–son bond, and a traumatic experience from early weaning with consequent feelings of abandonment by the mother (83). The devaluation of the mother in popular expressions involves a denial type of defense mechanism that is actually stating the opposite of what the person really feels:

> if anything is valuable to him, to the Mexican, it is precisely that—his mother. In some of his articulations and his popular expressions he is denying the object to whom he is profoundly attached. In other forms of expression the truth and the bond with the mother is more clearly manifested such as in songs or when an individual states: "they hit me in the mother" [equivalent to the English expression "They kicked my ass"] or "they broke my mother" [English equiv-

alent: "They beat me up badly"]. He is expressing that it is precisely that early bond with the mother that is important; without it he loses all contact and all strength. (114)

Ramírez's explanation seems logical. Of course, the devaluation of the mother in popular expressions is not strictly Mexican but is also found in other cultures. The United States has the popular expletive "motherfucker." Thus the devaluation of the mother must be perceived in terms of a widespread patriarchal ideology that devalues women.

It is important to recognize that the mother in Mexican corridos is consistently valued as an individual. The cultural landscape of Mexico obviously influences the corridista in the selection of the characters he chooses to depict in his narratives. The archetype of the Great Mother provides such structural support; it confers on the ballads mythic overtones and nuances and transforms many of these compositions into literary jewels with universal appeal.

❂ 2 ❂

THE TERRIBLE MOTHER
ARCHETYPE

The active, aggressive mother in the corrido exemplifies what Neumann (1974) denotes as the "Negative Elementary Character of the feminine," the Terrible Mother archetype. In this guise she implicitly or explicitly occasions the downfall or death of the hero.

The "Negative Elementary Character of the feminine" must not be taken literally and ascribed to women. Neumann warns: "The negative side of the elementary character originates rather in the inner experience, and the anguish, horror, and fear of danger that the Archetypal Feminine signifies cannot be derived from any actual and evident attributes of woman" (14). In other words, there is nothing inherently evil or fearful in women. It is a social construct of a patriarchal society that has categorized the feminine as destructive, harmful, bad, evil. In Spanish, for example, *death* is a feminine noun.

A psychological explanation for the recurrence of the Terrible Mother image may be inferred from theories posited by British psychologists Melanie Klein, Harry Guntrip, and D. W. Winnicott, who focus on object relations as primary processes in the formation of the individual.[1] They view the relationship between mother and offspring as the most significant factor in an individual's psychic and emotional maturation. Since the infant's contact with the mother persists for several years, a mother image or unconscious representation of the mother is internalized. The infant's experience with the mother, however, is of a dual nature, both positive and negative. The mother is perceived as the source of warmth, nourishment, and comfort. Owing to the nature of reality, however, the mother cannot be present at the infant's side all the time, thus frustrating the infant's needs and desires. Such frustration experienced early in life underlies the individual's unconscious representation of the negative mother.

In the corrido, the destructive, death-inflicting mother appears in direct confrontation with the protagonist, her son. Confrontations may arise out of the son's disrespect toward the mother (as in the "Corrido de José Lizorio"), the son's or daughter's disobedience (as in "Rosita Alvírez" and "Corrido de Lucío Pérez"), or the mother's jealousy toward her daughter-in-law (as in "Corrido de Belém Galindo"). In all three instances, death overtakes the protagonists.

16

THE CURSE-HURLING MOTHER

The "Corrido de José Lizorio," from the Guerrero Collection, demonstrates the Terrible Mother archetype in her destructive role.

Corrido de José Lizorio	José Lizorio Ballad
1. Un domingo fue por cierto el caso que sucedió que el joven José Lizorio con la madre se enojó.	It was a Sunday to be sure The event that occurred That young José Lizorio Became angry with his mother.
2. Señores, tengan presente y pongan mucho cuidado que este hijo llegó borracho y a su madre le ha faltado.	Gentlemen, take heed And pay close attention This son arrived home drunk And was disrespectful to his mother.
3. Señores, tengan presente y pongan mucho cuidado que porque era muy borracho a su madre la ha golpeado.	Gentlemen, take heed And pay close attention Because he was a drunk Hé struck his mother.
4. Señores, naturalmente la madre se enfureció alzó los ojos al cielo y fuerte maldición le echó.	Gentlemen, most naturally His mother was furious She raised her eyes to heaven And a strong curse did hurl.
5. La madre como enojada esta maldición le echó delante de un santo Cristo que hasta la tierra tembló.	The mother angrily This curse did hurl In front of a sacred Christ Even the earth did tremble.
6. Quiera Dios, hijo malvado, y también todos los santos, que te caigas de la mina y te hagas dos mil pedazos.	May God will it, evil son, And all the saints too, That you fall down at the mine And break into two thousand pieces.
7. El lunes por la mañana a la mina se acercó y le dijo a su ayudante no quisiera bajar yo.	On Monday morning He went near the mine And told his aide I don't want to go down.
8. Le pregunta su minero, ¿Por qué estás tan afligido? ¡ay! como no he de estar Mi madre me ha maldecido.	His miner asked him Why are you so worried? Oh! how can I not be My mother has cursed me.
9. Le contestó su minero pues no deberás bajar; anda y búscate un amigo que te quiera reemplazar.	And his miner responded You shouldn't have to go down Go and find a friend That will replace you.
10. Cuando miró la escalera	When he saw the ladder

pues él empezó a rezar
Madre mía de Guadalupe
que no me vaya a matar.

He began to pray
My dear Mother of Guadalupe
Please don't let me die.

11. A su casa fue José
muy triste y acongojado
pensando en la maldición
que su madre le había echado.

José went to his house
Very sad and gloomy
Thinking about the curse
His mother had hurled at him.

12. Cuando a la puerta llegó
allí se le arrodilló,
le dijo, Madre querida,
quítame tu maldición.

When he arrived at the door
He did kneel there,
He said, mother dear
Lift this curse from me.

13. Te ruego, Madre querida,
yo te imploro tu perdón,
soy hijo de tus entrañas
nacido del corazón.

I beseech you Mother dear,
I beg your forgiveness,
I am your son born from your womb
Born from your heart.

14. ¿Qué dices, madre, qué dices?
levanta tu maldición,
si no que traigan las velas
y que se traiga el cajón.

What do you say, Mother?
Do lift your curse,
If not bring on the candles
And bring the coffin.

15. De allí se salió José
muy triste y desconsolado,
nomás pensando en la madre
que no le había perdonado.

José left the house
Very sad and disconsolate,
Thinking only of his Mother
Who had not forgiven him.

16. Se negaron sus compañeros
a ayudarle a trabajar
y el pobre José Lizorio
su muerte allí fue a encontrar.

His friends refused
To help him at work
And poor José Lizorio
Found his death there.

17. En el nombre sea de Dios
dijo al mirar la escalera,
Jesucristo me acompañe
y la luz de la candela.

In the name of God
He said looking at the ladder,
May Jesus accompany me
And the light of the candle.

18. Al empezar la escalera
allí se desvaneció,
y el pobre José Lizorio
en el fondo se estrelló.

As he stepped down the ladder
He fainted there so
And poor José Lizorio
crashed at the floor.

19. Toditos los compañeros
muy pronto lo levantaron,
diéronle parte a su jefe
y a su madre le avisaron.

All of his co-workers
quickly picked him up
They notified the boss
And notified his mother.

20. Le avisaron a la madre
y un gran desmayo le dió,
alzó los ojos al cielo
y al momento se acordó.

They notified his mother
And she fainted away,
She raised her eyes to heaven
And quickly recalled.

21. La pobre madre lloraba

The poor mother did cry

muy triste y desconsolada	Very sad and disconsolate
pero eran ya todo en vano	But all was in vain
las lágrimas que regaba.	All the tears she cried.
22. La madre se confundió	The mother became confused
cuando lo miró tendido	When she saw him at the wake
te fuiste y me dejaste.	You have gone and left me
adios, hijito querido.	Good-bye my beloved son.
23. Perdóname, Padre mió,	Forgive me, my Father,
las faltas que he cometido,	The bad deeds I committed,
el demonio me tentó	The devil tempted me
y a mi hijo lo he maldecido.	And I cursed my son.
24. Cuando se cayó pa'bajo	When he fell down
cayó cruzado de brazos	He fell with his arms crossed
y su cuerpo lo sacaron	And they took out his body
por completo hecho pedazos.	Totally broken up.
25. Sus sesos los recogieron	Pieces of his brain they picked up
en la copa de un sombrero,	On the crown of a hat,
que sirvan para ablandar	Perhaps they will soften
los corazones de acero.	The hardened hearts.
26. Adios, todos mis amigos,	Good-bye to all my friends
adios, todos mis parientes,	Good-bye to all my relatives,
para que pongan cuidado	May you all pay attention
los hijos desobedientes.	All the disobedient sons.
27. Ya con esta me despido	I bid you farewell
después del triste velorio	After the sad wake
aquí se acaban cantando	I have finished singing
versos de José Lizorio.	The verses of José Lizorio.

The folk song narrates the tragic consequence of a mother–son confrontation. José Lizorio, a young man who works in the local mines, returns home from a drinking spree one Sunday and physically and verbally abuses his mother. The mother responds in the sixth stanza by angrily hurling a curse at her son:

Quiera Dios, hijo malvado,	May God will it, evil son,
y también todo los santos,	And all the saints too,
que te caigas de la mina,	That you fall down at the mine
y te hagas dos mil pedazos.	And break into two thousand pieces.

The young man, completely repentant by now, sadly and reluctantly goes to work, the curse weighing heavily on his mind. Upon arrival at the mine, he beseeches his co-workers to take his place that working day; however, none will do it. Finally, Lizorio begins his descent into the bowels of the mine. As he steps on the first rung, he faints and falls to his death. When his mother is informed of the tragic accident, she recalls the curse hurled in anger and immediately repents the deed. Toward the end of the song, she sorrowfully mourns the death of her son.

This corrido has twenty-seven stanzas. Almost two-thirds (sixteen stanzas) use the word *madre,* and three stanzas (6, 22, and 23) portray the mother speaking directly to her son and to God. The mother in this song is a dynamic character displaying a series of emotions and personality changes within the short span of the narrative. At the onset of the corrido, we encounter the figure of a woman victimized by her unruly, brutish son. This image is soon followed by the furious, imperious mother invoking the powers of heaven to strike the erring son. Toward the middle of the song, the mother is portrayed as a cold, unforgiving person deaf to the entreaties of her now contrite son. Finally, in the last stanza, she is the repentant mater dolorosa who grieves over the death of her son.

Several elements inform the mythic structure of this song. The first stanza situates the action on a sacred day, *domingo* (Sunday). The deeds that follow will be doubly blasphemous, for they take place on a holy day. The corrido, adhering to its reality principle, which is an important characteristic of this genre, supplies the exact day of the happening. The mythic structure predominates, however, for a more indefinite date is supplied, "un domingo." The opening verse does not dissolve time as completely as myth or *märchen* do ("Once upon a time. . . ."), but neither is it as specific as other legend or historical-type corridos are wont to be. The ballad also describes this particular incident as a "caso." *Caso* is defined by folklorist Joe Graham as:

> a relatively brief prose narrative, focusing upon a single event, supernatural or natural, in which the protagonist or observer is the narrator or someone the narrator knows and vouches for, and which is normally used as evidence or as an example to illustrate that "this kind of things happen." Importantly, the *caso* can assign meaning and value to the happening either explicitly or by its emplacement within a discussion. It uses past experience as a means of gaining knowledge. To mark, label, or otherwise identify a narrative as a *caso* is to make a statement about its reliability and therefore, about its value as useful information. (Graham, 1981:19)

Furthermore, Graham states, "*casos* have most frequently been associated with the supernatural or at least the very unusual" (20), and "the *caso* tells of experiences which are repeated—encounters with witches, *duendes,* wolfmen, etc." (14). The inclusion of the word *caso* in this corrido emphasizes the mythic atmosphere by associating it with the other world of semimythic elements, such as the devil, the witch, and the werewolf. The transgression takes place in the second stanza, the protagonist having broken the moral precepts of the community by being intoxicated and disrespectful to his mother. The state of being intoxicated, of course, is closely connected with Dionysus, god of wine. The cult of Dionysus and that of the Mother Goddess were intermingled. W. K. Guthrie elucidates in *The Greeks and Their Gods* (1971): "Thus the religions of Dionysus and of Kybele, the Asiatic Mother-goddess with her young attendant,

Attis, were of the same orgiastic type, and by historical times become inextrica-
bly mingled" (154).

What is even more astonishing is that ritual killing was associated with the
Dionysus cult. Strong opposition arose from various Greek states when the cult
was thought to practice ritual murder. Under the influence of Dionysus, women
were accused of killing their own sons:

> They have one universal feature, namely that the God's vengeance takes the
> form of visiting with madness the women of the land where he has been
> spurned. This usually leads to their tearing of a victim in pieces, either the king
> who has been the god's opponent, or, when the women themselves have been
> the offenders, one of their own children. The two motifs are combined in the
> Pentheus story, where the king who has forbidden the rites is butchered by his
> own mother. (166)

The corrido relates the story of how José Lizorio, due to his mother's *maldición*,
was broken into "two thousand pieces."

The state of being intoxicated, of being in the power of Dionysus, so to speak,
leads to loss of reason and human restraint. It is inevitable that tragedy will
follow, for

> no man can submit without a struggle to the experience of having his dis-
> tinctively human faculty of reason, and all that connects him with the normal
> world, overwhelmed and submerged by those animal elements which, nor-
> mally dormant or at least in subjection, are released and made dominant by the
> irresistible surge of Dionysiac power. (172)

In the fourth stanza of the "Corrido de José Lizorio," we find the mother
appealing to the cosmic forces of heaven and flinging her thunderbolt at her
son—"fuerte maldición le echó." In the fifth stanza we find the magical context
in which the powerful words were uttered: "In front of a sacred Christ / Even
the earth did tremble." The magical effect of a curse is doubly ensured if
pronounced under certain sacred conditions. The icon of the "sacrificed son"—
Santo Cristo—both ensures the efficacy of the curse and parallels the fate of the
son. Furthermore, we are explicitly informed of the cosmological forces involved in this tremendous confrontation: the earth trembles. The curse of a
mother in the presence of God (Santo Cristo) inflicts cosmological changes in
the universe; the magical force of the uttered words provokes an earthquake.
Again, the powerful Mexican folk belief that disrespect or disobedience to
parents will cause the earth to part and swallow the transgressor comes to mind
as the earth trembles. Of course, in the final stanzas of the corrido the protagonist meets death inside the bowels of the earth.

In the sixth stanza, the curse is actually uttered. The Terrible Mother
archetype depicted here is enhanced through the mythic motif of the curse.
The curse motif is no stranger to myth, folk tale, and folk beliefs. It was woven
into medieval narratives known as exempla. Exempla are still common among

the folk in Latin America, forming part of the repertoire of any good folk-tale informant (often narrated as *casos* that actually happened and were witnessed by the informant). The plot generally involves a disobedient offspring who physically or verbally attacks a parent and is subsequently severely punished. The punishment may involve a cataclysmic natural phenomenon such as an earthquake ("se lo tragó la tierra," the earth parts and swallows him/her) or a thunderbolt ("le cayó un rayo," he/she was struck by lightning) that castigates the offending individual with death or physical deformity or even a morphological transformation, such as changing the offender into an animal.[2] Gabriel García Márquez mentions two such cases in his novel *One Hundred Years of Solitude* (1976): a man transformed into a snake "for having disobeyed his parents" (39) and "The bartender, who had a withered and somewhat crumpled arm because he had raised it against his mother" (380).

Folklorist Frank Goodwyn underlined the significance and mythic nature of the curse in his study "A North Mexican Ballad: José Lizorio": "A curse is a command. It is addressed to some personified object or to the elements which are thereupon expected to visit calamity on the victim" (1947:240) Goodwyn mentions biblical examples of curse hurling and its occurrence in such diverse cultures as those of the Eskimo and of Macedonia. The Macedonian example, "Yanni's Mother," is particularly relevant to this study because of the personages involved in the curse: a mother and son.

> All the mothers were sending off their sons to prosper
> Except one mother, a bad mother, Yanni's mother.
> She sat at the window and uttered bitter curses:
> "Go to foreign lands, O Yanni, and mayst thou never return home!
> The swallows will come back year after year,
> But thou, O Yanni, mayst thou never appear, never return home!
> (Goodwyn, 1947: 246)

This, of course, parallels the stance assumed by José Lizorio's mother, with the same tragic results.

A motif associated with the curse motif further reinforces and parallels the archetype of the Terrible Mother: the mine motif. The mine or cave is tinged with a kaleidoscope of symbolism pertaining to both mythological and psychological realms. Neumann writes:

> The central symbolism of the feminine is the *vessel*. From the very beginning down to the latest stages of development we find this archetypal symbol as essence of the feminine. The basic symbolic equation woman = body = vessel corresponds to what is perhaps mankind's—man's as well as woman's—most elementary experience of the Feminine. (1974:39)

The principal symbolic elements assigned to this vessel are the mouth, the breast, and the womb. Neumann further amplifies the extent of the woman = body = vessel equation:

> We begin with the territory of the belly, which most strikingly represents the elementary containing character of the vessels; to it belongs the womb as symbol of the entrance into this region. The lowest level of this belly zone is the underworld that is contained in the "belly" or "womb" of the earth. To this world belong not only the subterranean darkness as hell and night but also such symbols as chasm, cave, abyss, valley, depths, which in innumerable rites and myths play the part of the earth womb that demands to be fructified.
>
> The cave, in its relation to the mountain that unites the character of the vessel, belly, and earth, also belongs to the dark territory of the underworld. (44)

Within the structure of the "Corrido de José Lizorio," the mine reinforces the death-provoking Terrible Mother figure.

> Thus the womb of the earth becomes the deadly devouring maw of the underworld, and beside the fecundated womb and the protecting cave of earth and mountain gapes the abyss of hell, the dark hole of the depths, the devouring womb of the grave and of death, of darkness without light, of nothingness. For this woman who generates life and all living things on earth is the same who takes them back to herself, who pursues her victims and captures them with snare and net. (179)

The mine is the "devouring" womb which "giveth and taketh away" and is an extension of the punishing mother. The mythic theme reverberating through patriarchally influenced world mythologies of the devouring-mother womb is revitalized in the humble "Corrido de José Lizorio." Within the simple lyrics and uncomplicated plot of disrespect and punishment are embedded mythic motifs shared by a multitude of cultures.

Lizorio, with the curse hanging over his shoulder, proceeds to the mine. His fear increases as he gazes into the dark interior of the gaping hole. At this juncture another mythic element appears: the Great Mother archetype in her Protective Goddess form, the Virgin of Guadalupe. Lizorio prays as he stares at the opening of the mine: "My dear Mother of Guadalupe / Please don't let me die." The Virgin of Guadalupe, "Madre de los mexicanos," always appears in a positive role. She is frequently summoned by the protagonist in the corrido to provide help or inspiration and is an incarnation of the Mother Goddess archetype (see chapter 3). Lizorio returns home to beg forgiveness and asks his mother to lift the curse. But his mother, in her Terrible Mother stance, is unforgiving.

In the seventeenth stanza, Lizorio invokes the name of God and of Jesus Christ. This stanza has the biblical overtones of the desperate, anguished cry of Jesus on the cross exclaiming: "My God, my God, why hast thou forsaken me?" And in the next stanza Lizorio falls to his death.

In the subsequent strophes a mater dolorosa is depicted. Now repentant and grieving over her son's death, the mother exclaims:

Perdóname, Padre mío,	Forgive me, my Father,
las faltas que he cometido	The bad deeds I committed,
el demonio me tentó	The devil tempted me
y a mi hijo lo he maldecido.	And I cursed my son.

A new mythic element, the devil, is introduced in this stanza. The appeal is made that a mythic force was responsible for the death of Lizorio.

The next to last stanza follows the formula of the exemplum:

Adios, todos mis amigos	Good-bye to all my friends
adios, todos mis parientes	Good-bye to all my relatives,
para que pongan cuidado	May you all pay attention
los hijos desobedientes.	All the disobedient sons.

It is an admonishment not to disobey one's parents.

Exemplum ballads are not limited to the mother–son dyad but often involve a father–son confrontation. Various folk songs actually portray the son as a parricide, with the father succumbing to the son's violence against him. Corridos reinforce the precept of respect for one's parents, for in all these compositions the son eventually dies in a tragic accident. Ballads portraying the father–son dyad include the famous "Del Hijo Desobediente," "Del Rayo de la Justicia," and "Del parricida" (see Mendoza, 1954).[3]

THE CASSANDRA MOTHER

The second category of Terrible Mother figures involves a woman in the guise of a Cassandra who, having a premonition of her child's impending death. warns him or her of the imminent danger.[4] I have classified the Cassandra mother with the Terrible Mothers not because she can predict her offspring's death—this in itself is not terrible—but because she couples her premonitions with strong interdictions. Furthermore, there is an implicit and often an explicit message in the corrido that it is the disobeying of the mother's advice that precipitates the death of her son or daughter. This type of mother figure is represented as a woman with extraordinary powers. She becomes a Terrible Mother when her offspring disobeys her. The impression conveyed is "Don't mess around with Mother Nature; if you do, you die." In other words, the moral of these corridos is that "mother knows best" and if you disobey her, you bring upon yourself the wrath of the cosmos.

The corrido generally begins at the juncture where the son (or daughter) is about to go out to a dance or "drinking with the boys." In formulaic phrases the mother implores her child to stay home:

| Su madre se lo decía | His mother would tell him |
| que a ese fandango no fuera. | Not to go to that fandango. |

And in formulaic phrases the corridista editorializes:

Los consejos de una madre	The advice from a mother
no se llevan como "quera."	Should not be taken lightly.

The scene is set. The mother's uneasiness and warnings foreshadow the protagonist's death.

The "Corrido de Lucío Pérez" from the Guerrero Collection is illustrative of this category.

Corrido de Lucío Pérez	The Ballad of Lucío Pérez
1. Eran las diez de la noche,	It was ten at night
estaba Lucío cenando	Lucío was having supper
cuando llegaron sus amigos	When his friends arrived
a convidarlo a un fandango.	Inviting him to a dance.
2. Su madre se lo evitaba	His mother forbade him
que a ese fandango no fuera,	To go to that dance;
los consejos de una madre	The advice of a mother
no se olvidan como quiera.	Should not be forgotten lightly.
3. Llegaron a la cantina	They arrived at the bar
y se pusieron a tomar,	And started to drink
pero Lucío no sabía	But Lucío did not know
que lo iban a traicionar.	He was going to be betrayed.
4. Lo sacaron a la orilla	They took him to the outskirts
por ver si quería pelear,	To see if he wanted to fight
le dieron tres puñaladas	They stabbed him three times
al pie de un verde nopal.	At the foot of a green cactus.
5. Los tres que lo apuñalaron	The three men that stabbed him
se sentaron a fumar,	Sat down to smoke
y se carcajeaban de risa	And cackled as they laughed
de oir a Lucío quejar.	Upon hearing Lucío moan.
6. Los tres que lo apuñalaron	The three men that stabbed him
se fueron para un potrero,	Left toward the corral
caminando muy despacio	Walking very slowly
los tres limpiando su acero.	The three cleaning their knives.
7. Madre mía de Guadalupe	Mother of Guadalupe
de la Villa de Jerez,	From the village of Jerez
dadme licencia, Señora,	Give me permission My Lady
de levantarme otra vez.	To get up once again.
8. Su pobre madre lloraba	His poor mother cried
debajo de unos jarales,	Underneath some reeds,
hijo, cómo te levantas,	Son, how do you expect to rise again,
si son heridas mortales.	They are mortal wounds.
9. Su hermano, de compasión,	His brother feeling sorry

la pistola le brindó;	Offered him his pistol;
hermano para qué la quiero	"My brother what do I need it for?
si el tiempo ya se pasó.	It is too late now."

10. Volaron los pavos reales	The peacocks did fly
del ciprés a los verjeles,	From the cypress trees to the orchard.
mataron a Lucío Pérez	They've killed Lucío Pérez
por causa de las mujeres.	Because of women.

11. Volaron los pavos reales	The peacocks did fly
para la Sierra Mojada,	Toward the Wet Sierra
mataron a Lucío Pérez	They've killed Lucío Pérez
por una joven que amaba.	'Cause of a young lady's love.

12. Y su familia lloraba	And his family did cry
lloraba sin compasión,	Cried without stopping
al ver así a Lucío Pérez	Seeing Lucío Pérez thus
llevarlo para el panteón.	Taking him to the cemetery.

13. Qué bonitas mañanitas,	What a pretty ballad,
no sé ni quién las compuso	I don't know who wrote it
aquí se acaban cantando	Here I end my singing
las mañanitas de Lucío.	The ballad of Lucío.

14. Ya con esta me despido	I now take my farewell
con tristeza y con pesar,	With sadness and grief
si en algo estuviera errado	If I have erred somehow
a mi me han de dispensar.	I beg your forgiveness.

This corrido has as its structural axis the mythic and biblical motif of betrayal and treachery by an intimate friend. The beginning of the stanza foreshadows the tragic events by situating the action in the night—"las diez de la noche," a formulaic phrase also used in other corridos. The dark, death-inflicting aspect of the cosmic forces is contrasted with the name of the protagonist, Lucío, signifying the opposite: light, the life-giving face of the universe.

The second stanza introduces the mother, offering her life-saving premonition of impending danger. Lucío disregards the warnings and precipitates the tragic events. The balladeer sets the stage by reminding the audience of the perils involved in disregarding a mother's advice.

The third stanza swiftly projects the action to a cantina—a dangerous place—where we see the trusting protagonist in the company of his "friends" ready to undertake a night of revelry. It is at this juncture that the ominous word *traición* is introduced. The action flashes quickly from the cantina to a second ominous setting—"la orilla" (an edge, a spatial location impregnated with sinister overtones)—and it is in this indefinite cosmological space that Lucío is stabbed three times. The corrido employs the mythic number three to indicate the cosmic character of the events taking place. Furthermore, the formulaic phrase "al pie de un verde nopal," where the heinous deed was committed, is contrasted with Mother Earth and her vegetative, fertile world of green, life-giving plants. In this instance Lucío serves as a sacrificial victim to the vegetative world. This is further reinforced by the nexus made between Lucío and "nopal" (cactus) and "espinas" (thorns), which bear the connotation of pain-inflicting instruments. Further inferences to the biblical scene of Jesus' crucifixion on Calvary appear in the next stanza. The "three friends" who stabbed Lucío sit beside the dead body and smoke a cigarette diabolically laughing at their deed. The smoke and "fire" of the cigarettes bring to mind the infernal fires of a hellish underworld. Furthermore, it must be recalled that during Jesus' crucifixion the Romans began to gamble at the foot of the cross, laughing at the sufferings of Jesus Christ. The animality and irrationality of the trio are underscored by the motif *potrero* (prairie), which connects this corrido with the "Hijo desobediente" ("The Disobedient Son") ballad (see Paredes, 1959:88–92).

Again paralleling Jesus' ordeal, Lucío implores the cosmic powers from above to aid him. In the seventh stanza he beseeches the Protective Mother, "Madre mía de Guadalupe," to succor him. A connection between the cosmic mother and physical mother is made within the stanza, for, while invoking the supernatural mother, the Virgin of Guadalupe, his natural mother responds in formulaic phrases: "Son, how do you expect to rise again, / They are mortal wounds."

The ninth stanza introduces Lucío's brother, who attempts to help but is too late. The two strophes that follow reiterate the animal and vegetative world with the *pavoreal* (peacock, symbol of pride) and *ciprés* (cypress, symbol of death) motifs and provide an explanation for the downfall of Lucío: women. Evidently Lucío was murdered by a rival for the love of a woman. The final two verses follow the traditional pattern of the corrido and supply the *despedida* (farewell) of the troubadour.

Many ballads incorporate the Cassandra mother whose premonitions are disregarded by the protagonist with the inevitable consequence of a tragic, violent end. The bard consistently editorializes that one should never disregard the advice of a mother because of the tragic denouement this act might bring. The corrido, therefore, exhibits the structure of the exemplum, which provides a concrete example of an offspring who disobeys an interdict and is severely punished for the transgression.

THE CRUEL MOTHER

The Cruel Mother motif is commonly found in the folklore of various cultures, including European, American, and Latin American folk tales.[5] This motif is also present, though not frequently, in corridos. In the "Belém Galindo" ballad from the Guerrero Collection, the Cruel Mother appears not in a mother–son or mother–daughter confrontation but in a mother-in-law–daughter-in-law dyad.

De Belém Galindo

Of Belém Galindo

1. En la población de Nieves
ha fallecido Belém,

In the town of Nieves
Belém has died,

el diecinueve de octubre
del año de ochenta y tres.

On the nineteenth of October
In the year 1883.

2. ¡Pobrecita de Belém,
ah, qué suerte le tocó!
Que por lengua de su suegra
su marido la mató.

Poor little Belém!
What bad luck she had!
That because of her mother-in-law
Her husband killed her.

3. Calle del Cinco de Mayo
¿por qué estás enlutecida?
Por la muerte de Belém,
que la mataron dormida.

Fifth of May Avenue
Why are you in mourning?
Because of the death of Belém,
They've killed her while sleeping.

4. Belém era muy bonita,
muy bonita y retratada,
y la mató su marido
a los diez días de casada.

Belém was very pretty,
Very pretty photographed,
And her husband killed her
After ten days of marriage.

5. Belém le dijo a la criada:
—No te vayas a tardar.
La criada se dilató
porque tuvo que lavar.

Belém told her servant:
"Don't be late."
The servant was late
Because she did the laundry.

6. —Belém, te vengo a decir,
te vengo yo a noticiar:
Don Marcos te quiere mucho,
te da plata que gastar.

"Belém, I've come to tell you
I've come to bring you the news:
Mr. Marcos fancies you,
He will give you money to spend."

7. Belém le dice a la suegra:
—No venga aquí a molestar,
que, mire que no soy de ésas,
no me doy ese lugar.

Belém told her mother-in-law:
"Don't come here to bother me,
I am not that type,
I don't like that behavior."

8. —Anda, Belém tan ingrata,
tú me la vas a pagar;
viniendo Hipólito, mi hijo,
algo le voy a contar.

"Listen, ingrate Belém,
You will pay for this;
When Hipólito, my son, comes,
I'll tell him a thing or two."

9. Sale Belém con la criada
a dar la vuelta al jardín,
no sabiendo la inocente
que esa noche iba a morir.

Belém leaves with her servant
To take a walk in the garden,
Not knowing the poor innocent
She was going to die that night.

10. La criada dice a Belém:
—¿Por qué llora sin cesar?
—La boca me sabe a sangre
y el corazón a puñal.

The servant asks Belém:
"Why are you crying so much?"
"My mouth has the taste of blood
And my heart the taste of dagger."

11. ¡Pobre de Belém Galindo,
cómo fue desventurada!
Su marido la mató
a los diez días de casada.

Poor Belém Galindo!
How unlucky she was!
Her husband killed her
After ten days of marriage.

12. ¡Qué Hipólito tan ingrato!
¡Qué Hipólito tan felón!

How cruel Hipólito was!
What a felon Hipólito was!

Le dió un tiro a Belemcita
en el mero corazón.

He shot little Belém with one bullet
Right in the heart.

13. Luego que ya la mató
se agachaba y la veía
y le decía:—¡Belemcita,
pedazo del alma mía!

After he had killed her
He would bend down to see her
And would say: "Belemcita,
Love of my life!"

14. Belém estaba tendida
en una mesa cuadrada,
Hipólito allí en la calle,
que lo aprehendió la Montada.

Belém was laid to rest
Upon a square table,
Hipólito was in the street,
Where he was apprehended by the
 police.

15. Llegaron los policías
y a Mendoza lo aprehendieron,
también vino el señor juez
y el cadáver recogieron.

The police arrived
And they apprehended Mendoza,
The judge also came
And took away the body.

16. Lleváronse ¡ay! a Belém
en una triste camilla,
y luego en el hospital
le hicieron la *aptosía*.

They took Belém away
In a sad stretcher
And then to the hospital
Where they did an autopsy.

17. Su blanco pecho le abrieron
para verle el corazón,
destrozado lo tenía.
¡Qué Hipólito tan traidor!

They opened her white chest
To check her heart.
It was destroyed.
Oh how cruel Hipólito was!

18. Cuando Hipólito nació,
¿qué planeta reinaría?
Su madre estaría en pecado

When Hipólito was born
What planet ruled his sign?
His mother must have been in a state of
 sin,

o no lo bautizaría.

Or must not have baptized him.

19. Ya Belém está en la gloria
dándole cuenta al Creador,
Hipólito en el Juzgado
dando su declaración.

Belém is in heaven now
Being judged by the Creator,
Hipólito is in court
Giving his declaration.

20. La declaración que ha dado:
—No, señor, no la he matado,
estando los dos durmiendo
la pistola ha disparado.

The declaration he gave:
"No, sir, I did not kill her,
When we were both sleeping
The gun went off."

21. Ya Belém está en la gloria,
Hipólito en el presidio,
ya el juez en el tribunal
leyéndole su martirio.

Belém is in heaven
Hipólito is in jail
The judge at the court
Reading him his punishment.

22. Ya con ésta me despido,
con mi sombrero de lado;
buenas nunca son las suegras
ni figuradas en barro.

I bid thee farewell
With hat in my hand
Mother-in-laws are never good
Not even sculpted in clay.

23. Ya con ésta me despido,	I bid thee farewell
al dar la vuelta a un *llantén*,	Upon circling a plantain
aquí se acaban cantando	Here I end my singing
versos de María Belém.	The verses of María Belém.

The first two strophes contain the kernel of the narrative: Belém died at the hands of her husband due to the false accusations of his mother. We are surprised to find in the sixth stanza Hipólito's mother trying to involve the young bride in a tryst with a lover, Don Marcos.

The ominous eighth stanza impregnates the corrido's atmosphere with the tragic events that are to come and parallels the curse explicit in the "Corrido de Lizorio" and the warning advice given by the mother in the "Corrido de Lucío Pérez." A premonitory feeling of unease and apprehension envelops Belém, who, unable to cease weeping, answers her maid's inquiries regarding her distress with a distich resembling the tragic poetry of Federico García Lorca: "La boca me sabe a sangre / y el corazón a puñal." The lines are permeated with mythic overtones. The cosmic force of a mythic element such as blood is to be "derramada" (spread) over the waiting Mother Earth. It is significant that these dramatic forebodings are expressed in a garden, symbolizing life, beauty, vegetation.

The corridista further implants an evil aura on the crime by establishing a connection between it and the spiritual state of the mother at the birth of the killer: "His mother must have been in a state of sin, / Or must not have baptized him." The relationship of cosmological forces and the heinous crime is implied by an association of the murderer's birth with the planetary motions of the sky: "When Hipólito was born / What planet ruled his sign?" Thus a mythic nexus is established between the unknown, cosmic workings of the universe and the human actions committed on earth. Ernst Cassirer has elucidated on the reasoning behind this type of mythic thought:

> In contrast to the *functional* space of pure mathematics the space of myth proves to be *structural*. Here the whole does not "become" by growing genetically from its elements according to a determinate rule; we find rather a purely static relationship of inherence. Regardless of how far we divide, we find in each part the form, the structure, of the whole. This form is not, as in the mathematical analysis of space, broken down into homogeneous and therefore formless elements; on the contrary, it endures as such unaffected by any division. The whole spatial world, and with it the cosmos, appears to be built according to a definite model, which may manifest itself to us on an enlarged or reduced scale but which, large or small, remains the same. All the relations of mythical space rest ultimately on this original *identity*; they go back not to a similarity of efficacy, not a dynamic law, but to an original identity of essence. This fundamental view has found its classical expression in astrology. For astrology every occurrence in the world, every genesis and new formation is fundamentally illusion; what is expressed in the world process, what lies behind it, is a predetermined fate, a uniform determination of being, which asserts itself identically throughout the moments of time. Thus, the whole of a

man's life is contained and decided in its beginning, in the constellation of the hour of birth; and in general, growth presents itself not as genesis but as a simple permanence and an explanation of this permanence. . . . by this "law of the whole" which dominates mythical thinking astrology can interpret coexistence in space only as an absolutely *concrete* coexistence, as a specific position of *bodies* in space; instead, all intuition of form is melted down into the intuition of content, into the aspects of the planetary world. (Cassirer, 1955:88–89)

These musings of the troubadour are impregnated with mythic connotations. The implication of not being baptized projects the killer into the realm of the irrational, the animal. According to Roman Catholic dogma, one does not achieve human status until one is baptized. Thus the mother's role at the time of the crime is reinforced in this distich and parallels the initial precipitating action (the mother's state of sin or her neglect in baptizing her son) that led to the tragic events.

Significantly, the name Hipólito resonates with mythological overtones. Greek mythology informs us that Hippolytos belonged to a group of giants:

They were born from Earth when the blood-drops from the mutilation of Uranus fell upon her. Hence they are often called Gegeneis i.e., earth-born. We do indeed find stories, some of them very early, in which the Giants, either under that name or under that of Gegeneis, are wild and savage men, something like the Kyklopes, whom in some way they resemble in their nature. (Rose, 1959: 56)

The mother of these giants goaded them into engaging in battle with the gods, possibly as a revenge against "some insult or wrong" directed at her. This plot certainly parallels the structure of "Belém Galindo": an avenging mother instigating her son to murder his wife.

Another myth associated with the name Hippolytos also has an underlying theme that somewhat parallels the corrido's dramatic structure:

After the death of [Hippolytos's] mother, Theseus married again, this time Ariadne's sister Phaidra. She fell passionately in love with her stepson, and in the absence of Theseus, at last let him know of her affection. He repulsed her, and she hanged herself, first writing a letter incriminating him. Theseus, returning, read the letter and cursed his son; now Poseidon had granted him three wishes, and the curse was one of them. Hippolytos, therefore, as he drove away from his father, who had banished him, was met by a huge sea-monster which frightened his horses; they bolted, threw him from the chariot, and dragged him to death. (266)

The name Hipólito is thus associated with the mythological hero Hippolytos, who in turn is associated with Terrible Mothers who, by their cunning, lies, and deceptions, cause death and destruction to those around them.

In the next to last stanza of "Belém Galindo" we encounter the satirical words

"Mother-in-laws are never good / Not even sculpted of clay." This verse, although intended as humor, recalls the Terrible Mother idols of clay of the Greeks, the Aztecs, and other cultures and thus repeats the negative image.

The mother-in-law appears infrequently in corridos. She is most commonly derided in the *bola*, a category of folk song closely related to the corrido.[6] In "Belém Galindo" the figure of the mother plays a double role, as mother and mother-in-law. Nonetheless, she functions as the archetype of the Terrible Mother and is the pivotal figure in the structure of this ballad, for her evil machinations bring about the death of an innocent young woman and the imprisonment of her own son.[7]

❋ 3 ❋

THE MOTHER GODDESS
ARCHETYPE

"It is no secret to anyone that Mexican catholicism is centered about the cult of the Virgin of Guadalupe," Octavio Paz asserts in *The Labyrinth of Solitude*.

> In the first place, she is an Indian Virgin; in the second place, the scene of her appearance to the Indian Juan Diego was a hill that formerly contained a sanctuary dedicated to Tonantzín, "Our Mother," the Aztec goddess of fertility. We know that the Conquest coincided with the apogee of the cult of two masculine divinities: Quetzalcoatl, the self-sacrificing god, and Huitzilopochtli, the young warrior-god. The defeat of these gods—which is what the Conquest meant to the Indian world, because it was the end of a cosmic cycle and the inauguration of a new divine kingdom—caused the faithful to return to the ancient feminine deities. (Paz, 1961:84–85)

Paz insists that this religious drive to find spiritual relief in the worship of goddesses parallels the desire to return to the safe and comforting warmth of the mother's womb. But a transformation has taken place in Tonantzín: through her linkage with Guadalupe she is no longer the fertility goddess of vegetation; "her principal attribute is not to watch over the fertility of the earth but to provide refuge for the unfortunate" (85).

The Virgin of Guadalupe indeed plays an immensely significant role in the cultural, political, and sociological milieu of the Mexican nation. Since the corrido is a cultural product, we should not be surprised to find the Virgin of Guadalupe present in many lyrics of Mexican folk songs. This chapter analyzes this sacred figure in the ballad as an artistic expression of the Protective Mother Goddess archetype. This archetype is another manifestation, a refinement, of the Great Mother archetype in her Good Mother guise. In Mexican songs and ballads she is a benevolent but generally passive and, most significantly, physically absent figure. The beleaguered hero of these songs often invokes the protection of the Virgin of Guadalupe and seeks her aid and blessing in various dangerous undertakings—battles, personal duels, journeys. But the Virgin never directly answers the hero's prayer; nor does she appear in person in the

33

song. This cosmic, luminous, sacred figure nevertheless envelops the corrido in which she appears in a spiritual, transcendental mist, thus conferring an aura of the sacred to the overall mythic configuration underlying the structure of many heroic compositions.

THE VIRGIN OF GUADALUPE LEGEND

According to tradition, in the early part of the sixteenth century (1531) an Indian peasant named Juan Diego was traveling toward Mexico City to seek help for an ailing uncle. On the way, an apparition in the form of the Virgin Mary appeared to the startled Juan Diego on the hill of Tepeyac near the city. He was directed by the beautiful brown Virgin to journey on and to acquaint the bishop, Juan de Zumarraga, of her special desire to have a church built in her honor on that particular hill. Juan Diego doubted that the bishop would take his message seriously; he was acutely aware of his status as a "lowly Indian." The heavenly apparition nevertheless assured him in a kindly manner that all would be well and to make haste and relay the message.

As Juan Diego had foreseen, the bishop was unimpressed. The young lad returned to the hill and conveyed the news to the Virgin Mary, who was waiting for him. The apparition insisted that Juan Diego return to the bishop and acquaint him of her wishes. The second trip proved equally fruitless, for the bishop did not believe the messenger.

On the fourth try the Virgin, realizing the bishop's stubbornness, instructs the young Indian to gather some roses from the hill and deliver them to the prelate as proof of her existence. This he grudgingly agrees to do, for it is the middle of winter (December 12) and he doubts that there will be any flowers growing at this time of year. To his surprise, he finds exquisitely formed roses blooming on the hill. He gathers a few and carries them in his tunic to present to the bishop.

After Juan Diego confronts the bishop with the repeated message and adds that he carries a gift from the Virgin of Guadalupe, he unfolds his tunic and a bundle of fresh, lovely roses spills to the floor. The bishop stares in amazement, for painted on Juan Diego's tunic is the image of the Virgin of Guadalupe. The church is built on the site requested by the Virgin.[1]

The term *Guadalupe* apparently derives from *guada*, an Arabic term for "river," and *lupe*, an Arabic word denoting "hidden." The combination yields "hidden river."[2] Indeed, there is a small river by this name near the province of Cáceres in Extremadura, the region of Spain where many of the conquistadors claimed their origin. A sacred image bearing the title Guadalupe was venerated there around the time of the Conquest and in the centuries that followed.[3] An alternative theory of the etymology of the word has been posited by other scholars. Marina Warner (1976) informs us that

in Nahuatl, the Indian language spoken by Juan Diego, the word might have been *coatalocpia* from *coatl* meaning "serpent," *tealoc* meaning "goddess" and *tlapia,* which means "watch over," i.e. the protective serpent goddess. Alternatively, a derivation from *coatl,* meaning "serpent," and *llope,* meaning "tread on," has been suggested. Both roots imply that Juan Diego, exposed to Jesuit and Franciscan missionaries' propaganda about the Immaculate Conception of the Virgin, had merged her with the native snake mother goddess of the Indians, who was worshipped locally at Tepeyac. (390)

Historical sources affirm that Fray Juan de Zumarraga, who eventually became the first bishop of Mexico, was the Catholic official to whom Juan Diego imparted the news of the miraculous appearance. After the first apparition an *ermita,* or small chapel, was built where the Virgin appeared.

Fray Bernardino Sahagún, in *Historia general de las cosas de Nueva España* (1568), was the first to intuit the connection between Guadalupe and Tonantzín: "Near the mountains there are three or four places. . . . One of these is here in Mexico where there is a hill called Tepeyac. In this place they [the Aztecs] had a temple dedicated to the mother of the gods whom they called Tonantzín, which means Our Mother. There they offered many offerings, [incense and flowers] in honor of this goddess, and many people came from far away places . . . and they brought many offerings. Men and women came to these festivals, as well as young men and young women. The attendance of people was great during these days and all said we go to the Feast of Tonantzín. Now that the church of Our Lady of Guadalupe is built there, they call her Tonantzín" (Sahagún, 1950, book 11, appendix).

The first "substantial" (adobe) church was erected in 1556 and credited to Archbishop don Alonso de Montufar (Martí, 1973:96). By 1622 this small church had expanded to such a point that it was officially considered a temple. Archbishop Juan Pérez de la Serna blessed and dedicated it that same year (109). Between 1640 and 1650 a second adobe temple was constructed under the auspices of Luis Lasso de la Vega, and it was here that the sacred image was worshiped (M. Rodríguez, 1980:28). By this time the cult of the Virgin was rapidly expanding.

The original *tilma,* or cape, belonging to Juan Diego and purported to bear the imprint of the sacred image of Guadalupe was the centerpiece at the new temple. It had been officially transferred from the old church to the new building by Archbishop Juan de la Serna.[4] By these actions the Catholic Church demonstrated its increasing acceptance of the new cult. The process of institutionalizing the worship of Guadalupe had begun. The cult to the new deity continued to spread, rapidly attracting great numbers of faithful. Toward the end of the seventeenth century (1695), church dignitaries were forced to construct a new cathedral to accommodate the continually increasing faithful. This building has weathered floods, earthquakes, and revolutions and still stands at the Cerro del Tepeyac in Mexico City (Martí, 1973:110).

By the beginning of the eighteenth century the basilica at the Cerro del Tepeyac was recognized as a great pilgrimage center for the worship of Guadalupe. Equally important were the festivities surrounding the celebration of the appearances. The yearly fiestas would begin as early as September and culminate on the twelfth of December, the last date on which the Virgin of Guadalupe was said to have appeared to Juan Diego. The yearly festivities were particularly impressive because of the great faith and fervor demonstrated by the Indians, who trekked from their villages to pay homage to the image. These native groups honored the image by presenting dances, rites, and music generally known as *mitotes* (Lafaye, 1976:255).[5]

The creole population of Mexico City and the surrounding area was equally devoted to the new deity. They donated gifts of money expressly for the construction of chapels, roads, gardens, and other monuments to honor the Virgin. Magnificent tree-lined boulevards connecting the cathedral to downtown Mexico City were built in this manner (ibid.:274–276). The beauty and prestige of the cathedral and the cult of Guadalupe became famous throughout the world.

A strong bond between the cult of the Virgin of Guadalupe and the *políticos* of central Mexico began to form. It soon became the custom of high-ranking politicians, bureaucrats, government officials, viceroys, and other functionaries to begin and end their tenure by paying homage to the Virgin of Guadalupe at the site of the basilica. Thus politics and the cult of Guadalupe began to merge at an early point (ibid.:255).

During the period before 1810, a strong competition arose between the Virgin of Guadalupe and the Virgin of Los Remedios (M. Rodríguez, 1980:56). From its inception, the Guadalupe cult was identified with the American population—the Indian masses, the creoles, the mestizos, blacks, and mulattoes—whereas the Virgin of Los Remedios, who was of Spanish origin and was a popular sacred image in the Iberian Peninsula, counted among her following the *peninsulares*, or *gachupines* (Spaniards), recently arrived from Europe. The political implications of the two Virgins and their respective cults became obvious during the Wars of Independence (1810–1821). Each warring party selected its sacred standard bearer. The American insurgents chose the Virgin of Guadalupe, while the Spanish battalions carried the image of the Virgin of Los Remedios to the battlefields. Corridos depicting this turbulent era demonstrate this partisanship:

> Divina Guadalupana   Divine Guadalupe
> con esos preciosos dedos   With those precious fingers
> échale la bendición   Give thy blessing
> al señor cura Morelos.   To Father Morelos.
>   (Guerrero Collection)

Early leadership in the Wars of Independence came mostly from the church. It was no surprise, therefore, to hear the priest Miguel Hidalgo y Costilla, "Father of the Independence Movement," in the famous Grito de Dolores (the call for arms against the Spaniards given in Dolores, Guanajuato), invoke the name of the Virgin of Guadalupe. Her image was prominent, flying high on the banners carried by the rebels (Vasconcelos, 1971:269).

Father Miguel Hidalgo's invocation of the Virgin of Guadalupe was not an isolated act. The hero of the Wars of Independence, Father José María Morelos, officially dictated an order in 1813 for all patriotic Mexicans to wear on their clothing the image of Guadalupe (M. Rodríguez, 1980:56). The emblem identified those supporting the revolutionary movement. Thus, loyalists and rebels became identifiable through their religious beliefs.

Since the insurgent forces from Mexico were victorious in the wars with Spain, the Mexican nation attributed their triumph in no small measure to their belief in the Blessed Virgin of Guadalupe. They believed her special protection emanating from heaven helped their cause.

The significant ramifications of the Guadalupe cult have been carefully researched by the French scholar Jacques Lafaye in *Quetzalcoatl and Guadalupe: The Formation of Mexican National Consciousness, 1531–1813*. This work examines the conditions in New Spain that nourished the soil in which the cult of Guadalupe flowered. Historians agree that the Conquest produced a four-caste system composed of peninsulares, creoles, mestizos, and Indians (and a few mulattoes and blacks). Political and economic power rested mostly in the hands of the peninsulares, with the creoles chafing under what they considered discriminatory conditions. This point proved to be the seed that germinated and finally exploded into revolutionary fervor in the Wars of Independence. The creoles and peninsulares nevertheless formed the ruling class in Mexico; it was the mestizos, Indians, blacks, and mulattoes who were disfranchised. The misgivings, distrust, and pervasive hatred with which each caste viewed the other was hardly conducive to the forging of a national spirit.

The cult of the Virgin of Guadalupe had its beginnings in a general climate of religious distrust and religious heterogeneity and syncretism. The early period of colonization, with its diverse ethnic populations, inevitably produced an explosive clash of religious beliefs. The intense missionary zeal of the Spaniard to Christianize the Indian and other *no creyentes* (nonbelievers) forced an underground movement of beliefs that fermented into a sputtering of fanatic prophets, visionaries, and other cult-oriented religious leaders who sought to liberate the masses from Spanish and creole political hegemony. No doubt both the political and religious instability of the times helped nurture the cult of the Virgin of Guadalupe. As Lafaye (1976) suggests:

> The dominant creole minority needed the decisive support of the rest of the population in order to free itself from Spanish tutelage; it had to elaborate an ideology capable of integrating the subjugated ethnic groups, first utilized as a labor force, later as a combat force. The oppressed state of the majority of the nation—a majority composed of the Indians and the *castas*—created a propitious terrain for the continual appearance of messianic movements of spiritual, political, and social liberation. As mythical responses destined to fulfill these aspirations, there appeared and developed beliefs in a pristine evangelization of Mexico by the apostle Saint Thomas, under the name of Quetzalcoatl, and the miraculous apparition of the virgin Mary of Guadalupe on the hill of Tepeyac, the former sanctuary of Tonantzin, mother-goddess of the Aztecs. (29)

The Guadalupean cult follows the pattern of the rise of messianic movements given certain sociological, historical, and political conditions. The Italian scholar Vittorio Lanternari (1963) studied the factors converging in the formation, acceptance, and spread of messianic religious movements. He cited two motivating forces in the populations that breed them, a desire for freedom and for salvation: "freedom from subjugation and servitude to foreign powers as well as from adversity, and salvation from the possibility of having the traditional culture destroyed and the native society wiped out as a historical entity" (239).

These reasons perfectly correspond to the cultural and political situation in the Colonial period in Mexico. The Mesoamerican Indians and other populations were chafing under the oppressive yoke of Spain. Furthermore, the intense cultural clash between the native American population and the Spanish implanted in Mexican soil fomented spiritual and psychological unrest.

Lanternari pinpointed the conditions in the nineteenth and twentieth centuries that were instrumental in the rapid rise of cults. Similar conditions obtained in the 1498–1810 period, and his insights can profitably be extrapolated to the Mexican situation in the sixteenth century:

> The increasingly close contacts between whites and natives that have developed in the course of the last hundred years, especially under the stress of two world wars, have given rise to nativistic religious movements in almost every part of the globe. Two factors have contributed most substantially to this: the intensified efforts of imperialism to bring the aborigines under control, and the growing awareness on the part of the native peoples of the economic and cultural lags in their own societies as compared to the civilization of the West. Therefore, it is the impact made upon the so-called "primitive" societies by the colonial powers that has brought about conditions favoring the rise of messianic movements. (242)

Most significantly, Lanternari noted a similarity between later messianic movements and the early ones from Western Europe. These similarities can be comprehended in terms of the underlying causes provoking their germination and the goals and aspirations of hope and salvation inherent in the movements. Caution should be taken, however, in completely equating the two:

> Beyond the similarities, it is also important to see the differences between movements generated by a conflict between societies or by the clash with external forces, and those generated by dissensions within the pattern of one society—even though we should view the distinction external and internal motivation in a dialectical sense and not as a static condition. Indeed, there is no messianic movement of external origin which does not also have certain internal motivations, since all of them are linked with one another within the historic process, even as there are no prophetic movements engendered by internal conditions which do not also have external repercussions. The impact from outside which produces a crisis within society compels the internal forces of that society to make a choice between clinging to traditions rendered obsolete by events, or developing new patterns of culture better able to meet

the new challenge. Although the messianic cults arising from conflict with Western culture are by far the most numerous, primitive societies have also produced movements to meet critical conditions of purely internal origin. (245–246)

The Virgin of Guadalupe cult arose at a time when the Indian populations were experiencing great doubt in their native gods. When the Spaniards arrived in Mexico proclaiming the "true" religion and making war with the native population, the Aztecs put all their faith and trust in their gods to vanquish the aggressive invaders. When the Aztecs were defeated, and saw their clay idols crumble at the feet of the conquistadors, the seeds of doubt began to grow. These doubts did not, however, manifest immediately when the Aztecs were finally defeated (1521). On the contrary, a strong defense of their gods was eloquently articulated by the Aztec priesthood, the respected *tlamatinime*, who before a large assembly of Spaniards and Indians voiced their anguish:

> Our Lords, our very esteemed Lords:
> great hardships have you endured to reach this level.
> Here before you,
> we ignorant people contemplate you. . . .
>
> Through an interpreter we reply,
> we exhale the breath and the words
> of the Lord of the Close Vicinity.
> Because of Him we dare to do this.
> For this reason we place ourselves in danger. . . .
>
> Perhaps we are to be taken to our ruin, to our
> destruction.
> But where are we to go now?
> We are ordinary people,
> we are subject to death and destruction, we are mortals;
> allow us then to die,
> let us perish now,
> since our gods are already dead. . . .
>
> You said
> that we know not
> the Lord of the Close Vicinity,
> to Whom the heavens and earth belong.
>
> You said
> that our gods are not true gods.
> New words are these
> that you speak;
> because of them we are disturbed,
> because of them we are troubled. . . .
>
> And, now, we are
> to destroy
> the ancient order of life

of the Chichimecs,
of the Toltecs,
of the Acolhuas,
of the Tecpanecs? . . .

Is it not enough that we have already lost,
that our way of life has been taken away,
has been annihilated.

                              (León-Portilla, 1978:63–67)

    As the fabric of autochthonous Indian societies was torn asunder, a syncretism of the old and the new commenced. Thus Guadalupe is perceived by various scholars as the reincarnated deity in the mestizo mold of two cultures, white and Indian. The Virgin of Guadalupe's indigenous roots can be traced to the female Nahuatl goddess of various names, all related to Tonantzín, signifying Nuestra Madre (Our Mother). It is not by coincidence that the main center of worship for Tonantzín was at the Cerro del Tepeyac, where Guadalupe made her appearance.

    Lanternari isolated a pivotal "moment" in the acculturation process: "All messianic or prophetic movements express a 'moment' in history in which the forces of innovation, anticonservatism and antitraditionalism come together to make a final break with tradition itself" (253–254). It is a special tension-filled time when the ancient and the modern converge to form a new spiritual structure that meets their needs and aspirations. This confrontation between the old and the new, the official and the popular, serves to awaken in the people the need to formulate their beliefs in order to effectively deal with the challenges of the constantly changing society into which they have been thrown.

    The effect of all this turmoil, adjustment, and readjustment was a drive for reform in all spheres of life. If the religious heterogeneity and clash of cultures provided a fertile climate for a new syncretic cult, the intellectual climate in Spain and in Europe as a whole predisposed the immigrant Spaniard not only to readily accept but to expect miraculous events in the New World. The discovery of America itself was viewed as a miraculous omen from God. It was often interpreted as the beginning of the third stage in Christian historical development, the final phase that was to see the rule of the "Holy Spirit and the Woman of Revelation 'clothed with the sun having the moon under her feet'" (Lafaye, 1976:33).

    The Aztecs, too, had a belief in their specialness as a chosen people, the guardians and keepers of the welfare of the universe:

El azteca es entonces un pueblo con una misión. Un pueblo elegido. El cree que su misión es estar al lado del Sol en la lucha cósmica, estar al lado del bien, hacer que el bien triunfe sobre el mal, proporcionar a toda la humanidad los beneficios del triunfo de los poderes luminosos sobre los poderes tenebrosos de la noche. (The Aztecs are therefore a people with a mission. A chosen people. They believe their mission is to be on the side of the Sun in his cosmic battle, to be on the side of Good; to ensure Good triumphs over Evil; to be able to give to humanity all the benefits derived from the victory of the Gods of Light over the Evil Gods of Darkness, of the night.) (Caso, 1964:234)

This belief on the part of both the immigrant Spaniards and the native Americans will be demonstrated in the corridos that I will examine.

Historians see the period 1728–1759 as the time when the cult of Guadalupe solidified in the imaginations of the ruling elite, religious leaders, and castas alike.[6] Various factors contributed to the crystallization and the increasing preeminence of the cult, not least of which was a series of earthquakes, volcanic eruptions, solar eclipses, and epidemics. Of course, the soil had been prepared by the belief in Mexican "specialness" that was rooted firmly in the minds of the people and was gaining acceptance both as a political weapon and as spiritual inspiration:

> The Virgin Mary in her image of Guadalupe, who first appeared to the native Mexicans represented by a humble Indian convert, had endowed the "Americans" with charisma. The identification of Mary with the Woman of Revelation made it possible by reference to prophecies attributed to the apostle Saint John to see in the Marian cult of Tepeyac the announcement of the last times, or at least the end of the Church of Christ, to be replaced by the church of Mary, the church of the last days. Just as God had chosen the Hebrews in order to incarnate himself in Christ his son, so Mary, the redeemer of the last times, she who was to triumph over Antichrist, had chosen the Mexicans. (Lafaye, 1976: 87–88)

Almost three centuries after the first appearance of Guadalupe, a creole priest from Michoacan, Miguel Hidalgo y Costilla, was destined to funnel discontent into the volcanic eruption of the Mexican independence movements. And it was Hidalgo who firmly implanted "the Star of the North," the Virgin of Guadalupe, as the Queen of the young Mexican nation. In the famous Grito de Dolores—"Viva México" ("Long live Mexico!"), "Viva la Virgen de Guadalupe" ("Long live the Virgin of Guadalupe!")—was encased the fuel that ignited the flames of revolt.

In the furious battles that ensued after independence, the Virgin of Guadalupe often served as the standard bearer for one political side or another. In the Guerras de la Reforma (1854–1857), the civil wars that were tearing the nation apart, troubadours sang (Mendoza, 1976:7):

Madre mía de Guadalupe   Mother of Guadalupe
que gane la Religión   Let our Religion win
que protestantes tenemos   We already have Protestants
y corrompen la razón.   And they corrupt reason.

During the explosive years of the Mexican Revolution (1910–1917), the feminine deity of Guadalupe was recruited anew to provide the pivotal moral force to succeed. Generals and ragtag soldiers proclaimed jubilantly the blessings and the protective mantle of Guadalupe as their very own. Guerrilla fighters seized the image of Guadalupe as a symbol of their righteousness; their legitimacy as soldiers and insurgents fighting for what they believed was a just and moral cause.

The corrido translates this phenomenon through marvelously constructed images of moral rightness and sacred intervention. There are no encrusted ornaments or exuberance of imagery in the lyrics of the songs; a tight, seamless cohesion of thought and syntax permeates the terse verses that articulate the powerful events unfolding in the Mexican landscape. An example is the "Tragedia original de los Maderistas dedicada al Sr. Don Francisco I. Madero" ("The Original Tragic verses of the Maderista Troops Dedicated to Mr. Francisco I. Madero," Campos, 1962, vol. 1:145–148):

Levantemos el grito	Let us raise our voices
viva Dios es lo primero	Glory be to God first of all
la virgen de Guadalupe	The Virgin of Guadalupe
Y don Francisco I. Madero. . . .	And Mr. Francisco I. Madero. . . .
Decía Antonio Nevares	Antonio Nevares would say
muchachos, no hay que temer,	Boys, there is nothing to fear
la Virgen de Guadalupe	The Virgin of Guadalupe
nos ha de favorecer. . . .	Will protect us. . . .
A la reina de los cielos	The Queen of the Heavens
es lo que éstos traían de guía	These men did have as a guide
ya cuando entran a pelear	When they begin to fight
se encomiendan a María.	They commend themselves to Mary.

A corrido from the Guerrero Collection underscores the racial nexus between Guadalupe and the Mexicans:

Viva la Guadalupana	Long live Guadalupe
gritaban los insurgentes	Yelled the insurgents
que es la Reina soberana	She is the Sovereign Queen
de los indios de occidente.	of the American Indians.

A threat of invasion by the United States in the second decade of this century propelled the Mexican folk singer to seek the intervention of the Mother of God:

Madre mía Guadalupana	Mother of Guadalupe
échame to bendición	Give me your blessing
ya me voy a la guerra,	I am off to war
ya viene la intervención.	The Intervention is here.
Con gusto daré mi sangre	With pleasure I shed my blood
te lo juro madre amada	I swear to you beloved mother
por no ver nuestra bandera	In order not to see our flag
de otra nación pisoteada.	By another nation defiled.

¡Oh hermosa Guadalupana	Oh beautiful Guadalupe
prenda sagrada y querida!	Sacred and beloved jewel
no permitas que el extraño	Do not let the foreigner
venga a quitarnos la vida.	Take our life away.

("Del peligro de la
Intervención Americana,"
Guerrero Collection)

When the Cristero Rebellion (1927–1929) erupted in peasant villages and towns in central and northern Mexico,[7] one of the most poignant corridos of the era, "Corrido de Valentín de la Sierra," painted the tableau (Bonfil, 1970:37):

Antes de llegar al cerro	Before reaching the hills
Valentín quiso llorar	Valentín wanted to cry
Madre mía de Guadalupe	Mother of Guadalupe
por tu religión me van a matar.	Because of your religion they're going to kill me.

Valentín, facing death, reminds the Virgin of Guadalupe, perhaps in a last effort to seek heavenly succor, of the reason for his precarious situation.

The political value of Guadalupe was still not exhausted. César Chávez, the Mexican-American union organizer, used the image of the Virgin of Guadalupe in the 1960s in his efforts to galvanize farm workers into forming a union. And a public opinion poll by the Instituto Mexicano de Estudios Sociales in Zamora and Saltillo in 1969 showed that 43.8 percent of working-class Mexicans considered the Virgin Mary their most important deity; only 23.1 percent chose God (M. Rodríguez, 1980:78).

THE ARCHETYPE

In the preceding pages I traced the strands of religious, political, and metaphysical thought that give form and substance to the cult of the Virgin of Guadalupe. I also gave a few examples to show how the image of the Virgin of Guadalupe is repeatedly invoked in the corrido. The frequency with which Guadalupe is cited affirms the major role this patron saint has played and continues to play in the development of the Mexican people. In this section I will examine more closely the archetypal appearances of this feminine deity in a supposedly thoroughly masculine genre.

Oral-Formulaic Function

The Protective Mother Goddess archetype appears vividly in classical antiquity in the poignant scene from Homer's *Iliad* that depicts a dejected Achilles summoning his mother, the goddess Thetis:

> But Achilleus weeping went and sat in sorrow apart from his companions beside the beach of the grey sea looking out on the infinite water. Many times

stretching forth his hands he called on his mother: "Since, my mother, you bore me to be a man with a short life, therefore Zeus of the loud thunder on Olympus should grant me honour at least. But now he has given me not even a little. Now the son of Atreus, powerful Agamemnon has dishonoured me, since he has taken away my prize and keeps it."

So he spoke in tears and the lady his mother heard him as she sat in the depths of the sea at the side of her aged father, and lightly she emerged like a mist from the grey water. She came and sat beside him as he wept, and stroked him with her hand and called him by name and spoke to him: "Why then, child, do you lament? What sorrow hath come to your heart now? Tell me, do not hide it in your mind, and thus we shall both know."

(Lattimore, 1951:68)

A more humble example from classical antiquity is found in a poetic invocation attributed to Catullus (1964, poem 63):

> Attis with the scream of a madman fled to the forest
> And there for ever and ever all his life's course
> He was a slave.
> O Holy Mother Lady of might . . .
> Grant that this house where I dwell
> May never know the madness thou canst send
> Drive other men to frenzy drive other men insane.

The gods of Greek and Roman mythology often intervened in the affairs of mortals, choosing sides now with one, now with another, and causing havoc not only in their earthly kingdom but in Mount Olympus as well. It should not be surprising, therefore, to find exquisite literary pieces in which Greeks and Romans call for the aid of their benefactors, be they male or female. In later centuries this legacy from antiquity continued to prosper and flourish in European literatures. The corrido reflects this ancient literary tradition of invoking the gods or goddesses in battle or at a particularly dangerous point of the hero's adventure.

Since the protagonist of the Mexican ballad is often in battle or undertaking dangerous conditions that lead to his death, the invocation or prayer to God becomes an oral-formulaic device. In line with Parry's definition of a formula as a "group of words which is employed regularly under the same metrical conditions to express a given essential idea" (Lord, 1981:4), I examine instances in which the Virgin of Guadalupe appears as a formulaic unit, fulfilling such formal functions as facilitating versification, helping the corridista at the level of line formation, and serving as a mnemonic element.

Close analysis of corrido verses reveals two significant strategies employed by the troubadours in structuring quatrains. One strategy is to use formulaic phrases, such as the following, to provide a ready-made eight-syllable line:

Madre mía Guadalupana	Mother of Guadalupe
Viva la Guadalupana	Long live Guadalupe
La Virgen de Guadalupe	The Virgin of Guadalupe

Divina Guadalupana	Divine Guadalupe
Ay, Virgen de Guadalupe	Oh, Virgin of Guadalupe
Y María Guadalupana	And Mary Guadalupe
Oh hermosa Guadalupana	Oh beautiful Guadalupe
Madre mía de Guadalupe	My mother of Guadalupe

The second strategy is to use the formulaic phrase for purposes of rhyme: Mañana—Guadalupana, Guadalupana—soberana, Indiana—Guadalupana, Guadalupana—Mexicana, Guadalupana—Tapana.

Examples of corrido strophes show some of these formulaic phrases used to structure line and meter:

Madre mía de Guadalupe,	Mother of Guadalupe
Señora mía de San Juan,	My Lady of San Juan
ten piedad de nuestras almas	Have mercy on our souls
¡pues en tus manos están!	For they are in your hands![8]

¡Viva México! Señores,	¡Long live Mexico, Gentlemen!
¡Viva la Guadalupana!	Long live Guadalupe!
y que viva para siempre	And may always live
la Bandera Mexicana.	The Mexican flag.[9]

¡Ay, Virgen de Guadalupe!	Oh, Virgin of Guadalupe!
Madre Nuestra del consuelo	Our Mother of consolation
En menos que se los cuento	In less [time] than I can relate this
Alberto estaba en el suelo.	Alberto was on the ground [dead].[10]

¡Ay qué Madero tan hombre,	Oh Madero was a real man
bonitas son sus *aiciones!*	Great were his actions
Mandó a los cabecillas	He sent all the leaders
echar fuera las prisiones.	To free the prisoners
Madre mía de Guadalupe,	Mother of Guadalupe
Llénalo de bendiciones.	Fill him with your blessings.[11]

Divina Guadalupana	Divine Guadalupe
con esos preciosos dedos	With those precious fingers
échale la bendición	Give your blessing
al señor Cura Morelos.	To Mr. Morelos.[12]

Al veintidos de febrero	The twenty-second of February
siempre se ha de recordar,	Will always be remembered
la Virgen de Guadalupe	The Virgin of Guadalupe
y Dios lo han de perdonar.	And God may forgive him.[13]

¡Viva la Guadalupana!	Long live Guadalupe!
¡Viva México ilustrado!	Long live illustrious Mexico!
¡Vivan las ligas sociales!	Long live the socialist leagues!
también los confederados.	And also the confederates.[14]

The most common epithet is "Madre mía de Guadalupe," an octosyllabic line. This is the preferred meter in corrido versification. It can be incorporated easily into the strophes to supply any line in a quatrain.

With respect to rhyme, it is a felicitous coincidence that *Guadalupana* rhymes with *Mexicana*, providing the corridista with two elements that inject unity and cohesion as well as tightness of structure in the conceptualization of the strophe. Thus with patriotic vehemence the the poet exults (in an ABBA pattern):

Reina mía Guadalupana	My Queen Guadalupe
Perdona nuestra maldad	Forgive our iniquities
ten de nosotros piedad	Have mercy on us
y de la nación mexicana.	And on the Mexican nation. [15]

Mythic Function

De Chasca (1970) amplified Milman Parry's definition of *formula* to encompass a more dynamic and flexible view of oral formula:

> A formula is a habitual device of style or of narrative mode: as verbal expression it is a group of words forming an identical or variable pattern which is used in the same, or similar, or dissimilar metrical conditions to express a given essential idea whose connotative meaning is frequently determined by the extent to which it is modified by poetic context; as narrative mode, it refers to the customary but variable manner in which the verbal matter is to tell a story. (254–258)

This reformulation is based on the premise that

> words are a dynamic not a static, a complex not a simple, a flexible not a rigid, element within any linguistic context, except in a context of scientific exposition. For this reason the habitual use of a phrase in an epic poem does not always cause it to lose its expressive flexibility, its capacity for aesthetic reference or for ironic reversibility. (263)

Chasca is correct in his reevaluation of the formula in the structure of oral poetry. In my analysis of the corrido, the "Madre mía de Guadalupe" formula is more than a mere octosyllabic device that completes a line. The Virgin of Guadalupe generally appears as a protective force in the corrido's mythic structure. In some songs she is an important component at the beginning of the hero's adventure as it was structured by Joseph Campbell in *The Hero with a Thousand Faces* (1973). According to Campbell, the hero's adventure monomyth has a tripartite structure based on *rites de passage*: separation–initiation–return. In this narrative model, the hero, having heard the call to adventure, goes forth into the world to seek knowledge. After many tests and tribulations he or she returns home, bringing the knowledge and wisdom found on the journey. Here Guadalupe can be pinpointed as one of the "helpers," or entities, that provide the hero with some type of aid, be it physical or psychological, in order to successfully continue his or her journey.

A second important role the Virgin plays in many folk songs is at the "final meeting with the Goddess" stage in the hero's journey. According to Campbell this point in the trajectory encompasses "the ultimate adventure, when all the barriers and ogres have been overcome." This stage

> is commonly represented as a mystical marriage . . . of the triumphant hero-soul with the Queen Goddess of the world. Thus is the crisis at the nadir, the zenith, or the uttermost edge of the earth, at the central point of the cosmos, in the tabernacle of the temple, or within the darkness of the deepest chamber of the heart. (Campbell, 1973: 109)

The "Corrido de Martín Díaz" ("Ballad of Martín Díaz," Bonfil, 1970: 26–27) exemplifies the first function, Guadalupe as helper:

1. En el nombre sea de Dios,
voy a empezar a cantar:
corrido de Martín Díaz
que no he podido arreglar.

In the name of the Father
I shall begin to sing
The ballad of Martín Díaz
That I haven't been able to arrange.

2. Que en esa Mesa Redonda
comenzaron a pelear
el veintinueve de octubre,
ni me quisiera acordar.

That in that Round Table
They began to fight
The twenty-ninth of October
I don't even want to remember.

3. Vinieron dos aeroplanos
queriéndonos bombardear:
soldados de Martín Díaz
comenzaron a pelear.

Two airplanes came
Wanting to bomb us
The soldiers of Martín Díaz
Began to fight.

4. ¡Qué vida la de Martín!
¡Qué vida tan arreglada!
de haberse visto en las balas
y ninguna le pegara.

What a life Martín had!
What a gifted life!
To be covered by bullets
And have none hurt him.

5. Sería por las oraciones
que su madre le rezaba,
¡Corre, caballo alzán,
no se te olviden las mañas!

Maybe it was the prayers
That his mother prayed for him,
Run, palomino horse!
Don't forget your tricks!

6. Qué pensarían los muchachos,
que no me sobraban ganas;
he podido con el tercio
cuanto más con las barañas.

What did those boys think?
That I didn't have the nerve?
I've taken care of heavy loads
The light ones are no problem.

7. Gritaba Pedro Velásquez
con una voz muy ladina:
—Nos subimos para el cerro
me llevo mi carabina.

Pedro Velásquez did shout
With a very rebellike voice:
"We will climb the hill
I will take my carbine."

8. La Virgen de Guadalupe
me ha de servir de madrina
otro día por la mañana
ya viene alboreando el día.

The Virgin of Guadalupe
Shall be my godmother
On the following day
The day's dawn does come.

9. Ya no llores mamacita,

Do not cry dear mother

ya estoy en tu compañía.	I am in your company
Aquí termina el corrido	Here ends the ballad
del capitán Martín Díaz.	The ballad of Captain Martín Díaz.

This corrido is a good example of the classic structure delineated by Duvalier (see Introduction). The introductory phrases "En el nombre sea de Dios, / voy a empezar a cantar" give a religious, supernatural aura to the lyric. The invocation, "In the name of the Father," establishes the patriarchal hierarchy evident in most corridos. In the second distich of the first strophe we meet the hero, Martín Díaz.

The second stanza provides the place (Mesa Redonda) and date (twenty-ninth of October), followed by the formulaic phrase "ni me quisiera acordar," which rhymes with "pelear" to provide an ABCB rhyme scheme.

The third strophe describes the action: airplanes bombing the hero's battalions. But in spite of the great danger spoken of in this strophe, the next one situates the hero in an almost supernatural atmosphere, since Martín is not harmed by the bullets. In this aspect the lyric adheres closely to the corrido tradition in which the protagonist is involved in numerous battles but is able by some mysterious force to evade bodily harm.

The fifth stanza further connects the hero with the supernatural by implying that he may be under the special protection of his mother's prayers: "Sería por las oraciones / que su madre le rezaba." Paredes (1971:97–108) demonstrated through the analysis of Mexican legends that during the nineteenth century the mestizo personality evolved from a miraculous, supernatural-oriented world view to a more pragmatic, reality-oriented position. That helps us understand why, just after a supernatural speech act is enunciated, a second one implicitly tries to cancel it: "¡Corre, caballo alazán, / no se te olviden las mañas!" This second distich in the strophe contains two kernels of information that can explain, without recourse to the supernatural, the reason for the hero's multiple escapes: a fast, cunning horse. Furthermore, since hero and horse are often perceived as one entity, the parallel imagery horse = hero implies that the hero also is quick and full of cunning and can evade anyone. The sixth strophe verifies this analysis, since the hero brags about his bravery and prowess.

It is not until stanza eight that we encounter the Virgin of Guadalupe. Here the hero articulates Guadalupe's role as the godmother or helper (madrina), an epithet that falls within the established conventions of traditional myths and fairy tales. As Campbell states:

> The helpful crone and fairy godmother is a familiar feature of European fairy lore; in Christian saints' legends the role is commonly played by the Virgin. The Virgin by her intercession can win the mercy of the Father. . . . The hero who has come under the protection of the cosmic Mother cannot be harmed. . . . This is the guiding power that runs through the work of Dante in the female figures of Beatrice and the Virgin, and appears in Goethe's Faust successively as Gretchen, Helen of Troy, and the Virgin.

Campbell further states that such a figure represents

> the benign, protecting power of destiny. The fantasy is a reassurance—a promise that the peace of Paradise, which was known first within the mother womb, is not to be lost; that it supports the present and stands in the future as well as in the past (is omega as well as alpha); that though omnipotence may seem to be endangered by the threshold passages and life awakenings, protective power is always and ever present within the sanctuary of the heart and even immanent within, or just behind, the unfamiliar features of the world. (1973:71–72)

This view corresponds with the "Ballad of Martín Díaz," for a connection with the mother is made in the last strophe: "Ya no llores mamacita, / ya estoy en tu compañía." The distich is ambiguous, since in most corridos the formulaic phrase "ya estoy en tu compañía" refers to joining God in heaven or joining the dead. Here the verses may be understood to say either that the hero is safe and sound back in his mother's house or that he has died and joined his deceased mother in heaven.

Be that as it may, this corrido demonstrates how the Virgin of Guadalupe appears in the image of the Protective Mother Goddess archetype. Corrido heroes repeatedly invoke this figure to aid them in their trials and tribulations, as is readily seen in other songs:

Madre mía de Guadalupe	Mother of Guadalupe
Tu me haz de favorecer	You shall favor me
para no rendir mis armas	So as not to surrender my weapons
hasta morir o vencer.	Until I win or die.[16]
Con mi "huinche," mi caballo	With my "Winchester," my horse,
y dos canunas	and two belt cartridges
y de escudo la Virgen del Tepeyac	And as shield the Virgin of Tepeyac
he de hacer que se respete el Plan de Ayala	I shall make them respect the Plan of Ayala
o que sucumba cual valiente liberal.	Or let those brave liberals fall dead.[17]

And when death overtakes the hero, the Virgin of Guadalupe is reproached for having failed in her specific function of aiding the hero:

Madre mía de Guadalupe	Mother of Guadalupe
por qué no fuiste mi escudo	Why were you not my shield
de las balas traicioneras?	From those treacherous bullets?
Ahora el crimen mejor pudo.	Now crime has done me in.[18]

The second role of Guadalupe in the corrido, which comes in the meeting with the Goddess stage of the hero's journey, is generally introduced toward the close of the song, when the hero is dying and begs Guadalupe's help in crossing the threshold between the living and the dead. She is sought as a benevolent intermediary between the hero and God. For example, when Valentín de la Sierra dies, his final words are

—¡Madre mía de Guadalupe,	Mother of Guadalupe
a tu amado hijo	To your beloved son
encomiendo mi alma!	I commend my soul![19]

This example shows the theme of dying used to structure poetic closure. Herrnstein Smith (1968), found that the thematic use of death was particularly appropriate for compositions having a "paratactic" structure, "where the coherence of the poem will not be dependent on the sequential arrangement of its major thematic units" (99). Among such compositions she included nursery rhymes, traditional lullabies, and folk songs.

Although the corrido generally does follow a sequence of events in a temporal order (the beginning of the hero's adventure, the trials, death), in theory the verses could continue indefinitely, since the balladeer could compose strophes concerning all aspects of the hero's life. Therefore, to prepare the audience for the conclusion of the ballad, some warning that the death of the hero is at hand is necessary. Such closure in many of these compositions is secured by having the protagonist verbalize his desperate situation, often invoking the help of the Virgin of Guadalupe in his final hour. This technique provides the composition with what Herrnstein Smith terms "a sense of finality, of stability, and integrity" (viii).

CORRIDO AND CANCIÓN

A brief comparison of the Mexican canción, which in general does not exhibit a mythic structure, and the corrido, which follows Campbell's hero monomyth pattern, provides us with significant information regarding the two genres. The lyrics of canciones that contain references to the Virgin of Guadalupe are permeated with intense feelings of nationalism and patriotism. They depict a strong relationship of the Mother of God (Guadalupe) with the Mexican nation as a whole, rather than with one specific individual, as the corrido often does. In the "Ofrenda Guadalupana" canción, for example, the protagonist brings a birthday gift to the Virgin of Guadalupe and implies that she is representative of the Mexican nation. In "Plegaria Guadalupana," the protagonist gives thanks to the Virgin for curing his mother and asks that the Mexican nation be in peace. And in "Virgencita Ranchera," the protagonist proclaims the Virgin to be Queen of Mexico. (For these songs, see the discography, part D in Works Cited and Consulted.)

Two major themes permeate the canción: personal sufferings and nationalistic sentiments about the Virgin of Guadalupe and the Mexican nation. Thus the canción further substantiates Lafaye's thesis that the Guadalupana has been and continues to be an important element in the formation of national consciousness and the perception of "chosen people" status of the Mexicano and the Mexican nation. The two, of course, go hand in hand.

CONCLUSION

The Protective Mother Goddess archetype manifested through the image of the Virgin of Guadalupe in the corrido is an indispensable element in the conceptualization of both the mythic and the formal structure of these songs. At the level of line formation the various formulaic phrases associated with the Virgin of Guadalupe supply the folk poet with splendid ready-made verbal constructions that may be easily incorporated for purposes of meter, rhyme, and strophe formation. At the more transcendental level of mythic structure, the Virgin of Guadalupe archetype assumes the function of helper on the hero's journey to self-knowledge and expansion of consciousness.

Since my rationale for applying archetypal criticism to Mexican ballads is predicated on the assumption that archetypes arise out of a specific historical context and are not inevitable products of the unconscious, a critical question resulting from the incorporation of a female deity into a male-oriented milieu is unavoidable, for Mexico is accused of being a macho country par excellence. This conundrum is not easily explained. Marina Warner offers a plausible explanation for the persistence, acceptability, and popularity of the Virgin Mary:

> But it is this very cult of the Virgin's "femininity" expressed by her sweetness, submissiveness, and passivity that permits her to survive, a goddess in a patriarchal society. For her cult flourishes in countries where women rarely participate in public life and are relegated to the domestic domain. In countries like Ireland, Spain, Portugal, Italy, and Belgium, women are not rallying for her comfort to a symbol that holds out hope of something different from their lives. Mary is worshipped in places where the symbol of the subject housewife applies readily, and therefore both reinforces and justifies the ruling state of affairs, in which women are expected to be, and are, men's devoted mothers and wives. (Warner, 1976:191)

The Virgin of Guadalupe in the Mexican ballad, however, is not necessarily perceived as a frail, submissive, subservient, weak-hearted female. On the contrary, she is conceived as a warrior (indeed, Father José Morelos granted her the rank of general) who can aid the various battalions to achieve victory over their enemies (M. Rodríguez, 1980:56). Guadalupe also is a celestial aristocratic figure (albeit of Indian descent) who has been crowned with monarchical terminology, "Reina de los Mexicanos" ("Queen of the Mexicans"), "Reina de las Américas" ("Queen of the Americas"), and "Emperatriz de América" ("Empress of America"). In paintings and other art work Guadalupe is resplendant in her star-studded robe. She is depicted suspended in the heavens, the sun streaming behind her serving as a backdrop to illuminate her figure and the crescent moon a footstool for her delicate but obviously powerful feet.

Several historical and cultural strands have converged in the figure of Guadalupe to effectively weave her image into the tapestry of politics and become all things to all people. Guadalupe can be perceived as a modern link in the long chain of goddesses who have ruled the earth. As Merlin Stone writes (1978:xii): "In prehistoric and early historic periods of human development, religions existed in which people revered their supreme creator as female. The Great Goddess—the divine Ancestress—had been worshipped from the beginnings of the Neolithic period of 7000 B.C. until the closing of the last Goddess temple, about A.D. 500." Astarte, Isis, Ishtar, Tiamat ruled supreme. Echoes of this memory must reverberate in the collective unconscious with a force too difficult to erase. The early fathers of the Catholic Church realized this attraction and used it for their own purpose: to strengthen the power of the church as an institution. The archbishops of Mexico, with a rebellious, half-Christianized flock on their hands, seized upon the emblem of the Virgin of Guadalupe to bring the masses into mainstream Catholicism and to consolidate their own power in Mexico.

Creole politicians, too, appropriated the symbol of Guadalupe and used it as a powerful political tool in the crystallization of national consciousness. They saw in the emblem of Guadalupe a rallying point for the masses against foreign elements and eventually for coalescing them into a bona fide nation. Once established as a political weapon capable of unifying a nation, the Virgin of Guadalupe was seized repeatedly as the standard bearer for various political causes, fromMiguel Hidalgo y Costilla to Emiliano Zapata to César Chávez.

The Indians, for their part, having lost their gods, sought in the syncretism of Guadalupe-Tonantzín refuge from the onslaughts of Spanish subjugation and oppression, while the newly created mestizo population perceived in Guadalupe the reflection of its own image. Guadalupe soon encompassed the reincarnation of two ancient cultures revitalized and renewed in her image. M. Rodríguez (1980) adds that, to the present-day Mexican, living next to the most powerful and wealthiest country in the world, the Virgin of Guadalupe continues to serve as a psychological defense against pervasive feelings of inferiority that invade the masses because of their poverty-stricken situation. The rationalization runs thus: the United States may have riches, a powerful war machine, and scientific and athletic superiority, but it does not have the most precious gift humans could possibly desire: the Mother of God, Guadalupe (79–80).

The folk poet, cognizant of this awesome power, interlaces the corrido lyrics with the luminous image of the Virgin to interject moral and divine support for the song's hero. This mythic aura parallels that of the Greek hero of antiquity, whose special rapport with a goddess invested the mortal human with invincible prowess and elevated him to a semidivine status. The supernatural presence of the Virgin links modern-day heroes with those of antiquity, underlining the classical heritage of the corrido hero.

At the literary level, the Virgin of Guadalupe archetype provides an important structural component in the mythic conceptualization of the corrido. At the level of strophe formation it supplies a needed octosyllabic line. And at the societal level these folk songs confer dignity and power on women. The Protective Mother Goddess archetype manifested in the corrido is based on solid historical experience and reflects the multifaceted role of women in Mexican society.

❂ 4 ❂

THE LOVER ARCHETYPE

The two important vectors of patriarchal ideology and social class converge in the formation, flowering, and dissemination of the Lover, or Eve, archetypal image in Mexican folk songs. In addition, literary tradition—which was heavily influenced by patriarchal ideology—and the events that transpired in the making of the Mexican nation contributed to the formation of this *"mala mujer"* ("evil woman") image found in Mexican corridos.

Mexico inherited from Spain the general conceptualization of women in Western society. Included among the many negative views of women in Western civilization is the Eve mystique, the woman's role in the loss of paradise for humanity. To this concept Mexico added one of its own. Historians agree that the Mexica-Aztec empire was conquered by the Spaniards with the help of a native woman: La Malinche, or Doña Marina, as Hernán Cortés christened her. La Malinche was Cortés's mistress and political adviser. Seared in the Mexican mind is the image of a woman betraying her nation, her people.

Mexico's historical origins, therefore, specifically involve a woman as betrayer, as traitor to her race, as whore to the conquerors, and as the sullied and tainted mother of the mestizo race that was to surface after the holocaust of the Conquest. The image of the evil, tainted woman inherited from Western conceptualizations was thus given form and substance in the historical specificity of Mexico. Eve and La Malinche became inexorably intertwined, reinforcing each other in the Mexican national consciousness. It is not surprising, then, to find the archetypal image of Eve in the corrido in various manifestations as "La Belle Dame sans Merci" (i.e., coquette and seductress), the disobedient mate or the traitor.

"LA BELLE DAME SANS MERCI"

The motif of "La Belle Dame sans Merci" is firmly anchored in Western literary and artistic expressions, appearing not only in Keats's "La Belle Dame sans Merci" but also in folk tales, legends, and folk poetry.[1] Stith Thompson associated the motif with witches, the feminine incarnations of evil par excellence, declaring that "sometimes witches are pictured as beautiful and attractive women enticing lovers and then deserting them. . . . Such was Keats's La Belle Dame sans Merci and such, indeed, is a whole legion of Circes and Calypsos in both popular and literary tradition" (Thompson, 1977:251).

The dangerous and deadly connotations of the Belle Dame link her image to the Terrible Mother archetype analyzed in chapter 2. The women to be discussed here, however, are young and generally unmarried. They are not technically mothers, as were the women in chapters 1 and 2, but are frequently represented as flirtatious maidens whose coquettish behavior leads inevitably to a tragic denouement. That indicated to me that a separate category was necessary for the beautiful woman who kills or destroys.

The Eve construct is indeed a variation of the Terrible Mother archetype. We can verify this assertion by reviewing some essential characterizations of the Terrible Mother. Neumann informs us that the ominous feminine figure incarnating life-producing and life-destroying properties is associated with Mother Earth itself:

> Disease, hunger, hardship, war above all, are her helpers [Mother Earth's], and among all peoples the goddess of war and the hunt expresses man's experience of life as female exacting blood. This Terrible Mother is the hungry earth, which devours its own children and fattens on their corpses; it is the tiger and the vulture, the vulture and the coffin, the flesh-eating sarcophagus voraciously licking up the blood seed of men and beasts and, once fecundated and sated, casting it out again in new birth, hurling it to death, and over and over again to death. (Neumann, 1974b:149–150)

The terror of death, in a patriarchal culture, is projected onto the figure of a woman; thus we have the nightmarish appearance of the witch, the siren, the femme fatale, the seductress, the devouring vagina:

> The destructive and deathly womb appears most frequently in the archetypal form of a mouth bristling with teeth. We find this symbolism in an African statuette where the tooth-studded womb is replaced by a gnashing mask, and in an Aztec likeness of the death goddess, furnished with a variety of knives and sharp teeth. This motif of the *vagina dentata* is most distinct in the mythology of the North American Indians. In the mythology of the other Indian tribes a meat-eating fish inhabits the vagina of the Terrible Mother: the hero is the man who overcomes the Terrible Mother, breaks the teeth out of her vagina, and so makes her into a woman. (Ibid.:168).[2]

Biologically speaking, the sex act has the potential of producing life; concomitantly, this newly conceived life at its very inception encapsulates within its nucleus the germ of death. It is axiomatic that that which is born dies. Hence at the first sproutings of intellectual musings humanity intuited the strong bond between sexuality and death, between birthing and killing. Thus the objectification of women who kill, maim, and eat other beings appears in numerous world mythologies.

The Greeks had countless deadly feminine figures in their mythological pantheon. Among them were the Poine, who preyed on children. These women were artistically conceptualized with snakelike hair and talons. Another deadly group was the Maenads—also known as "the Mad Ones"—who purportly tore a young boy limb from limb and ate him raw during the annual festival of Dionysus. The Lamia seized infants and fed upon them. Another group targeted unsuspecting young men; their modus operandi was to lure them with their beauty, to seduce them with their sexuality, and finally, after transforming themselves into horrible monsters, to kill these love-struck lads. Medusa's serpent-filled hair inspired terror in those who dared look at her and turned men to stone. The Sphinx meted out punishment to those who failed to decipher her riddle. The Sirens' sensuous singing lured sailors to their death. Scylla, once beautiful, became dog-faced and monsterlike; Echidna, half-woman, half snake, had the reputation of destroying all men who ventured to her side; Charybdis, a voracious young lady, sucked men down her fathomless whirlpool; and Chimera, who had the attributes of goat, lion, and dragon, terrorized all who saw her.

The Middle East had Ishtar, who annually killed her son-lover. The Hebrews write of Lilith, Adam's first "Eve," who was castigated for refusing to acknowledge her mate as her lord and master; deprived of her children, she roams the world abducting and murdering infants. In Brittany, Dahut is famous for killing her lovers, and in Celtic-French folklore the *Dames Vertes* ("Green Ladies") are cruel and seductive forest deities much feared for luring unsuspecting travelers to their death (see Monaghan, 1981; Guthrie, 1971; and Rose, 1959).

In America, the Aztec pantheon likewise is filled with violent, destructive goddesses. Ferdinand Anton, who provides a summary of various pre-Hispanic goddesses in his anthropological study *La mujer en la América antigua* (1973), states that among the Aztec goddesses were such figures as "Coatlicue, 'The Goddess of the Serpent Skirt' also called 'Devourer of Wastes.' She is the goddess of Earth and fertility who gives birth to all and devours all. . . . She devoured everything alive including the stars and planets. Her temple was known as 'The House of Darkness'" (70). Another was Chicomecoatl, or "Seven Serpents Goddess of Corn," to whom human sacrifices were offered. Izapapalotl, "Obsidian Butterfly," was a demonic goddess associated with death, and Mictlanciuatl was the goddess of the world of the dead. Anton includes among these menacing ladies the goddess Tlazolteotl, "Devourer of Wastes":

> She shares many characteristics with Coatlicue and at times are one and the same. She was the goddess of the Huastec region along the gulf coast of Mexico. Later she was worshipped in the highland areas as well. In its Mexican form she had four major attributes which were related to the phases of the moon (also closely related to witchcraft). Under her third attribute she represented purity; the one who cleansed the sins of the impure. The name "Tlazolteotl" itself was associated with the impure; it was commonly used to denote or signify sexual excesses. (70)

We also encounter evil goddesses in the Maya pantheon. Ixcel was "the mother or grandmother of the gods. . . . She had many negative attributes (mostly hostile to man) and symbolized darkness" (71). Another Mayan group was the Ixtabai, "who although exhibiting a feminine appearance, could transform themselves into any figure or object":

> Frequently they metamorphosed into trees (Yaxche) and when men accidentally stumbled upon them they were wont to cause their death. One of these ladies' favorite pastimes was to sit on tree branches, combing their hair, thus attracting young men wandering into the depths of the forest. At other times the Ixtabai transformed themselves into serpents and devoured men by either sequestering them into the underworld or throwing them into a well *(cenote)*. (71)

A mythical figure of more recent vintage is La Llorona, the Weeping Woman. Notorious for her beauty, she wanders in a vain search for her lost progeny, whom she is accused of having murdered. La Llorona is frequently found near bodies of water screeching, "¡Ayyy, mis hijos!" ("Ohhh! My children!"). The legend of La Llorona is one of the most popular and widespread tales in Mexico and the southwestern United States. Its theme of unrequited love and feminine violence against progeny has captured the imagination. Many Chicanos identify themselves as orphans of La Llorona, and her representation often appears as a political symbol in Chicano art and literature.[3]

La Belle Dame appears in the Mexican ballad in two modes. In one she is a Mexican beauty who disobeys a high authority and is punished with death and the death of others. In the other mode she is a young woman who, through her beauty and two-timing nature or treacherous actions, causes the death of a male protagonist and frequently her own. Corridos such as "El 24 de junio" ("The 24th of June"), also known as "Micaela," and "Rosita Alvírez" exemplify the first mode, while corridas such as "La Güera Chabela," also known as "Juan Cadenas," "Los dos hermanos" ("The Two Brothers"), and "Rafaelita" exemplify the second mode.

The Disobedient Eve

"El 24 de junio" has as its underlying theme the disobedient Eve motif. The central conflict in this drama is a confrontation between a rebellious woman, Micaela, and an authority, a man. Juan, the male protagonist, is symbolic of the Law as structured by the patriarchal system.[4] The name *Juan* originally signified "sun" (Amades, 1956:19). In patriarchal mythology the sun is represented by the figure of Apollo, who in turn is equated with "reason."

The initial disobedient act—Micaela's unwillingness to remain in the private domain of the home—precipitates a series of actions that terminate in her death as well as the death of her lover, Simón. The lyrics recapitulate Eve's original disobedient act against male authority—Jehovah's and Adam's—and the subsequent punishment of death—spiritual in the Edenic myth, physical in the corrido.

<table>
<tr><td>

Corrido de Micaela
(El 24 de junio)

1. El 24 de junio,
el mero día de San Juan
un baile se celebraba
en ese pueblo de Ixtlán.

2. Micaela desde temprano
sonriendo le dice a Juan:
"Por ser el día de tu santo
al baile me haz de llevar."

3. —No quiero hacerte el desaire
pero algo presiento yo,
de que esta noche en el baile
se te amargue la función.

4. Te lo diré por claro,
que le recelo a Simón,
Y no permito que bailes
ni le hagas mucho jalón.

5. —Adios, chatito, ya vuelvo

le dijo para sailir.
—Me voy con unas amigas
ya que tú no quieres ir.

6. —Oye, Micaela, que te hablo
no vayas a esa reunión
que me está tentando el diablo
de echarme al plato a Simón.

7. Se fue Micaela primero
se puso luego a bailar
y se encontró de compañero
al mero rival de Juan.

8. Alegres pasan las horas,
las doce marca el reloj,
cuando un tiro de pistola,
dos cuerpos atravesó.

9. Vuela, vuela palomita,
para por ese panteón
donde ha de estar Micaela
con su querido Simón.
(Mendoza, 1964:309–310)

</td><td>

Micaela's Ballad
(The 24th of June)

It was the 24th of June
On the very feast of St. John
A dance was taking place
In that town of Ixtlán.

Micaela, early in the morning
Smilingly said to Juan:
"'Cause it's your saint's day
You have to take me to the dance."

"I don't want to turn you down
But I have a premonition
That tonight at the dance
Your festivity will turn to bitterness.

"I will tell you plainly
I don't trust Simón,
And I don't want you to dance with him
Or lead him on."

"Good-bye, pugnosed-one, I'll be
    back,"
She said as she left.
"I am going with some friends
Since you don't want to go."

"Listen, Micaela, I am speaking to you
Do not go to that dance
For the devil is tempting me
To kill Simón."

Micaela left first
And began to dance
And she found as partner
Juan's very rival.

The hours pass by happily
The clock strikes twelve
When a pistol shot
Pierced two bodies.

Fly, fly little dove
Pass by that cemetery
Where Micaela must be
With her lover Simón.

</td></tr>
</table>

The lyric is permeated with mythic elements and elevated to a cosmic plane through the substratum of sacred rites. These rites, associated with sacrifice, death, and regeneration, infuse more tension into the already electrically charged atmosphere in which the calamitous events transpire.

The folk poet situates the tragic drama in an ambiance saturated with connotations of the sacred. This cosmogonic drama takes place on the twenty-fourth of June, a date impregnated with biblical overtones as the feast day of Saint John the Baptist, Jesus' cousin, who was beheaded at the request of Salome after she performed a sensuous dance for King Herod. The corrido establishes a link between Salome and Micaela since it is a dance that in both cases precipitates the death of a man (and in the corrido the death of the female protagonist as well). The corrido presents the archetypal image of Eve in the guise of flirtatious, disobedient Micaela.

June 24 also reflects an important point in the planetary system: the summer solstice, or midsummer day. On this day the sun is seen at its highest point in the sky. Frazer (1975) suggested that people could not help but experience awe, wonder, and a certain helplessness coupled with fear at this climactic moment in the sun's odyssey:

> But the season at which these fire-festivals have been most generally held all over Europe is the summer solstice, that is Midsummer Eve (the twenty-third of June) or Midsummer Day (the twenty-fourth of June). A faint tinge of Christianity has been given to them by naming Midsummer Day after St. John the Baptist, but we cannot doubt that the celebration dates from a time long before the beginning of our era. The summer solstice, or Midsummer Day, is the great turning-point in the sun's career, when after climbing higher and higher day by day in the sky, the luminary stops and thenceforth retraces his steps down the heavenly road.
>
> Such a moment could not but be regarded with anxiety by primitive man so soon as he began to observe and ponder the courses of the great light across the celestial vault; and having still to learn his own powerlessness in face of the vast cyclic changes of nature, he may have fancied that he could help the sun in his seeming decline—could prop has failing steps and rekindle the sinking flame of the red lamp in his feeble hand. (Frazer, 1975:720–721)

Frazer noted the prevalence of Midsummer Eve rites throughout Europe and Russia and even among the Muslim peoples of North Africa, particularly Morocco and Algeria (719–723, 731–732). Three main features of these summer rites have been observed: "the bonfires, the procession with torches round the fields, and the custom of rolling a wheel." Smoke supposedly "drove away certain noxious dragons which at this time, excited by the summer heat, copulated in the air and poisoned the wells and rivers by dropping their seed into them," while the custom of "trundling a wheel meant that the sun, having now reached the highest point in the ecliptic, begins thenceforward to descend."

In addition to the preoccupation with the sun and its celestial trajectory, the folk linked the date and its astronomic phenomenon with the fertility of the soil, of animals, and of humans themselves. In Swabia, for example, "lads and lasses, hand in hand, leap over the midsummer bonfire, praying that the hemp may grow three ells high, and they set fire to wheels of straw and send them rolling down the hill. Sometimes, as the people sprang over the midsummer bonfire they cried out 'Flax, flax! May the flax this year grow seven ells high!'" Frazer pointed out that

> the belief of all the people that by leaping thrice over the bonfires or running thrice between them they ensured a plentiful harvest is worthy of note. The mode in which this result was supposed to be brought about is indicated by another writer on Welsh folk-lore, according to whom it used to be held that "the bonfires lighted in May or Midsummer protected the lands from sorcery, so that good crops would follow. The ashes were also considered valuable as charms." Hence it appears that the heat of the fires was thought to fertilise the fields, not directly by quickening the seeds in the ground but indirectly by counteracting the baleful influences of witchcraft or perhaps by burning up the persons of the witches.

Celebration of the feast day of John the Baptist is widespread in Spain. The Spaniards helped disseminate the tradition throughout the American continent along with other religious beliefs:

> although this festival originates from antiquity—is of mythic origins—coincid-ing with the spring solstice, with the adoration of the sun, it has become a religious celebration, in which all of Spain pays homage to the birth of the precursor of the Good News, to the messenger of the Eternal. This form is reminiscent of those celebrating pagan rites and superstitions rejected by Catholics, but accepted without thinking by the townspeople. All the regions celebrate the eve of St. John, and it is without a doubt the holiday that has a greater variety of elements and forms of celebrating it. The principal forms of celebrating it are fire and water: the first symbolizes the burning sun, which beats on the fields, toasting the wheatfields, while we see the water returning to refresh them, preparing them for the new sprouts. We have in this night all kinds of bonfires, games, and songs. (De Hoyos Sainz, 1985:396)

The connection between sensuality, fertility rites, and this feast day is reiter-ated in the dancing and young lovers' activities that transpire on this night:

> The garlands are another element pertaining to this night belonging to lovers. Here the young lads show their love interests by adorning with garlands the doors or windows of their beloveds. The verdant garlands, arc shaped, are decorated with flowers, with unripened cherries and apples. In other places they leave baskets full of candies and fruits, handkerchiefs or ribbons, or some other piece of adornment. (397)

Sex and death, too, are intimately linked here: "The mocking personality of the Aragonese punishes on this night the pride and coquetry of some young maidens by placing on their windows instead of garlands, a skeleton or a bone from an animal."

All these connotations of rites and sacrifice offered to the cosmos resonate in the happenings narrated in the "Corrido de Micaela." The audience, sharing the cultural background of the balladeer, receives the encoded message and intuits the tragedy that will unfold.

The confrontation between the two strong wills of the protagonists is delineated through the first four strophes. Micaela, willful and coquettish, announces her plans to attend the dance that is scheduled in the town of Ixtlán in honor of the feast day of Saint John. Two sacro-mythic aspects appear in the first stanza. Here Micaela is construed in the double role of Eve the Rebel and Eve the Seductress who, with coquettish smile, *orders* Juan—note the imperative *haz*—to escort her to the dance. Mythic and sacred themes are reiterated in the elements of the día de santo as well as the dance motif. A día de santo in Hispanic culture is for the most part the day a person celebrates his or her birthday. Hence we have in the lyrics the juxtaposition of death—rapidly and inexorably approaching—with the phenomenon of birth; the two are linked in a dynamic chain underscoring the cyclical nature of the biological rhythm of life. The birth and death processes, the two most transcendental points in a person's life, are impregnated with mythic connotations and intimately bound from the very beginning of the narrative, transforming the corrido into a magico-cosmic ritual similar to that found in classical Greek tragedy.

Anthropological studies have demonstrated the mythic elements informing the dance motif, which is suffused with affectivity, sensuality, and sexuality. Cirlot (1950:721) points to its significance as a symbol of the coming and passing of time. For Eliade the dance constitutes an archetype:

> All dances were originally sacred; . . . they had an extrahuman model. The model may in some cases have been a totemic or emblematic animal, whose motions were reproduced to conjure up its concrete presence through magic, to increase its numbers, to obtain incorporation into the animal on the part of man. In other cases the model may have been revealed by a divinity . . . or by a hero. The dance may be executed to acquire food, to honor the dead, or to assure good order in the cosmos. It may take place upon the occasion of initiations, of magico-religious ceremonies, of marriages, and so on. . . . What is of interest to us is its presumed extrahuman origin (for every dance was created *in illo tempore*, in the mythical period, by an ancestor, a totemic animal, a god, or a hero). . . . a dance always imitates an archetypal gesture or commemorates a mythical moment. In a word, it is a repetition, and consequently a reactualization, of *illu tempus*, "those days." (Eliade, 1974:28–29)

The dance motif in this corrido functions as a significant element in the structuring of a mythico-cosmic universe.

The third stanza foreshadows the shedding of blood. Juan confides to Micaela his premonition of an impending catastrophe, of unfortunate events to unfold that will mar the happy festivities. And in the fourth strophe Juan is forthright in forbidding Micaela to dance with his "rival," Simón. Here the authoritative voice of the male forcefully articulates the interdiction we know Micaela will transgress.

Paredes clearly stated the unenviable dilemma in which a young girl may find herself at dances owing to the stringent patriarchal code:

> Taking a girl out for a dance was the most common cause for violence. The girls sat with their mothers or with other older women, and it was not until the music started that men crossed over and asked the girls of their choice for that particular dance. Being refused a dance was considered as much of an affront as a slap in the face. On the other hand, custom gave a girl's true love the right to prohibit her from dancing with anyone else, or to keep her from dancing with certain persons only. Her brothers or other close male relatives had the same privilege. So a girl often found herself in a position where she could start an uproar whether she danced or not. (Paredes, 1953:111)

Micaela, however, is not an innocent maiden but feels free to go out with her girlfriends—not her mother or other older relatives—and seems to have a second admirer on the side. She is not a shrinking violet but an aggressive, flirtatious woman.

In the fifth strophe that parallelism between Eve and Micaela becomes apparent: both are rebellious, disobedient women who deliberately challenge male authority. In both cases they are severely castigated for their temerity. Micaela, not content with openly disobeying the male, includes a calculated insult in her leavetaking. "Adios, chatito, querido" implies more than it says, for cleverly masked inside the diminutive epithet "chatito"—supposedly a term of endearment—is the greatest of affronts to a male. The term *chato*—meaning a person with a flat, short nose—is usually applied to women. The roles here have been reversed; encoded in Micaela's "chato" is a taunting message: "I am the one that rules in this house. You are the female here." The suffix -*to*, which denotes "little," "small," or "insignificant," is equally charged with pejorative connotations when hurled at the male. The mocking tone of the whole line was a direct challenge to Juan's patriarchal authority.

The sixth stanza depicts Juan recuperating from the attack on his masculinity and his authority by reiterating: "Do not go to that dance." The interdiction "For the devil is tempting me / To kill Simón" conjures up two threatening mythic elements that should have frightened Micaela into submission: death and the devil. The devil, of course, is an archetypal image that incarnates the essence of evil. As Satan, or Lucifer, he is closely associated with Eve, for it was he in the guise of a serpent who tempted the biblical first mother into tasting the forbidden fruit, the disobedient act that led to humanity's mythical expulsion from paradise. Again, a reversal of roles is seen: the devil is now tempting the male protagonist in this drama. The appearance of the maleficent figure of Satan increases the tension in the narrative, and the lyric becomes infused with the smell and taste of blood, the odor of impending death. A series of parallel incidents foreshadows the catastrophic denouement: Lucifer, for instance, was victorious in tempting Eve to taste the forbidden fruit, and Eve was likewise successful in tempting Adam; the parallel structure of the temptation motif becomes apparent, and we can deduce that the devil will again be successful in tempting Juan.

The spilling of blood is now inevitable. The phrase "echarme al plato" (literally, "to put in my plate"; figuratively, "to kill") invites an association of the ritual killing that is to take place with other primitive rites, such as cannibalism: "To eat the enemy; to ingest his/her flesh is to ritually devour the violence that the enemy signifies" (Girard, 1984:277).

Micaela, strong-willed and independent, wantonly disregards Juan's order and proceeds to the dance. Upon arrival she breaks his second order: "Do not dance with Simón."

The introductory line of the eighth strophe describes the happy, carefree rhythm of time passing by. The second line of the distich, however, abruptly halts time forever and catapults it into eternity: "las doce marca el reloj." All of a sudden time is dissolved into its true mythic nature, infinity. For as long as these lyrics are sung time will forever be twelve o'clock—midnight, that special interval when it is neither day nor night but infinity. It is the sacred hour of the cosmos when death (the death of the previous day) and birth (the birth of a new day) meet and merge in a moment of timelessness, the time of *illo tempore*, before the creation of the stars and planets, before the creation of the universe.

And it is precisely at this magico-sacred hour that the murder is enacted: "When a bullet from a pistol / Pierced two bodies." In the terse, matter-of-fact style of the corrido the violent scene of love and death, of eros and thanatos, is consummated. One clean shot traverses two bodies and rivets them in the final embrace of death.

The earlier happiness, joy, and energy of the dancers contrasts sharply with the events that follow. The cosmic dancers, totally enveloped in their ecstatic dance, live a moment of plenitude, in complete innocence of the approaching chaos. The pistol fire that engulfs them annihilates the verve and energy emanating from their bodies. The tension is magnified by the juxtaposition of the two dynamic energies opposed and yet in rhythm with each other— temporality and biological life symbolized in the rhythmic movement of the dance. Life is completely in tune with the temporal aspects of the universe; yet time eventually extinguishes life, and death overtakes the dancers. The bard then ends his narrative on a triumphant note, on the side of the lovers, Micaela and Simón. Breaking the barriers between life and death, the troubadour offers an image of the lovers side by side, their atoms commingling forever, joined in an ultimate embrace beyond death.

In this corrido the archetypal image of Eve, the woman who disobeys Jehovah and tastes the forbidden fruit, thus serves as a structuring element. The woman once again is depicted as the instigator and perpetrator of tragic deeds. With her beauty and her coquetry, woman (Eve) is able to subvert patriarchal order. Micaela's disobedient, rebellious self is analogous to Eve in the Garden of Eden. Both women transform the equilibrium in the patriarchal universe. According to patriarchal conceptualizations of women, Eve and Micaela are both guilty of seducing males into a series of nefarious and destructive actions that bring death and violence into the world.

The Two-Timing Eve

The corrido "Los dos hermanos" tells a mythological story of fraternal strife, a conflict initiated by love for the same woman. The "enemy brothers" motif appears frequently in myth, folklore, and literature. The biblical Cain and Abel are the archetypal pair representing the most extreme form of sibling rivalry, which ends in violent death. The confrontation between Cain and Abel was said to be the first crime, the mythical origin of killing and murdering one's "brother." The Bible recounts other examples of fraternal rivalry. Esau and Jacob, Isaac's two sons, vie for the blessings of their father; Joseph is sold to strangers by his eleven jealous brothers.

In classical Greek literature, Sophocles' *Oedipus at Colonus* tells of the fraternal conflict between Eteocles and Polyneices, two secondary characters in the drama, who fight to their death over the right to rule Thebes. In folklore we generally have three brothers competing against each other, with the youngest frequently being victorious in the quest for riches, a princess, or other goals.[5]

In "Los dos hermanos," we see the archetypal image of the woman as evil two-timer coming between two brothers and causing their death.

Los dos hermanos	The Two Brothers
1. Este es el nuevo corrido que yo les vengo a cantar, de dos hermanos muy buenos que tuvieron que pelear.	This is the new corrido That I've come to sing About two good brothers Who had to fight.
2. Juan Luis uno se llamaba y el otro José Manuel y empezaron las discordias por una mala mujer.	One was named Juan Luis The other was José Manuel And the conflict began Over a bad woman.
3. Iba Juan Luis a una fiesta con la mujer que quería, esto presente lo tengo, el año treinta corría.	Juan Luis was going to a party With the woman he loved This I remember well The year '30 it was.
4. Y en eso llegó su hermano con la guitarra en la mano, y empezó cantando versos como retando a su hermano.	Suddenly his brother arrived With a guitar in his hand, And he started singing verses As if challenging his brother.
5—Mira, Juan Luis, que te digo que esa mujer ya fue mía. —No tengo la culpa, hermano, eso yo no lo sabía.	"Listen, Juan Luis, to what I say That woman was mine already." "It is not my fault, brother, I did not know that."

6. A su muy buena pistola	For his trusty pistol
José Manuel echó mano,	José Manuel reached
de dos balazos mató	And with two bullets killed
a la mujer de su hermano.	His brother's woman.

7. —José Manuel, lo que has hecho	"José Manuel, what you've done
hoy mismo te va a pesar,	You will regret this very day
mataste lo que quería,	You've killed the one I loved.
con tu vida has de pagar.	You will pay with your life."

8. Se salieron para afuera	The two went outside
y se oyeron dos disparos,	And two shots were heard,
y en el quicio de una puerta	And in a doorway
los dos hermanos quedaron.	The two brothers fell.
(Mendoza, 1964:308)	

The anonymous two-timing woman is blamed for the tragic events that transpire. The juxtaposition between the two "good brothers" and the "bad woman" is made in the introductory strophes. The archetypal function of the "evil" feminine is highlighted in the contrast between the named, individualized brothers, Juan Luis and José Manuel, and the anonymous female—called only by the pejorative adjective *bad* and the generic *woman*. As in the "Corrido de Micaela," a mythic atmosphere surrounds the killing; events transpire at a fiesta. The term *fiesta* derives from *festival*, which in archaic times had as its primary function the sacrificial rite ("sacrifice and festival are one and the same rite," Girard, 1970:196). Freud (1950:135) stated that "there is no gathering of a clan without an animal sacrifice, nor . . . any slaughter of an animal except on these ceremonial occasions."

The connotation of mythic time is conveyed in the ballad by its lack of temporal specificity. Although a year apparently is cited ("el año treinta corría"), the failure to identify the century in which the confrontation took place hurls events into indefinite, mythic time. Erasing the boundaries of space and time, the corrido enters the realm of the sacred.

The fourth stanza underscores the power of words. *Homo logos*, reasoning man, has structured a world in which words can kill. Thus the confrontation begins with language; more specifically, with an artistically created form of speech: musically articulated verses. The *reto*, or challenge, is transmitted ritually through the formulaic medium of the poetic expression. A linkage thus is accomplished between the corridista and José Manuel, the singing protagonist. One is the mirror image of the other, forming a chain of fraternal violence.

The theme of culpability appears in the fifth strophe. The dyad guilty–innocent is constructed on the biblical commandment "Thou shall not covet thy neighbor's wife." In this instance it carries even more weight, since it is a brother's "woman" who is involved and the incest taboo comes into play. But Juan Luis, although involved in a relationship with his brother's woman, is not completely guilty; like Oedipus, who marries his mother, he was not cognizant of the kinship tie. Juan Luis parallels the tragic hero described by Freud:

> The Hero of tragedy must suffer; to this day that remains the essence of a tragedy. He is to bear the burden of what was known as "tragic guilt"; the basis of that guilt is not always easy to find, for in the light of our everyday life it is often no guilt at all. As a rule it lay in rebellion against some divine or human authority; and the Chorus accompanied the Hero with feelings of sympathy, sought to hold him back, to warn him and to sober him, and mourned over him when he had met with what was felt as the merited punishment for his rash undertaking. (Freud, 1950:156)

Juan Luis insists on his innocence by invoking his lack of knowledge of the facts, the preexisting sexual relationship between his beloved and his brother. By thus stating his case Juan Luis implies that had he been aware of the relationship he would not have touched his brother's lover. This assertion in turn connotes a knowledge of the incest prohibition, and no doubt Juan Luis realizes the danger he is in. Freud is clear on this point:

> The prohibition of incest . . . has a practical basis as well. Sexual desires do not unite men but divide them. Though the brothers had banded together in order to overcome their father, they were all one another's rivals in regard to the women. Each of them would have wished, like his father, to have all the women himself. The new organization would have collapsed in a struggle of all against all, for none of them was of such overmastering strength as to be able to take on his father's part with success. Thus the brothers had no alternative, if they were to live together, but . . . to institute the law against incest, by which they all alike renounced the women whom they desired and who had been their chief motive for dispatching their father. (144)[6]

The guilt directed at Juan Luis is deflected and now centers on the woman previously characterized by the precognizant balladeer as "bad." From the folk poet's perspective she must have known of her involvement with the two brothers and therefore was classified as a "bad woman." José Manuel, upon learning who the guilty party is, takes his instrument of violence—his pistol— and with two shots kills "his brother's woman." The pistol parallels the guitar in the fourth strophe; the guitar was the instrument with which the verbal duel began, and the gun serves as the instrument with which the second duel commences. The two bullets that kill the woman foreshadows the death of the two brothers; the numerical adjective *two*, reiterated throughout the lyrics, links this death scene with the impending death of the two brothers.

The final verses recount the death of the two men. Death is transmitted by auditory stimulation: the sound of the two shots. The action, therefore, takes place in the imagination of the audience, where the two shots reverberate with the ominous blast of death. The final death scene is imbued with mythical connotations and most significantly meshes the murder site with the feminine, as the two brothers fall "in a doorway." Cirlot (1982:85) notes that the door is "a feminine symbol which, notwithstanding, contains all the implications of the symbolic hole, since it is the door which gives access to the hole. . . ." The door as a hole may symbolize either an entrance to life or an exit from life.

Here again we see the corrido providing a multifaceted perspective on the role of women in Mexican society. Although these two examples of the Eve archetype present women who deviate from the patriarchal code and become victims of male aggression, I should point out that in the corrido women are not always portrayed as the victims of male violence. In many instances they are the perpetrators of violent acts themselves. Some corridos, such as "Juanita Quiroz" and "Camelia La Tejana," show women cold-bloodedly murdering their husbands or lovers. I selected these two corridos because of their popularity and the mythic structure underlying the framework of the songs. They are classic ballads which the people have particularly embraced and made their own. That implies, of course, a certain attitude toward women, i.e., these folk feel more comfortable with male violence toward women than its opposite.

THE TRAITOR EVE

The archetypal figure of Eve as betrayer derives from her role in the Garden of Eden. Biblical scriptures recount how Eve betrayed the trust and love of Jehovah and sided with his archenemy, Lucifer, in the guise of a serpent. She again "betrays" Adam, her mate, by knowingly seducing him into eating the forbidden fruit and thereby relinquishing the right to live in paradise.

Mexican history has been bedeviled by traitors. Santa Ana is perceived as a traitor for selling what is now the southwestern United States in 1848; Francisco I. Madero was betrayed by one of his trusted men and shot to death; Emiliano Zapata was killed by a treacherous bullet; and Francisco Villa was ambushed and murdered.[7]

But the Mexican figure par excellence signifying betrayal has been a woman—Doña Marina, La Malinche, accused of selling out to the Spaniards, of betraying her countrymen, the Aztecs, to the European conquerors. Bernal Díaz del Castillo, the soldier-historian, recounted in his down-to-earth style the origins of Cortés's lover:

> Que su padre y madre eran señores y caciques de un pueblo que se dice Painala, y tenía otros pueblos sujetos de Guazcacualco; y murió el padre, quedando muy niña, y la madre se casó con otro cacique mancebo, y hubieron un hijo, y según pareció, queríanlo bien al hijo que habían habido; acordaron entre el padre y la madre de darle el cacicazgo después de sus días, y porque en ello no hubiese estorbo, dieron de noche a la niña doña Marina a unos indios de Xicalango, porque no fuese vista, y echaron fama que se había muerto. Y en aquella sazón murió una hija de una india esclava suya y publicaron que era la heredera; por manera que los de Xicalango la dieron a los de Tabasco, y los de Tabasco a Cortés. (Her father and mother were lords and rulers of a town called Painala, and held other towns as subjects from Guazcacualco; and the father

died while she was very young, and the mother married another young chief
and they had a male child, and it seems they loved him well; the mother and
father decided to make him their heir after he came of age, and so as not to
have any impediment they gave away in the night the little girl Doña Marina to
some Indians from Xicalango, so as not to be seen and sent word she had died
and during that time a slave's daughter died and they [Doña Marina's mother
and stepfather] announced the heir [Doña Marina] had died; so it was that the
people from Xicalango gave her to the people from Tabasco and the people
from Tabasco gave her to Cortés.) (Díaz del Castillo, 1967:56–57)

Thereafter Malinche becomes "La Lengua"—"The Tongue," or interpreter
for Cortés. Doña Marina proves to be a sagacious and brilliant diplomat who
cleverly counsels Cortés in the intricacies of Aztec and other Mesoamerican
Indian political and military strategies. It is readily admitted by most historians
that Doña Marina was instrumental in helping Cortés achieve his diplomatic
and military victories over the local populations.[8] For this role La Malinche has
been reviled in history, her name associated with betrayal and treason.

Earlier I discussed how many Mexican intellectuals, the most prominent
being Octavio Paz, feel about this historical figure. A reevaluation of Malinche
has been undertaken by Chicana scholars, most notably Adelaida del Castillo,
who views her as a much maligned figure. Del Castillo (1975:124–149) sees
Malinche not as a betrayer of her race but as one who had converted to the
religion of the conquerors and was thereafter a Christian activist who wished to
share Catholicism with her countrymen.

Be that as it may, the *traidora* figure has a pivotal role in many corridos. The
internal structure of the valiant-hero corridos may be represented by a circle
that begins and ends with the death of the hero. The narrative unfolds and
evolves between the two axial points of death; as we trace the path of this circle,
it is obvious that the dramatic thread of the narrative reaches its pivotal axis at
the point of betrayal. The process of ascent and descent of the hero is inter-
changed in a dynamic and vertiginous zigzag of emotionally charged scenes that
are masterfully orchestrated to elicit an affective response in the listener. Thus
the significant planes that structure the action follow the pattern Death—
Adventure—Betrayal—Death.

The axis on which the action rotates toward its inevitable finale and through
which the tragic destiny of the hero is accomplished is the treachery and
betrayal of the protagonist by a woman. In this manner, the women who appear
in the lyrics, although playing a secondary role in the sociohistorical drama,
serve the function of anti-heroes, or anti-heroines to be more precise.

A fine example of the schema is the "Corrido de Valentín Mancera" (Guerrero, 1924), which begins:

Escúchame prenda amada	Listen, my beloved one
hermosa flor de Jasmín	Beautiful jasmine flower.
escucha los tristes versos	Listen to the sad verses
del valiente Valentín.	Of the valiant Valentín.

Día lunes, trece de marzo
que desgracia sucedió
se balearon con la escolta,
Cipriano Méndez murió.

It was Monday, March the 13th,
What a tragic day it was.
In a shootout with the Army
Cipriano Méndez died.

Era Cipriano el segundo
de la gente de Mancera
que odiaba a los gachupines
en Acámbaro y por fuera.

Cipriano was the second one
The second Mancera man to die.
He hated gachupines
In and out of Acámbaro.

Su madre triste decía
—Válgame Dios, Valentín,
¿hasta cúando te reduces?
¿Cúal será tu último fin?

His poor mother would say,
"My dear God, Valentín,
When will you settle down?
What will your end be?"

Valentín le contestó:
—No llores, madre adorada,
vale más morir peleando
que correr de la acordada.

Valentín answered her:
"Do not cry dear mother.
It is better to die fighting
Than to run from the federal soldiers."

The corridista's invitation to listen to the "sad verses" of Valentín immediately transports the audience into the tragic path of the hero. In addition, the omens and premonitions that envelop the hero (the death of Crispín; the premonitions felt by Valentín's mother, the date [March 13], the words *sad, tragedy, death*) all prepare the audience for Valentín's death.

The danger awaiting Valentín is reiterated with great dramatic impact in the ninth stanza:

Pero un amigo le dijo:
—No quieras a esa mujer.
Le contestó Valentín:
—Pues es todo mi querer.

But a friend warned him:
"Do not love that woman."
Valentín answers:
"She means everything to me."

Should there be any doubt left about Valentín's impending danger, the verses that follow erase it:

Llegó y le tocó la puerta
con muchísimo contento
y le dijo la muy ingrata
—Pasa, Valentín adentro.

He arrived and knocked
A very happy man was he;
And the ingrate woman said,
"Come on in, Valentín."

The circle is closed, and Valentín is catapulted toward the tragic end that awaits him. In the eighteenth stanza we find Valentín unarmed:

La San Juana le decía:
—¿Qué dices, ya lo entregamos
Trecientos pesos nos dan,
con ellos nos remediamos.

San Juana repeatedly says to her:
"Shall we turn him in now?
Three hundred pesos we get;
They sure will come in handy."

The two female conspirators proceed to get Valentín drunk and then drug him
with opium. Thereafter, death does not tarry. Valentín is delivered into the
hands of his enemy, the hated Catalán:

Luego llegó Catalán	Then Catalán arrived
a la casa de San Juana	At San Juana's house
y mandó darle balazos	And ordered Valentín shot
cual perro, de una ventana.	Like a stray dog.

Toward the close of the ballad, the corridista restates the betrayal motif:

Mancera nació en San Juan	Mancera was born in San Juan
y en San Juan de Dios quedó	And it was in San Juan he died
Y se nombraba San Juana	And the woman was San Juana
la infame que lo entregó.	The wretch that betrayed him.

This corrido, which appeared circa 1882, is one of the first to portray the
death of a hero who rebels against the established social order. It belongs to the
guerrilla fighters cycle. Social conditions in Mexico stimulated the flowering of
the genre. It was the period preceding the Mexican Revolution when the
dictator Porfirio Díaz was in power and ruled with iron-fisted cruelty. The
masses, chafing under this politically repressive regime and rampant poverty,
applauded anyone who challenged the ruling class.[9] This type of song, in which
the feats of revolutionary heroes are extolled, peaked during the Revolution.

It was also during this tumultuous period that the "Corrido de Benito
Canales" (Mendoza, 1976:184–188) appeared. The lyrics depict the circumstances surrounding the death of Canales, a rebel fighting against the Federales
(the Federal soldiers). We again confront hero and anti-hero, the latter in the
form of a woman, playing their tragic roles.

Año de mil novecientos	It was in the 1900s
en el trece que pasó	1913 that just ended
murió Benito Canales	That Benito Canales died
el Gobierno lo mató.	The government killed him.

This sparsely written stanza immediately informs the audience of the death of
the hero. The theme of love is then added to the theme of death, for Benito
Canales was meeting his lover, Isabel, in the town of Surumuato, Guanajuato
state:

Andaba tienda por tienda	He was going store by store
buscando tinta y papel	Looking for pen and ink
para escribirle una carta	In order to write a letter
a su querida Isabel.	To his beloved Isabel.

It is not Isabel who betrays him but an anonymous "mujer tapatía," a woman
from the Tapatía (Guadalajara) region:

Una mujer tapatía	It was a Tapatía woman
fue la que les dio razón.	Who betrayed him.
—Ahorita acaba de llegar.	"He has just arrived!
Váyanse sin dilación.	Go without delay!"

Cuando la tropa eso oyó	When the troops heard the news
pronto rodearon la casa	They surrounded the house
esa ingrata tapatía	That ingrate Tapatía
fue causa de su desgracia.	Was the cause of his death.

Treachery and betrayal seal the fate of the hero, and the battle between Benito and the Federales ends as promised with his death:

Aquí termina el corrido	Here this ballad ends
de Don Benito Canales	Benito Canales' song
una mujer tapatía	It was a Tapatía woman
lo entregó a los federales.	Who betrayed him to the Federal troops.

The archetypal figure of the traidora, or Treacherous Woman, also appears in corridos written after the 1930s. Once again there are numerous ballads in which the theme of treachery plays an important role in the fall of the hero. An example is a drug-smuggling song entitled "El regio traficante."[10] The protagonist's lover betrays him to the *rinches* (Texas Rangers), archenemies of the Chicano population and the northern counterparts of the hated Federales.[11]

Al lugar donde el llegaba	At the place he used to go
ella lo fue a recibir	She went to meet him
y los rinches lo rodearon	And the Rangers surrounded him.
ya no era posible huir.	It was impossible to flee.

Rodolfo pensó en rendirse	Rodolfo thought of surrendering
cuando rodeado se vio	When he was surrounded
pero prefirió morirse	But he preferred to die
y fue quien el fuego abrió	So it was he who opened fire
llevándose por delante	Taking with him
a la que lo denunció.	She who betrayed him.

Close examination of these corrido lyrics reveals why this particular figure plays such a prominent role in Mexican balladry. The scene of betrayal in the songs is indispensable. The hero must exhibit almost supernatural powers of skill, bravery, and ability to demolish his enemies. Therefore, since the corrido's subject matter is the death of the hero, a plausible explanation of his defeat must be given.

A hero may lose his luck in various ways: sometimes through a self-destructive quality in himself, expressed by such words as *fey* or *hybris*, sometimes through the kind of accident that is clearly not quite an accident, such as the death of Achilles through a wound in his vulnerable heel. Most commonly,

however, the hero is brought down by some form of *froda,* usually some
magical or other power which may be physically weak but is strong in other
areas that the hero cannot control. Such a power is often wielded, or symbolized, by a treacherous woman. (Frye, 1976:68)

The corridista, however, does have an option as to the gender of the person
selected to betray the hero. There are many male traitors in Mexican ballads.
The principal difference between the two figures is the erotic factor connected
with the female. The male generally betrays for money, whereas the female may
do it either for money or for some other reason not explicitly stated by the folk
poet. The archetypal image of the Treacherous Woman is obviously negative.
Corridos depicting the heroic exploits of Mexican fighting men need such a
negative figure, male or female, to precipitate the hero's descent. The folk poet,
cognizant of this fact, avails himself of the Treacherous Woman archetype,
inherited from both archaic and modern cultures.

CONCLUSION

Although the Mexican lovers, or Eves, I have discussed in this chapter are
portrayed as harbingers of death, on closer examination we see that the songs
actually illuminate the ideological constructs on which these images are based:
they are socializing agents designed to instruct, coerce, and frighten rebellious
and unruly young women into "proper" behavior. The ballads are literally
ejemplos, or exempla, designed to instill conformity in young maidens who
might be foolish enough to transgress the social norms instituted by the
patriarchal order.

The very need to structure such corridos indicates that Mexican women were
not as submissive and passive as we have been led to believe. If they had been,
there would be no need for such songs. Furthermore, these corridos' strong
appeal to the popular imagination points to the multivalent meaning encoded in
the lyrics.

The Treacherous Woman in the Mexican ballad differs from the two other Eve
figures in that although it is again a young, usually attractive woman who
catapults the hero to his death, the literary figure is a construct of poetic
invention, poetic license, and actual historical events. Although in the Mexican
historical and political landscape the majority of recorded traitors have been
males, La Malinche, as we have seen, provides an important exception. The folk
poet utilizes the *traidora* motif based on literary tradition, on the ever-present
Eve archetype which is shared by many cultures, and on actual historical
experience. History has tended to judge harshly the deeds of male traitors, and
their actual names are recorded in song when they are real historical persons,
e.g., "La traición de Guajardo" in the Guerrero Collection. The troubadour
uses the *traidora* motif when he or she wishes to add a love interest or a note of
eroticism, or to capture the imagination of the audience. But even in this

negative image the balladeer offers the audience a different perspective on Mexican women—a perspective that is more well-rounded than most other sources have provided.

Not only do the corridos I have examined here present archetypal images of women in their negative aspect of the femme fatale; they also provide a perspective on the personality and social status of women in Mexican society. Much has been written about Mexican women and their oppression by their male counterparts. Although undeniably this genre adheres to patriarchal ideology, the songs indirectly afford us a different profile of these women. By depicting recalcitrant, rebellious, indeed subversive women, these folk songs challenge much of the past portrayal of the submissive, passive Mexicana and are in accord with revisionist scholarship of the past few decades on machismo, the family, and male–female power structures in Mexican and Chicano society.[12]

The position of Chicano scholars Alfredo Mirandé, Maxine Baca Zinn, Miguel Montiel, María Nieto Senour, Richard Griswold del Castillo, and others is that the Chicana has been cast in a stereotypical image derived from impressionistic, nonscientific observations. This image has not been substantiated by empirical data.[13] Sociologist Zinn boldly asserts that

> Chicanas are variously portrayed as exotic objects, manipulated by both Chicano and Anglo men, as long-suffering mothers subject to the brutality of insecure husbands, whose only function is to produce children; and as women who themselves are childlike, simple, and completely dependent on their fathers, brothers, and husbands. Regardless of the specific characterization, Chicanas have been depicted as ignorant, simple women whose subservience and dependence results in the inability to make the home a productive unit for their families. Social scientists correctly analyzed Chicano social organization in terms of patriarchal-authoritarian principles, but they have incorrectly assumed this to mean that women are insignificant, and that they exert power only by manipulation. (1975:19–31)

Glenn R. Hawkes and Minna Taylor summarized the traditional social science view of Mexican male-female relationships:

> The Mexican-American family structure is described as a traditional patriarchy. It is supposedly modified only slightly from the structure found in Mexico, in which women are put on a pedestal, while being despised for their weakness and passivity. Husbands dominate their wives and carry out their family obligations as they see fit.
>
> In the United States this set of patriarchal relations continues to exist. While the man may be a second-class citizen outside the family circle, at home he is a king, demanding and receiving unquestioning obedience from his wife and children. The husband is the authority figure in the family making all the decisions and disciplining the children. It is he who decides on financial matters and represents the household in dealings with the outside world. The wife, on the other hand, is expected to be submissive, chaste, and unworldly.

She is expected to acknowledge her husband's authority, to place his needs and desires before her own and to carry out his decisions. (Hawkes and Taylor, 1975:807)

The term most aptly describing this relationship is *machismo*. It is a concept that is widely accepted by social scientists and has widespread popularity in the American mass media and even with the general public. Scholars expounding the machismo paradigm include Margaret Clark, William Madsen, Robert Staples, and Robert C. Jones.[14] Theories promulgated in the 1940s, 1950s, and 1960s on the Mexican-American family structure were based on the male dominant–female submissive construct.

Américo Paredes (1967) was one of the first scholars to question the concept of machismo. More recently, Ronald E. Cromwell and Rene A. Ruiz (1979) stated that "the patriarchal Hispanic family structure characterized by macho dominance in marital decision making is a myth which prevails in social science literature." They concluded that "based on an intensive analysis of four major studies on marital decision making within Mexican and Chicano families . . . the available data fail to substantiate the hypothesis of Mexican and/or Chicano male dominance in marital decision making" (355). Indeed, decisions ranging from where to live to the family budget were in general arrived at jointly in the working-class families surveyed.

Revisionist scholars do not, however, deny the oppression of Mexicanas and Chicanas. Zinn (1975) elucidates:

> Though numerous recent studies have challenged macho male dominance in the realm of family decision making, there is also evidence that patriarchal ideology can be manifested even in Chicano families where decision making is not male dominant. . . . findings of both male dominant and egalitarian families revealed also that the ideology of patriarchy was expressed in all families studied. . . . (39)

Feminist scholars have also begun questioning the pervasive belief that men have totally dominated women throughout history and in all cultures.[15] Recent anthropological studies have discovered various levels of male–female relations vis-à-vis the degree of power wielded by each. Sanday (1981) describes three categories of male dominance: mythical male dominance, systems of unequal relationships, and systems of equal relationships. The existence of one or the other, Sanday states, is directly dependent on female economic or political power:

> In discussing the basis for male dominance, it is essential to distinguish male aggression against women from the exercise by women of political and economic power. Where the former exists in the presence of the latter, the term mythical male dominance will be employed to describe the relationship between the sexes. Where males turn aggression against women and/or women are excluded from economic and political decision making, the relationship

between the sexes will be defined as unequal. Finally, where males do not display aggression against women and women exercise political and economic authority or power, the relationship between the sexes will be defined as equal. (165)

In analyzing several cultures, Sanday found that in the first category of male–female relations, where women have economic and political power, male aggression toward women tends to be high. Where inequality exists and women are excluded from the political and economic sphere, male aggression also is significant. But where equality between the sexes exists, aggression against women is practically negligible.

The concept of mythical male dominance was developed by anthropologist Susan Carol Rogers (1975), who found, in her study of peasant societies, a "balance between formal male authority and informal female power" (165). Rogers detected in some peasant societies a situation where women outwardly showed deference to men, particularly in public places, and allowed men to hold positions of power and prestige. This "acting out" of male dominance, according to Rogers, "is in the interests of both peasant women and men because it gives the latter the appearance of power and control over all sectors of village life, while at the same time giving to the former actual power over those sectors of life in the community which may be controlled by villagers" (129). However, neither males nor females actually believed that males were dominant.

Corridos depicting the archetypal image of Eve fall within the constructs formulated by patriarchal ideology, where the feminine is perceived as evil and associated with death and destruction. Furthermore, they form part of the body of knowledge that is instrumental in the socialization process of men and women about their respective roles in society. These folk songs in effect function as exempla did in the Middle Ages. Such exempla were employed by the clergy to instruct the faithful on matters of proper social and religious behavior.[16]

The love–death corridos serve to legitimate male domination. Sociologists Peter L. Berger and Thomas Luckmann (1967) proposed that

> Legitimation produces new meanings that serve to integrate the meanings already attached to disparate institutional processes. The function of legitimation is to make objectively available and subjectively plausible the "first-order" objectivations that have been institutionalized. . . . Legitimation "explains" the institutional order by ascribing cognitive validity to its objectivated meanings. Legitimation justifies the institutional order by giving a normative dignity to its practical imperatives. (92–93)

They distinguished between various levels of legitimation, noting that "incipient legitimation is present as soon as a system of linguistic objectifications of human experience is transmitted" (94). Kinship vocabulary is given as an example.

Folk songs are assigned to the second level of legitimation. At this level linguistic expressions

> contain theoretical propositions in a rudimentary form. Here may be found various explanatory schemes relating sets of objective meanings. These schemes are highly pragmatic, directly related to concrete actions. Proverbs, moral maxims and wise sayings are common on this level. Here, too, belong legends and folktales, frequently transmitted in poetic form. (94)

Thus the love–death corridos function as mediators in transmitting the proper code of behavior to future generations by presenting the tragic consequences of violating the code. Concomitantly, however—and possibly without being aware of it—the corridista presents the rebel woman who challenges the legitimacy of the mores extant in a culture. By opposing them she becomes a hero and role model.

The primary socialization of the female protagonists in love–death corridos obviously failed. As the perceptive Paredes (1953:114) succinctly put it: "It is doubtful, however, if the tragedias accomplished their job, which was to keep the girls from dancing." Instead of the passive woman, we witness the struggle of the rebellious individual seeking to restructure the social canon and rupture those codes that stifled her freedom.

Soldadera gallops with the Revolutionary Army, furiously seeking an enemy in the startled presence of other *calaveras*, or skulls. This José Guadalupe Posada drawing inspired the *corrido* "La Coronela" ("The Woman Colonel"). From *Posada's Popular Mexican Prints*, selected and edited by Roberto Berdecio and Stanley Applebaum, 1972. Used with permission of Dover Publications, New York.

Young *soldadera* in the Mexican Revolution. This photograph and others on these pages are from the famed Agustín Casasola Collection in the National Institute of Anthropology and History, Pachuca, Mexico, and are used with permission (Fondo Casasola, Fototeca del INAH).

Woman soldier dressed in male uniform.

Women on train tops accompanying soldiers.

Women cooking on train tops.

Women with soldiers, celebrating. Dated Tuesday, April 23, 1912.

Woman with revolutionary soldiers.

Soldadera with friend.

Middle-class women supporting the Revolution.

Young woman posing as *soldadera*.

Women with revolutionary troops.

❊ 5 ❊

THE SOLDIER ARCHETYPE

Mexico inherited the Soldier, or Woman Warrior, archetypal image from classical tradition. The ancient Greeks believed in a land beyond their city-state borders, on the banks of the river Thermodon, that was inhabited solely by women, though controversy exists about whether this realm was real or merely a sexual fantasy of the male imagination.[1]

The inhabitants of this country of the Amazons were said to mate once or twice a year. The products of their unions were selected and retained as citizens on the basis of their sex: the male child was either discarded or given away; the baby girls were raised as future Amazons. This all-female principality was organized with two heads of state, one in charge of military affairs, the other dedicated to domestic issues. Classics scholar Patricia Monaghan (1981) elaborates this point, declaring that "under their military queen the Amazons were a mighty army of mounted warriors bearing ivy-shaped shields and double-bladed axes" (13).

The Amazon state is said to have lasted some four hundred years, until 600 B.C., but was finally overcome by Hercules, who, under assignment to perform the twelve impossible tasks, stole the golden girdle from the Amazon queen's waist. This action, along with the possible abduction of the queen herself, initiated a war ending in defeat for the Amazon kingdom.

The mental construct of the fearless, militaristic woman is firmly entrenched in the mythology of the Greeks. Pallas Athena, for example, was viewed as a great warrior, while Artemis, the virgin goddess who roamed the forests with her band of nymphs, "bearing the bow and quiver, avoiding men and killing any male who looks on her," is very much in the tradition of the Woman Warrior (Monaghan, 1981:27).[2]

Needless to say, the conceptualization of the Woman Warrior is not limited to the Greeks. In Scandinavian mythology we encounter the archetype in the Valkyries, who are artistically represented with helmets on, riding horseback over the carnage left after bloody battles. They are awesome figures, indeed (ibid.: 298–299). Medieval literature of the knight errant type was imbued with fantastic stories, such as the existence of a fabulous land where the Amazons still lived.[3]

The Spanish conquistadors, avid readers of the genre, thought they saw in the exotic newly discovered American continent glimpses of these mythical female warriors among the native Indian tribes. Thus the largest river in Brazil got its name from these mighty women who had captured the imagination of the Spaniards.

The natives of Mesoamerica also had the concept of the Woman Warrior—with an added twist. The Azteca-Mexica considered women who perished while giving birth to a child to be honorable soldiers who had died in combat or in ritual sacrifice. As Soustelle writes:

> The destiny of the "valiant woman" in the hereafter was therefore exactly the equivalent, the counterpart, of that of the warriors who died in battle or upon the sacrificial stone. The warriors accompanied the sun from its rising to its height, and the women from the zenith to its setting. The women had become goddesses, and therefore they were called the *ciuateteo* "the divine women." Their suffering and their death earned them apotheeosis. (1964:195)

The concept of the *soldadera*, therefore, although not strictly conceptualized as women engaged in actual battles, existed in the religious structure and the minds of the Aztec nation.

The historical specificity of the Americas itself was perhaps conducive to the creation of a female Soldier archetype. Since mental constructs have an ultimate basis in reality, we may deduce that the constant battles between Spaniards and native Americans encouraged the surfacing of valorous women who were forced by necessity to fight alongside the male soldiers.

The Spanish conquistador and poet Alonzo de Ercilla y Zuñiga incorporated into his literary epic *La Araucana* of 1569 the concept of the valiant frontier woman who seeks to motivate the troops to stand firm and to fight the fierce incursions of the Araucanian Indians to the bitter end. With splendid poetic sensitivity Ercilla (1977:102–103) celebrates a woman warrior:

> Doña Mencía de Nidos, una dama
> noble, discreta, valerosa, osada
> es aquella que alcanza tanta fama
> en tiempo que a los hombres es negada:
> estando enferma y flaca en una cama,
> siente el grande alboroto, y esforzada,
> asiendo de una espada y un escudo,
> salió tras los vecinos como pudo.

> Doña Mencía de Nidos, a lady
> Noble, discreet, valorous, daring
> She is the one who gained great fame
> At that time denied to men:
> While ill and emaciated in her bed,
> She hears the great commotion and forcing herself
> Grabs a sword and a shield,
> And runs after the townspeople as well as she could.

The conquering Spaniards are suffering a great setback against the Araucanians in Concepción, Chile. They are at a point where fleeing is the only rational course. Nevertheless, with great courage and sword in hand, Doña Mencía exhorts the Spaniards not to surrender but to stand firm and fight for their honor and their homes.

Rough conditions on many frontiers undoubtedly induced many women to grab gun or rifle and fight for their very survival. Certainly the tradition of the valiant fighting woman has been a consistent part of Latin American revolutionary upheavals, from the struggles for independence from Spain to the Nicaraguan Revolution in the 1970s.[4]

WOMEN IN MEXICO'S INDEPENDENCE MOVEMENT

Mexico officially honors several heroines who were involved in revolutionary struggles. The most famous is La Corregidora, Doña Josefa Ortiz de Domínguez, whom the Mexican nation immortalized by putting her image on the nation's currency. History books effusively praise the valor and patriotic mettle of Doña Josefa, who was a leading figure in the Wars of Independence (1810–1821).

Married in 1791 to Don Miguel Domínguez, a lawyer from a well-to-do family, Doña Josefa moved to Queretaro when her husband was promoted to be *corregidor* (chief magistrate) of that state. This appointment afforded the Domínguez family access to the upper echelons of creole society as well as to the military elite and the church intelligentsia. Josefa's home became the center of popular *tertulias* (parties) in which philosophical and political issues were frequently discussed. Father Miguel Hidalgo y Costilla, the progenitor of Mexican independence, was a frequent guest, as were Juan Aldama and other liberals who now grace the pages of Mexican history (see Kentner, 1975:45–94; Uroz, 1972:254–256; and Romero Aceves, 1982:139–141). The conspiracy to overthrow Spanish rule began to germinate in the republican confines of Doña Josefa's living room.

Doña Josefa eventually was to play a key role in the movement to free Mexico from the Spanish yoke. It was Josefa herself who relayed an urgent message to Father Hidalgo y Costilla warning him that their plans for the uprising were in danger of being discovered by authorities. Fearing the worst, Father Hidalgo y Costilla could wait no longer. He began the revolutionary fight by inciting the Indians, the mestizo peasants, and other interested citizens of the town of Dolores in Guanajuato to take up arms. This initial call to battle is now celebrated as the Grito de Dolores (midnight, September 15, 1810).

Doña Josefa participated actively in the uprising. Unfortunately, her role was uncovered and she was incarcerated in a convent for several years. She remained to her death a staunch defender of liberal ideals and stood firm in her quest for freedom for the young Mexican nation.

The grateful nation heaped many honors upon Doña Josefa. The poet Rafael Nájera (1957) named one of his poems "La Corregidora" in memory of her role. In this poem he enumerates the leading figures of the insurgent movement and then exclaims:

y aun el alcalde	and even the sheriff
Ignacio Pérez, el héroe	Ignacio Pérez, the hero
de quien se sirvió no en balde	Whom Doña Josefa called upon
la noble doña Josefa,	With great foresight
para dar en breves frases,	To deliver in brief phrases
el grito de alarma al cura	The sound of alarm to the priest
y a los bravos capitanes.	And the other brave captains.

Another woman revolutionary, Doña Leona Vicario, worked diligently for the defeat of the Loyalists and donated her estate to the revolutionary cause (see García, 1979). But women's participation in the conflict was not limited to these two.[5] Indeed, historians acknowledge that women were heavily involved but find it difficult to document their feats owing to the omission of their full names from the annals of war and historical archives. Even with these limitations, Kentner (1975) identified 250 women as having been active. But Kentner noted that

> a problem arises . . . in that many more women were involved than can be identified. The camp followers and those who remained with their husbands throughout the battles, tending the wounded, preparing food, making cartridge, are almost impossible to identify. Even though several women were accompanying Father Hidalgo when he was captured on March 19, 1811, none of their names was recorded, although there are long lists of the names of the men captured at the same time. (1–2)

Nevertheless, diligent research in the diaries, court-martial records, newspaper accounts, private correspondence, and memoirs of the insurgents has yielded valuable information on the activities of the women who were committed to Mexican independence.

Women's participation, Kentner stated (95), included at least eight major roles: soldiers actually engaged in battle, some of whom led female or male battalions; spies and couriers; "seductresses" who got enemy soldiers to defect; wives, sweethearts, and daughters who followed their male kinfolk into war; cooks; nurses; fund raisers—many upper-class and middle-class women donated their estates to the movement; and camp followers—women who followed the soldiers and performed various services, such as cooking, cleaning, and scavenging for food (we may include in this category the many so-called prostitutes).

Of special interest to this study are those women Kentner cited who actually brandished weapons and rode into battle. They include La Barragana, who conscripted several Indians from her hacienda, formed a regiment armed with bows and arrows, then joined Father Hidalgo in Guanajuato, and Doña

Teodosea Rodríguez ("La Generala"), who was at the helm of an Indian army of bowmen and supposedly fought with Miguel Allende and other revolutionaries.

During the second phase of the independence movement (1812–1815), women continued to distinguish themselves, some becoming instant legends. One such woman was María Manuela Molina. Originally from Taxco, María was of Indian descent. Her fierce, independent spirit quickly embraced the revolutionary ideals. She is reputed to have raised an army of men and to have fought successfully in seven battles. The Suprema Junta officially granted her the title "La Capitana" in April 1812. She died as a result of numerous wounds (see Romero Aceves, 1982:131–133).

Women's role as couriers and spies was just as important for the success of the revolutionary endeavor as engaging in battle. Many of these women were caught and imprisoned; some were summarily executed. They suffered harsh punishments and indignities for their beliefs and participation in the liberal cause (Kentner, 1975:243–249).

The interesting group of women labeled "seductresses" seduced, by whatever means possible (mostly mental, not physical), Loyalist soldiers into joining the rebel forces. Kentner quoted a *fiscal*, or district attorney, from Valladolid who laments the activities of one such "seductress," María Bernarda Espinosa:

> One of the greatest evils which we have had from the beginning of this war . . . are the women who, on account of their sex, have been the instrument of seducing all classes of persons. . . . The chance presents itself to us today to be able to make a public example of Bernarda Espinosa, although she does not admit that she had seduced any directly. But she has spewed forth propositions in favor of those who, forgetting the sacred oath which they made to the best of monarchs, take arms, violating the rights and the peace and tranquility which we enjoy. (255)

The custom of women's involvement in war efforts must have remained firmly entrenched after independence, for we read in Frances Calderón de la Barca's journal of 1843 her impressions regarding a ragtag army she was observing:

> We have just returned after a sunny walk, and an *inspection* of the *pronunciados*—they are too near Mexico now for me to venture to call them *the rebels*. The infantry, it must be confessed, was in a very ragged and rather drunken condition—the cavalry better, having *borrowed* fresh horses as they went along. Though certainly not *point-device* in their accoutrements, their good horses, high saddles, bronze faces, and picturesque attire, had a fine effect as they passed along under the burning sun. The sick followed on asses, and amongst them various masculine women, with *sarapes* or *mangas* and large straw hats tied down with coloured handkerchiefs, mounted on mules or horses. The sumpter mules followed, carrying provisions, camp-beds, etc.; and various Indian women trotted on foot in the rear, carrying their husbands' boots and clothes. There was certainly no beauty amongst these feminine followers of the camp, especially amongst the mounted Amazons, who looked like very ugly

men in semi-female disguise. The whole party are on their way to Tacubaya, to join Santa Anna! (Calderón de la Barca, 1982:433–434)

An early literary source also depicts soldadera involvement. The historical novel *Los Insurgentes*, published in 1869 by Juan A. Mateos, waxes poetic over what Mateos perceives to be the Mexicanas' singularity in fighting valiantly in war (19):

> Fuera de nuestro país no se conoce esa benemérita clase que forma la mitad del soldado, es decir, su mujer. No entraremos en la cuestión si las tienen con arreglo al Concilio de Trento ó al Registro Civil, el hecho es que el soldado, sobre todo en campaña, nada vale sin una compañera.
>
> Esas infelices mujeres son una especie de langosta que caen tanto sobre las fincas, como sobre los sembrados, como sobre los muertos, á quienes desnudan piadosamente.
>
> En la época de la insurrección, *realistas é insurgentes* entraban en las fincas á ejercer el derecho de conquista; de aquí la ruina de tantas *haciendas* y pueblos que han desaparecido, y cuyos escombros apenas se perciben en medio de la desolación de los campos y de las comarcas.
>
> En la época que se refiere nuestra historia, los insurgentes caminaban en familia; así es que á la hora de una derrota las mujeres y los niños caían prisioneros de guerra y entraban en el botín del vencedor, hasta que podían escapar de la esclavitud á que las condenaban en las fincas de campo, dándoles un trato duro é inhumano.
>
> El general había prescrito que las mujeres se quedasen á una gran distancia del campo de batalla, pero cuando menos se esperaba ya se las veía dando de beber á los soldados, y cargando á los heridos y ofreciendo algo que comer á los oficiales, aquello, como hoy, no tenía remedio.
>
> Nosotros les tributamos un sentimiento de ternura, porque en esos momentos solemnes ejercen la caridad con noble desinterés; nosotros hemos visto morir á algunas infelices, víctima del plomo en los momentos de socorrer á sus maridos agonizantes.

(That wonderful class that forms the other half of the soldier, that is, his wife, is not known outside our country. We will not enter into a discussion as to whether they have their women with the consent of the Council of Trent or the Civil Register, the fact is that the soldier, especially when on the battlefield, is not worth anything without his mate.

(Those unhappy women are a type of locust who fall upon the large estates as well as upon the planted crops, and upon the dead and proceed to charitably disrobe them.

(At the time of the Insurrection, both *Realists and Insurgents* would enter the large landed estates by right of conquest; herein lies the ruin of so many *haciendas* and towns that have disappeared, and whose ruins one can hardly discern among the desolation of the fields and villages.

(At the time referred to by our narrative, the Insurgents walked with their families; therefore at the time of a defeat in battle women and children would fall prisoners of war and were part of the booty of the victorious forces and would remain thus until they were able to escape from this slavelike state which condemned them to the agricultural fields of the estate where they were harshly and inhumanely treated.

(The General had ordered that the women should remain at a great distance from the battlefield, but when least expected one could see them giving water to the soldiers and carrying off the wounded and offering a bite to eat to the officials. That type of behavior is still with us today and cannot be avoided.

(We offer them here a tribute of tenderness, because in those solemn moments they carry out their charitable deeds with a noble unselfishness; we have seen some of these unfortunate women die, victims of a bullet at the precise moment they were aiding their dying husbands.)

WOMEN IN THE MEXICAN REVOLUTION

When the Mexican Revolution of 1910–1917 exploded, women joined the struggle. But opposition to the dictatorship of Porfirio Díaz began as early as the 1880s through small liberal presses (Alatorre, 1961:29). Many journalists were imprisoned or forced to flee to the United States to continue their feverish revolutionary activities. It was among these voices of the liberal press that women's leadership began to surface.

Juana B. Gutiérrez de Mendoza with her small but powerful newspaper *Vésper*, Guadalupe Rojo de Alvarado with the stingingly mordant *Juan Panadero*, and Carlota Antuna de Borrego with *El Campo Verde* were three of the many women involved in journalistic endeavors too numerous to mention. They distinguished themselves in valiantly offering their voices to the cause of freedom and their fierce opposition to tyranny and despotism (ibid.:30–35). In powerful articles they called for action and exhorted the nation to battle the dictatorship. These women demonstrated their pluck and mettle in entering the political fray, which entailed extreme danger to their own lives and to the safety of their loved ones.

The editors of the radical newspaper *Regeneración*, the brothers Ricardo and Enrique Flores Magón, lauded one of these pioneers:

> Ahora que muchos hombres flaquean y por cobardía se retiran de la lucha, por considerarse sin fuerzas para la revindicación de nuestras libertades; ahora que muchos hombres sin vigor retroceden espantados ante el fantasma de la tiranía y llenos de terror abandonan la bandera liberal para evitarse las fatigas de una lucha levantada y noble, aparece la mujer animosa y valiente, dispuesta a luchar por nuestros principios, que la debilidad de muchos hombres ha permitido que se pisoteen y se les escupa. La señora Juana B. Gutiérrez de Mendoza acaba de fundar en Guanajuato un periódico liberal, *Vésper*, destinado a la defensa de las instituciones liberales y democráticas. (Today, when many men cowardly weaken and leave the struggle, not considering themselves strong enough for the revindication of our freedom; today, when many men without vigor retreat, scared at the phantasm of tyranny, and full of terror abandon the liberal flag in order to avoid the strain of battling for a noble cause,

there appears a woman with dynamism and valor willing to fight for our principles, which many weak men have allowed to be trampled and spit upon. Mrs. Juana B. Gutiérrez de Mendoza has just founded in Guanajuato a liberal newspaper *Vésper* destined to defend our liberal and democratic institutions.) (Alatorre, 1961:32)

The most spectacular form of female participation in the Revolution was in actual armed conflict. Movies, pulp literature (comic books such as "La Coronela" from the series *Leyendas de Pancho Villa* [Turner, 1971:614], dance (particularly the Ballet Folklórico de Mexico), paintings (i.e., Diego Rivera and Clemente Orozco), the novel and short story, photography (see the Agustín Casasola Archive Collection), and, of course, the corrido have all immortalized the soldadera.

The conceptualization of women as warriors is based on actual historical facts. One of the first heroines of the 1910 upheaval, Carmen Serdán, sister of the first martyr of the Revolution, Aquiles Serdán, is reported to have appeared rifle in hand on the balcony of her house to exhort the population to take up arms against the Díaz regime. She did this in spite of the fact that the conspiracy had been uncovered and a rain of Federal bullets was blanketing the house (Romero Aceves, 1982:262–265). Later, Aquiles Serdán's mother and wife, as well as his sister, were killed for their revolutionary activities.

Several soldaderas attained the rank of general or colonel. Coronela Carmen Amelia Robles, from the state of Guerrero, joined the Zapatistas and fought against both the Porfiriato and the later Huerta government. It is said that she generally wore male attire and distinguished herself by winning many important battles. Historian Antonio Uroz (1972:264) asserts:

> Pocas personas se podían ufanar de ser tan buenas caballistas como era la Guerra [sic] Amelia en la Revolución. Como una real saeta salía a caballo en lo álgido del combate y siempre dejó una huella imborrable de lealtad, valentía y sentido humano. Con verdadera energía tomó parte en la toma de Iguala, Chilpancingo, Cuernavaca y otras muchas ciudades de nuestro país. (Few persons could state they were as good horsewomen as the Guerra Amelia was during the Revolution. Like a veritable arrow she would dart on her horse during the heat of the battle; and she always left evidence of her unimpeachable loyalty, valor, and human sensibility. With great energy she took part in the Battle of Iguala, of Chilpancingo, of Cuernavaca, and many other cities in our country.)

La Coronela Alaniz—Carmen Parra Alaniz (1885–1941)—was officially recognized by the Mexican government and granted the prestigious Al Mérito Revolucionario title. Her deeds are recorded in the "Relación del Personal Femenino del Archivo de Veteranos de la Revolución." She is reputed to have fought in numerous important battles, including those of Juárez City, Chihuahua, and Ojinaga (Alatorre, 1961:77–78).

Two women of high rank achieved fame not only for their valor but also for their cruelty. One of them, "La Coronela" Pepita Neri, alias Ricarda Centeno and Benita Banderas, belonged to the Zapata troops. The newspaper *El Nacional* in Mexico City recounted in 1959 the story of Neri's involvement with the Zapatistas:

> Repartiendo proclamas y entusiasmando labriegos, para convertirse al cabo en la terrible "Coronela," Pepita Neri, con dos cananas repletes de balas, cruzadas sobre el pecho a la granadera, pistola y puñal al cinto y jefaturando un puñado de hombres con los que hacía temblar hasta los más desalmados. (Distributing proclamations and recruiting laborers and later becoming the terrible "Colonel" Pepita Neri, with two bullet belts full of ammunition slung across her chest like a grenadier, with a gun and a knife at her belt and leading a bunch of men of whom she made even the meanest individuals tremble.) (Alatorre, 1961:92)

The other, Jovita Valdovinos, "The Generala," from Jalapa, Zacatecas, was also famous for her valor and warring skills but infamous for her cruelty (ibid.).

An interesting story surrounds the soldadera Petra Ruiz, alias Pedro Ruiz, nicknamed "Echa Bala," who achieved the rank of lieutenant. Alatorre (91) reports:

> Ataviada tan perfectamente con los indumentos varoniles y cortado el pelo, que nadie sospechó su sexo y fue tan grande el azoro por su sed de aventuras, que al disputarse el amor de las mujeres, cedíanle el puesto muchos de sus compañeros, temerosos de su destreza en el manejo del cuchillo o en la celeridad de los disparos. Naturalmente que al poco las abandonaba. (Dressed so perfectly with male attire and with her hair cut short, nobody suspected her sex; and her thirst for adventure was so great, that she would fight over the love of women with her comrades; they would step aside afraid of her skill with the knife and her ability with bullets. Naturally she would abandon [the ladies] shortly.)

It was not until toward the end of the war that she revealed her true nature. It is said that when President Venustiano Carranza was reviewing the troops a young "man" stepped to the front and shocked everyone by disclosing: "Señor presidente, como ya no hay pelea, quiero pedirle mi baja del ejército; pero antes quiero que sepa usted que una mujer le ha servido como soldado" ("Mr. President, since there is no more fighting, I want to ask you for a discharge, but before that I want you to know that a woman has served you as a soldier").

SOLDADERA ROLES IN THE CORRIDO

Three types of soldaderas are represented in the corrido. These types vividly demonstrate the historical process in the fashioning of an archetypal image. Some corridos depict the soldadera in her true historical dimension. Some romanticize the soldadera and transform her into a love object. In others the soldadera is transformed into a mythic archetypal figure. I have collected thirty-seven folk songs with soldaderas mentioned in their lyrics and will analyze several of them in this chapter.

Historical

As we have seen, the historical record confirms the involvement of Mexican women during periods of armed conflict. The heroic corrido corroborates the participation of Mexicanas on the battlefields. For the most part, however, the women appear as anonymous entities, at times denominated solely by their first names, at other times as "Juanas" or "galletas" ("cookies"), the names usually given to soldaderas. Some are simply labeled "mujeres."[6] This practice contrasts with the customary use of both names when males are extolled in corridos.

One of the few women exalted in the corrido by both her first name and patronymic is Petra Herrera in the "Corrido de las hazañas del General Lojero y la Toma de Torreón por el ejercito Liberador" ("The Ballad of the Feats of General Lojero and the Capture of Torreón by the Liberation Army"). This song (Campos, 1962, vol. 1:105–106) tells of the confrontation between General Lojero's soldiers and the Maderista battalion in the city of Torreón, Coahuila, on May 13, 1911. The Maderista followers fought valiantly, many of them perishing in the assault. At the conclusion of the engagement they were victorious against the Porfirista forces.

During the heated exchange of bullets and artillery fire, Petra Herrera supposedly was the first to lead the soldiers into the fray and was apprehended by enemy forces and taken prisoner. The corrido admiringly recounts:

La valiente Petra Herrera	The valiant Petra Herrera
en el fragor del combate	In the heat of the battle
aunque cayó prisionera	And even though she was taken prisoner
ni se dobla ni se abate.	She doesn't surrender or give up.

The fearless Petra does not bend, but on the contrary is aggressive and bellicose. Defiant to the end, she dares to shout, in the very presence of General Lojero, "¡Viva Madero!":

La llevaron los rurales	The Rural Soldiers took her
ante el general Lojero	To General Lojero
y sin temores cevales	And without deerlike fear
le dijo: ¡Viva Madero!	She said: "Long live Madero!"

Two other ballads, the "Corrido de la Toma de Torreón" ("Ballad of the Taking of Torreón") and the "Corrido del combate del 15 de mayo en Torreón" ("Ballad of the Combat of May 15 in Torreón") depict the same events and verify Petra Herrera's outstanding feats of valor. The "Toma de Torreón" (Campos, 1962, vol. 2:106–107) intones:

El día 14 a medianoche	On the 14th at midnight
entraron con gran violencia	They entered with great violence
Petra Herrera en adelante	Petra Herrera in front
a la mera presidencia.	Straight to the Presidential Office.

The Maderistas deliver a resounding defeat to the Federal troops, who are forced to flee in the middle of the night, having sustained heavy casualties:

La noche vino lluviosa	The night came upon us rainy
en la ciudad de Torreón	In the city of Torreón
los federales huyeron	The Federales fled
dejando la población.	Leaving the town.

The confrontation had been fierce and bloody:

El domingo sostuvieron	On Sunday they sustained
la guerra por todo el día	The battle the whole day through
matándose unos con otros	Killing each other
con bastante valentía.	With great bravery.

The routing of the Federales sealed the defeat of Porfirio Díaz. Petra Herrera's actions are doubly impressive, since this confrontation not only was one of the most important battles between the Maderistas and the Federales but also was led by outstanding professional military school men commanding several divisions. That Petra is singled out for praise is indeed an honor.

The "Combate del 15 de Mayo" (Campos, 1962, vol. 2:108–109) reiterates Petra Herrera's involvement in the bloody strife:

La valiente Petra Herrera	The valiant Petra Herrera
al combata se lanzó	To battle she entered
siendo siempre la primera	Always being the first
ella el fuego comenzó.	To start the exchange of fire.

At the ballad's close special attention and praise are heaped on this intrepid woman soldier:

¡Que viva Petrita Herrera,	Long live Petra Herrera
qué vivan los maderistas,	Long live the Maderistas!
qué mueran con los pelones	Let the "baldies" [Federales] die!
los cobardes porfiristas!	With the cowardly Porfiristas!

Only three other corridos depicting actual battle scenes mention women soldiers by name. The woman's first name is supplied in two; in the third song the soldadera is identified by her nickname. These three songs are "De Agripina," "Corrido de la toma de Papantla" ("Ballad of the Taking of Papantla"), and "El Coyote" ("The Coyote").

"De Agripina" narrates the events of a particularly bloody clash between the

Cristeros, who were fighting for the rights of the Catholic Church, and the Agraristas, who were seeking land reform and were backed by government forces representing the Revolution and its limits on the power of the Catholic Church (Ankerson, 1984). This ballad dates to the late 1920s, the days of the Cristero Rebellion, and describes how Doña Agripina, an Agrarista, fought and won a battle against the enemy forces. Evidently Agripina situated herself with other sympathizers on a hill, where they were being held and under siege by Cristeros. Fortunately for Doña Agripina, reinforcements arrive in time to save her and her people.

This corrido (Mendoza, 1976:89–91) adheres to the classic structure of the genre, with an introductory formula:

Señores, con el permiso,	Gentlemen, with your permission,
prestándome su atención,	Lend me your attention,
Voy a contar el corrido	I am going to sing a ballad
de la tal Revolución.	About the so-called Revolution.

A formulaic phrase then introduces the main character and hero of the corrido:

—¡Ay!—decía doña Agripina	"Oh!" said Doña Agripina
con sus armas en la mano:	With her weapons in her hand:
—yo me voy con esta genta	"I am going with these people
para el cerro Zamorano.	To the Zamoran Hills."

"Con sus armas en la mano" is a formula reminiscent of the heroic corridos, which have the hero "con su pistola en la mano" (Paredes, 1957). Agripina is thereby transported to the realm of the heroic, and we expect her henceforth to behave heroically in the most dangerous situations. Her Roman name itself is associated with strong women of the past. Agripina the Elder, for instance, was exiled by Emperor Tiberius, and her daughter, also Agripina, was Emperor Nero's mother who, through treachery (she poisoned Emperor Claudius), helped her son inherit the throne. But of course the corrido's succinct description of a woman with weapons in her hand and yelling aggressively place our Agripina in a special dimension.

The next three stanzas elaborate on the various factions engaged in mortal conflict, each ready to exterminate the other. Formulaic phrases in the stanzas that follow refocus attention on the Woman Warrior. The forces of nature provide help to the beleaguered soldadera as she holds off the enemy forces:

Vuela, vuela, palomita	Fly, fly, litle dove
con tus alitas muy finas;	with your very delicate wings;
anda llévale a Agripina	Here take to Agripina
estas dos mil carabinas.	These two thousand carbines.
Vuela, vuela, palomita	Fly, fly, little dove
con tus alitas doradas;	With your golden wings;

anda, llévale a Agripina Here take to Agripina
este parque de granadas. These grenades of ammunition.

There is a startling contrast between the dove, a symbol of peace, and the mission it is assigned: to deliver weapons of war. Moreover, the rhyming verses depict incongruous elements: "con tus alitas muy finas" and "estas dos mil carabinas," "con tus alitas doradas" and "este parque de granadas." The juxtaposition of the delicate, golden wings of a dove with the harshness of the instruments of war and death parallels the involvement of women in the ugly business of war as would be conceived in a patriarchal society. In ballad tradition the palomita is usually a messenger of love or of unfortunate news, such as the demise of a hero. Here the dove motif is the means of salvation for Doña Agripina. These strophes reaffirm Doña Agripina's importance and leadership position in the battle, since the shipment is being sent directly to her and not to the male generals.

The next stanza nonetheless displaces Doña Agripina from her exalted position of fearless leadership to the role of damsel in distress:

—¡Ay!—decía doña Agripina, "Oh!" said Doña Agripina,
que estaba ya en desatino: Who was very anxious,
—¡Divisa para aquel cerro "Look toward that hill
a ver si viene el auxilio! To see if help is on the way."

Even though Doña Agripina was introduced in a heroic stance, we now find her vacillating, doubting, showing some fear of impending death if aid is not near. Of course, male corrido heroes are also known to exhibit fear, but only in rare cases; this facet of human psychology usually is not allowed in lyrics about heroic men. Thus Doña Agripina varies from the male heroic model and is permitted a weakness that is taboo for male protagonists.

Fortunately, help is on the way and the next strophes recount the arrival of reinforcements and the blood bath that ensues:

De ese cerro del Pino From that Pino Hill
bajó la caballería The cavalry did descend
iban a ver a Agripina They were coming to see Agripina
que sitiada la tenían. Who had been laid siege.

Se fueron los agraristas The Agraristas did go
con muchísimo valor, With great valor,
formándole un sitio grande Forming a great siege
a Agripina alrededor. All around Agripina.

The Agraristas at a great price rescue Doña Agripina. The ballad's close follows the classic corrido structure outlined by Duvalier, with the *despedida,* or farewell, of the troubadour:

Ya con esta me despido With this I bid you farewell
parándome en una esquina, Standing by a corner,

aquí termina el corrido	This is where the corrido ends
de la señora Agripina.	The corrido of lady Agripina.

The ballad of "La toma de Papantla" (Campos, 1962, vol. 1:390–391) narrates the retaking of the town of Papantla in the state of Veracruz in 1913 by the Constitutionalist soldiers of Venustiano Carranza. The lyrics underscore the bravery of a woman named Chabela (derived from the proper name Isabel):

¡Ay! Chabela la mujer	Oh! Chabela the wife
de Juan Tapia se ha ganado	Of Juan Tapia has earned
el cariño de su pueblo	The love of her people
y en el ejército un grado.	And in the army a promotion.

Ironically, one notes that while the valor of Chabela is highlighted, she is perceived not in her own right but as the wife of Juan Tapia, whereas the husband, who is not acknowledged as having distinguished himself in battle, is cited with both his given name and his surname.

The inferior conceptualization of women, even though they are fighting side by side with males, is reiterated, albeit unconsciously, in "El Coyote," a ballad collected by Celedonio Serrano Martínez from Guerrero and appearing in Campos's collection (1962, vol. 1:217–218). The song tells of the Zapatistas, armies from southern Mexico, preparing and planning their strategies for an impending multipronged attack on the town. It begins with a series of exquisite lyrical strophes describing how the night protects the insurgent armies:

Camino arriba se mira	Road up ahead we can see
cabalgar una columna,	A column galloping
por capa lleva a la noche	The night serves as its cape
y por escudo la luna	And as its shield the night
va tras el triunfo y la gloria	It goes after triumph and glory
para ennoblecer su cuna.	So as to ennoble its heritage.
El secreto de la noche	The secret of the night
lo guarda el monte enlutado,	The black forest keeps
y el rumor de los caballos	And the sound of the horses
el barranco lo ha guardado;	The canyons have kept
mientras cantan los soldados	While the soldiers sing
con el corazón templado.	With a stout heart.

The male leaders of these forces are enumerated:

Ceballos está en su puesto	Ceballos is in his post
lo mismo Felipe Armenta;	The same for Felipe Armenta;
se mira a Custodio Hernández	One can see Custodio Hernández
acariciando sus treinta;	Caressing his rifle;
Don Epigmenio García	Mr. Epigmenio García
sus elementos recuenta.	Counts his gear.

But when we come to the woman leading her troops we are introduced to her only as "La Güera":

La Güera y su gente	Blondie and her people
improvisa sus trincheras,	Make their trenches,
aunque es mujer, tiene el grado	Even though a woman, she has the rank
de coronel, y sus trenzas	Of Colonel and her braids
no han impedido que ostente	Have not impeded her wearing
con orgullo sus estrellas.	Her stars with pride.

Again we are deprived of the soldadera's full name, although she was obviously in a leadership position—the corrido acknowledges that she was a colonel. The lyrics nevertheless support the historical records that indeed soldaderas achieved high positions within the revolutionary forces.

The anonymous soldadera appears in four other corridos, including "Las mañanitas de la Toma de Zacatecas" ("The Ballad of the Battle of Zacatecas"). This corrido narrates a decisive confrontation that dealt the death blow to the hated Victoriano Huerta government.[7] The tragic and bloody struggle began to unfold as troops from the 89th and 90th Battalions headed by Generals Juan G. Soberanes and Alberto Rodríguez Cerrillo arrived to the aid of Zacatecas. On June 16 the famous and highly respected General Benjamín Argumedo brought his forty-six hundred men. These forces, together with those led by Generals Antonio Rojas, Jacinto Guerra, Juan N. Vázquez, and Marcelo Caraveo, brought the total number of Federal soldiers to more than twelve thousand (Esparza Sánchez, 1976:67). On the Revolutionary side, the renowned Army of the North (Divisón del Norte) headed by Francisco Villa was trekking forward from the city of Torreón. The Villista troops left on June 19 for their rendezvous with the Federales.

The contending armies were well armed on both sides; the Federales, for instance, counted nineteen cannons in addition to rifles and machine guns. Casualties were heavy on both sides: six thousand dead for the Huertista forces, fifteen hundred for the Villa contingent, and two thousand civilians. In addition, five thousand Federales were taken prisoners.

The battle at once became a popular theme for corridos. The version of "La Toma de Zacatecas" that includes women in its lyrics was written by Arturo Almanza. It is a relatively long corrido—in the manner of the more traditional corridos, which tended to be very long—consisting of seventy-eight stanzas. It begins with the classic formula:

Son bonitos estos versos	These verses are pretty
de tinta tienen sus letras	Its letters are written in ink
voy a contarles a ustedes	I am going to tell you
la Toma de Zacatecas.	About the Battle of Zacatecas.
Mil novecientos catorce,	Nineteen hundred and fourteen
las vísperas de San Juan	The eve before St. John

fue tomada Zacatecas	Zacatecas was taken
como todos lo sabrán. . . .	As all of you know. . . .
La toma de Zacatecas	The Battle of Zacatecas
por Villa, Urbina y Madero,	By Villa, Urbina, and Madero,
el sordo Maclovio Herrera	The deaf one Maclovio Herrera,
Juan Medina y Ceniceros.	Juan Medina, and Ceniceros.
Salió don Francisco Villa	Mr. Francisco Villa left
de la ciudad de Torreón,	From the city of Torreón,
con toda su artillería	With all his artillery
hasta el último escuadrón.	To the very last squadron.

The next seventeen strophes narrate the strategic plans and positionings of Villa's soldiers and the beginning of the battle. As soon as the bullets begin to rain on the fighting men the blood starts its inexorable flow. And it is at this juncture that the women appear:

Andaban las pobres "juanas"	The poor soldier women were
empinadas de los cuerpos,	Bending down their bodies,
recogiendo a los heridos	Picking up the wounded
y rezándole a los muertos.	And praying for the dead.
Unas eran de la sierra,	Some were from the Sierra,
las más de las poblaciones,	Most of them from the town,
eran todas muy bonitas,	All were very pretty,
y de muchos pantalones.	And were very brave.

The gallant note introduced by the bard that "all were very pretty" is followed by the admission that they were also very brave. That, however, is the extent of the information provided regarding the soldaderas' participation in this decisive battle. The lack of recognition is even more deplorable considering that of the many versions of "La Toma de Zacatecas" only this one makes any reference at all to women.

In some corridos, women's roles as spies in wartime are recounted. One corrido provides a vivid example of a woman who, aware of the plot to assassinate Emiliano Zapata, warns him of the impending danger. The lyrics of the "Corrido de la Muerte de Emiliano Zapata" (Campos, 1962, vol. 2:269–273) mournfully intone:

Una mujer se acercó	A woman came toward
A Zapata desmayada,	Zapata almost fainting
diciéndole que Guajardo	Telling him that Guajardo
quería hacerle una celada.	Wanted to ambush him.
Zapata oyó los consejos	Zapata heard the advice
de su amiga sin igual,	From his very good friend,
y también formó sus planes	And made his plans
para evitar cualquier mal.	So as to avoid trouble.

Women's involvement in arms contraband is recorded in the corrido "Combate de San Clemente," which details the extent to which women were willing to compromise their very existence for a cause. This corrido (Campos, 1962, vol. 2:364–365) belongs to the Cristero Rebellion period.

Flores don Luis se llamaba,	Flores was Don Luis' name
un siñor de muncho ingenio,	A man of great ingenuity,
que con muncho y gran trabajo	With a lot of work and effort
y arriesgando muncho el cuero	And risking his skin
formó con muchachas güenas,	Formed with some nice girls
Brigadas y Regimientos.	Brigades and regiments.
Y ya bien aconsejadas	And then well advised
las mandó pa' las ciudades,	Sent them to the cities,
las haciendas y los pueblos	The haciendas and the towns
pa' que compraran cartuchos	To buy bullets
con los del destacamento,	At the supply store,
y con orden terminante,	And with a final order
que cuando obtuvieran éstos,	That when they obtained them
en canastos o costales,	In baskets and bags
o mejor en los chalecos	Or better yet in their vests
los lleveran ellas mesmas,	They themselves should take them
hasta nuestros campamentos.	To our camps.
Muchas mujercitas de esas	Many of these young women
perdieron su joven vida	Lost their young lives
en aquella lucha cruenta;	In that cruel struggle
otras prisión y martirio,	Others to prison or torture
y munchas, compadre Agruelio	And many, *Compadre* Agruelio
el utlraje de sus cuerpos.	Their bodies were violated.
Y créame asté, compadrito	And believe me, *Compadrito*,
que pa' estas mujeres güenas	That for these good women
a que me estoy refiriendo,	Of whom I am referring
hay un lugar en la Historia	There is a place in history
y una corona en el cielo.	And a crown in heaven.
Yo era pobre sosteniente	I was a poor lieutenant
que poca cuenta me daba	Who was not aware
de los hechos tan heroicos	Of the heroic feats
de las gloriosas brigadas;	Of these glorious brigades;
pero recuerdo unos nombres	But I remember some names
que llevo en mi alma grabados	That are imprinted in my soul
y hoy los menciono en mis versos	And today I cite them in my verses
pa'que sean bien recordadas.	So that they will be well remembered.
Luisa Ubiarco era una de ellas,	Luisa Ubiarco was one of them,
a ella colgaron los guachos	The *guachos* hung her
para ver si delataba;	To see if she would inform;
pero la valiente joven	But the valiant young woman
aguantó los sufrimientos	Submitted to the torture
sin decir una palabra.	Without saying a word.

Otra era María Gallardo,	Another was María Gallardo,
con caridad franciscana	Who with Franciscan charity
llevaba parque y vestidos	Took ammunition and clothing
a los soldados alteřnos;	To the soldiers in the hill;
y dándose tiempo a todo	And making time for everything
iguales cosas hacía	Did the same deeds
con los del Sur de Jalisco,	To those in South Jalisco,
de Colima y Michoacán.	And Colima and Michoacán.
Y doña Elodia Delgado,	And Doña Elodia Delgado,
grande mujer de verá,	Great lady in truth she was
de una mordia cortó	With a bite she cut
la oreja de su verdugo	The ear of a torturer
que la pretendía ultrajar.	Who tried to rape her.
Las hermanitas Castillo	The Castillo sisters,
Carmen, Toña, Concha y Lola	Carmen, Toña, Concha, and Lola
en unión de muchas más,	In the company of many others
nos llevaban muncho parque,	Brought us a lot of ammunition
alguna vez golosinas,	Sometimes even candy
y abundante ropa limpia	And plenty of clean clothes
pa' nuestras garras cambiar.	So we could change our rags.
Estas valientes muchachas	These valiant girls
unidas a las Mireles	Together with the Mireles
las Velasco y García de Alba	The Velascos and the García de Albas
trabajaban en verdá.	Worked very hard indeed.
y era tan grande su audacia	And their audacity was so great
y las argucias que empleaban	And also the tricks they used
que hasta sus perseguidores	That even their enemies
de su valor se admiraban.	Admired their valor.

Many women, of course, joined the struggle simply because their husbands, fathers, brothers, or lovers were deeply committed to the ideals of the revolutionary movement. Still others were drawn to the battleground by a combination of motives. The "Corrido de la Muerte de Emiliano Zapata" mentions the Guerrillero's wife subscribing both to the love of her husband and to the Revolution's goals. She, no doubt, exemplifies many soldaderas who were drawn into combat for love and ideals.

"Emiliano Zapata" (Campos, 1962, vol. 1:265–267) first recounts the happenings of the night before the fateful day Zapata was treacherously assassinated:

Zapata durmió esa noche	Zapata slept that night
con la dueña de su amor	With his beloved
que andaba también luchando	Who was also fighting
para la revolución.	For the Revolution.

Cassandralike, Mrs. Zapata warns her husband of the danger:

La mujer le dijo entonces:	The woman then said to him:
"Ayer te avisé que tengo	"Yesterday I warned you

el negro presentimiento	That I have this black premonition
de que te quebre el Gobierno.	That the Government will break you.

"Vete lejos d'estas tierras	"Go far away from this area
porque después será tarde,	Because later might be too late,
pues si te quebra el Gobierno	If the Government kills you
Los indios se mueren de hambre."	The Indians will die of hunger."

Dijo Emiliano Zapata:	Emiliano Zapata said:
"Ya'stás como la mujer	"You are just like that woman
que por creer que me mataban	Who, thinking they were going to kill me,
vino desde Cuautla ayer."	Came all the way from Cautla."

Zapata, paralleling the heroes of Greek mythology who were filled with hubris, dismisses the warning as superstition:

"Esas son supersticiones	"Those are just superstitions
que nadie las debe creer	That no one should believe
Guajardo es de pantalones	Guajardo is a real man
y con él voy a vencer."	And with him I shall win."

Women at times joined the movement voluntarily, as exemplifed in "La Toma de Torreón" ("The Battle of Torreón"), in which a soldier invites his girlfriend to follow him in battle (Campos, 1962, vol. 2:112–115).

¿Qué dices, chata, nos vamos?	What do you say, Pug-Nose, shall we go?
Yo si me voy con usted	Yes I will go with you
pero me lleva a caballo	But take me on horseback
porque no sé andar a pie.	Because I don't like walking.

On the other hand, many women were innocent victims of war. In "Domingo Arenas" there unfold the tragic events visited upon a town caught in the grip of the violence of the Revolution. The rebel Domingo Arenas from Tlaxcala was one of the early advocates of agrarian reform and social justice. He caught the imagination of the people and is the subject of many corridos. This ballad (Campos, 1962, vol. 2:170–173) narrates the early peaceful life of Arenas as a baker, his problems with his girlfriend, his teaming up with the rebels, and finally the violent attack on his hometown. The townspeople, alarmed at the attack, warn each other of the impending danger to their daughters. In a poignant series of stanzas we hear of the parents' concern:

—Compadre: Domingo Arenas	"*Compadre:* Domingo Arenas
ya viene cerca del río,	Is coming by the river
meta a sus hijas al pozo,	Put your daughters in the well
no importa que tengan frío.	No matter if they're cold."

—Compadre: Mis hijas son	"*Compadre:* my daughters are

en el pozo ya escondidas.
El agua del pozo está
llena de estrellas caídas.

In the well already hidden
The water in the well is
Full of fallen stars."

A las ocho de la noche
el miedo atrancó las puertas;
por las rendijas entraba
la luz de las bayonetas. . . .

At eight o'clock at night
Fear locked the doors;
Through the cracks entered
The light from the bayonets. . . .

Domingo Arenas ha hincado
su garra en carne tabaco;
su novia tiene en el pecho
un trébol ensangrentado. . . .

Domingo Arenas has pricked
His weapon on tobacco-colored flesh;
His girlfriend has in her chest
A blood-filled clover. . . .

Las manos siembran incendios
y destrozan la ciudad;
a las muchachas decentes
desnudan su honestidad.

The hands sow fires
And destroy the city
And the decent girls'
Innocence is laid bare.

A las seis de la mañana
la tropa se va a los cerros;
Domingo Arenas se lleva
el nardo de los luceros.

At six o'clock in the morning
The troops leave for the hills;
Domingo Arenas takes with him
The lilies of the morning stars.

La ciudad se queda sola,
sonora de cartucheras.
—Compadre: ¡Ya no tengo hijas,

The city is left alone
Sonorous with cartridges.
"*Compadre:* I don't have any daughters
any more!

se las llevó el manco Arenas,
prendidas en las espuelas!

The crippled Arenas took them
Pinned to his spurs!"

Romanticized

In the preceding examples the representation of women participating in armed conflicts, particularly in the Revolution of 1910, adheres to the reality principle in that the lyrical constructs are based on historical models. The women cited in the songs are rarely the main topic of discourse, except in "De Agripina," which was probably written in the 1920s. The archetype of the Soldier as a full-fledged subject for the Mexican ballad was still in its embryonic stages. As I have emphasized, archetypes arise in specific historical contexts. The soldadera, as a mythic figure, was bound to appear sooner or later, given the historical conditions.

Not surprisingly, the appearance of the Soldier archetype and its consequent mythification began to surface in close connection with the love theme. A patriarchal society such as Mexico's could not readily accept the fighting woman as reality was presenting her. She was therefore rarely if ever the subject of heroic corridos. Historical reality was knocking on the corridista's door, however, and, true to corrido tradition, the bard had to recognize these women fighters and their work and commitment in the front trenches of the Revolution. Two alternatives were presented to the balladeer aside from completely ignoring women's involvement in the conflict: to neutralize the woman by making her a love object and thus presenting her in a less threatening manner or to transform the soldadera into a mythic figure. In this section I consider the first alternative. The second will be considered in the next section.

The transposing of the soldadera into a love object became problematic for the troubadour since he or she could not employ the classic form of the heroic corrido; a more flexible structure, a more lyrical framework, had to be employed to fit the romantic contents of the ballad. The songs depicting the love for a soldadera therefore took a different structure from Duvalier's classic formula for corrido construction. The love songs resemble more the canción's structure and style. Nonetheless, most corrido collections, recorded versions of these ballads, anthologies, and the people themselves generally classify these songs as corridos. Thus we have "La Adelita," "Joaquinita," "La Valentina," and "La Rielera"—all songs reflecting the male–female love relationship in time of war. Most importantly, the women in these corridos are perceived as soldaderas, although little mention of their participation in battle is made. I will analyze "La Adelita" (Guerrero Collection) in detail.

La Adelita

1. Adelita se llama la joven
a quien yo quiero y no puedo olvidar,
en el mundo yo tengo una rosa
y con el tiempo la voy a cortar.

2. Si Adelita quisiera ser mi esposa,
si Adelita fuera mi mujer,
le compraría un vestido de seda
para hacerla reina en mi cuartel.

3. Adelita, por Díos te lo ruego,
calma el fuego de esta mi pasión,
porque te amo y te quiero rendido
y por ti sufre mi fiel corazón.

4. Si Adelita se fuera con otro
le seguiría la huella sin cesar,
en vapores y en buques de guerra
si por tierra, en un tren militar.

5. Toca el clarín de campaña a la
   guerra,
salga el valiente guerrero a pelear,
correrán los arroyos de sangre;
que gobierne un tirano jamás.

6. Y si acaso yo muero en campaña
y mi cuerpo en la sierra va a quedar,
Adelita, por Dios te lo ruego,
con tus ojos me vas a llorar.

7. Ya no llores, querida Adelita,

Adelita

Adelita's the name of the maiden
That I love and cannot forget;
In this world I have a rose
And with time I shall cut it.

If Adelita wanted to be my wife
If Adelita would be my wife,
I would buy her a silk dress
And make her queen of my barracks.

Adelita, in God's name I beg you
Calm the fire of my passion
Because I love and like you completely
And my faithful heart suffers for you so.

If my Adelita left with someone else
I would follow her tracks unceasingly
By steamboat or battleship
And by land on a military train.

The clarinet sounds the war battle cry

Let the brave warrior come out to fight
The streams will run with blood
But a tyrant will never rule.

And if I should die in battle
And my body be left in the Sierra
Adelita, in God's name I beg you,
That your eyes shed tears for me.

Please don't cry, my beloved Adelita,

ya no llores, querida mujer,
no te muestres ingrata conmigo,
ya no me hagas tanto padecer.

8. Me despido de mi querida Adela,
ya me alejo de mi único placer,
nunca esperes de mí una cautela
ni te cambie por otra mujer.

9. Soy soldado y la patria me llama
a los campos que vaya a pelear,
Adelita, Adelita de mi alma,
no me vayas por Dios a olvidar.

10. Por la noche andando en el campo,

oigo el clarín que toca a reunión,
y repito en el fondo de mi alma:
Adelita es mi único amor.

11. Si supieras que ha muerto tu
amante
rezarás por mí una oración,
por el hombre que supo adorarte
con el alma, vida y corazón.

12. Ya me despido de mi querida Adela,
de tí un recuerdo quisiera llevar,
tu retrato lo llevo en mi pecho
como escudo que me haga triunfar.

13. Conque quédate, Adela querida,
yo me voy a la guerra a pelear
la esperanza no llevo perdida
de volverte otra vez a abrazar.

Please don't cry, my beloved lady,
Don't be hardhearted with me,
Please don't make me suffer so much.

I bid farewell to my beloved Adela
I take leave from my only pleasure.
Never fear from me any reticence
Or that I should change you for another
woman.

I am a soldier and my country calls me
To the battlefield to fight,
Adelita, Adelita, my very soul,
Please, in God's name don't forget me.

At night, while walking in the
battlefields,
I hear the clarinet calling us in
And I repeat in the depths of my soul:
Adelita is my only love.

If you find out your lover has died

Say for me a prayer;
For the man that adored you
With soul, life, and heart.

I bid farewell to my beloved Adela
From you a token I wish to take
Your picture I carry in my heart
As a shield that'll bring me victory.

So stay, my beloved Adela,
I take my leave to fight the war.
I shall not lose hope
To once again embrace you.

This corrido adheres to medieval love lyric conventions: a lovelorn supplicant entreating his lady to love him and be faithful while he marches to the distant battlefields.

The first distich acquaints us with the beloved's name and the soldier's love for her, while the second uses a sexual metaphor common in the canción—the cutting of a flower, in this instance a rose—to connote sexual conquest.

The second strophe introduces the theme of war. The suitor desires to show off his wife and, by lavishing finery on her, elevate her to "queen of my barracks." Adelita's status is unclear. We do not know whether she is a soldadera living in the barracks already or whether she lives elsewhere and her boyfriend will bring her to his military quarters.

The topoi of the love-sick swain characteristic of courtly love poetry is evident in the third strophe. The invocation to the heavens to soften his lady love's heart, the supplicant stance of the lover ("te lo ruego"), the inflamed nature of the love expressed connoting sexual desire ("el fuego de esta mi pasión"), the "rendido" (surrendered) status of the enamorato, and the plaintive allusion to his "suffering heart" are all elements characteristic of the European tradition.

The fourth strophe introduces another traditional theme dear to Mexicans: the neurotic fear men have of being abandoned by their women. (Ironically, empirical studies demonstrate that the opposite is the rule: it is the Mexican male who frequently abandons the woman [Ramírez, 1977:82].) The strophe also is filled with military terminology ("war ships" and "military train"), reiterating the status of the lover as soldier.

Oddly, the fifth strophe is infused with patriotic fervor; the theme of love is put aside, and the valiant warrior is underscored. The rationale for the bloody war is articulated in the interlocutor's firm insistence that blood will flow but tyranny will not rule.

That death is ever present in the soldier's mind is verbalized in the sixth stanza. Perhaps using his precarious position as a soldier to convince Adelita that life is short and they should take advantage of the moment for tomorrow may be too late, the poet-lover introduces the possibility of being mortally wounded in combat—"Y si acaso yo muero en campaña." His pathetic last request would be for Adelita to cry at his grave. This pathos-filled scene possibly makes Adela weep, for immediately in the seventh strophe the enamorato implores his lady love to cease crying and give in to his amatory requests.

In the eighth stanza he bids farewell to Adelita and reiterates the medieval convention of swearing fealty and unending love to his ladyship as he marches off to war.

The first distich of the ninth strophe perfunctorily returns to the theme of patriotism—"Soy soldado y mi patria me llama." The second distich charmingly returns to the forget-me-not theme, and the tenth stanza reaffirms the soldier-lover's own fealty to his lady love, even at the battlefront.

A presentiment of death permeates the eleventh strophe, bringing the two lovers back to the realities of war and of death in battle.

In the twelfth and thirteenth stanzas poetic closure is achieved through the introduction of a formulaic line bidding farewell. The theme of war predominates in both strophes. The interlacing of the themes of war and love is accomplished in the twelfth stanza through the metamorphosis of a prized photograph of Adela into a love shield placed above his heart. Implicit in the lyrics is the magical belief that this portrait will protect the soldier from a bullet.

The last stanza indicates that Adela is not actively joining in the fray, for the soldier distressingly alludes to Adelita's staying behind ("Conque quédate, Adelita querida") while he goes to war ("yo me voy a la guerra a pelear").

A second, later version of "La Adelita" is more explicit about the status of Adela as a soldadera.

La Adelita	Adelita
1. En lo alto de un abrupta serranía acampado se encontraba un campamento,	In the high sierras Camped were the soldiers

y una moza que valiente los seguía,

locamente enamorada de un sargento.
Popular entre la tropa era Adelita,
la mujer que el sargento idolatraba,
porque además de ser valiente, era
    bonita.
Y hasta el mismo coronel la respetaba.

2. Y pues sabía que decía, aquel que
    tanto la quería:
—Que si Adelita quisiera ser mi novia,
que si Adelita fuera mi mujer
le compraría un vestido de seda
para llevarla a bailar al cuartel—.

3. Una noche en que la escolta
    regresaba
conduciendo entre sus filas al sargento,
y la voz de una mujer que sollozaba,

la plegaria se escuchó en el
    campamento.
Al oirla el sargento, temeroso

de perder para siempre a su adorada,
ocultando su emoción bajo el esbozo
a su amada le cantó de esta manera.

4. Y después que terminó la cruel
    batalla
y la tropa regresó a su campamento,
por las bajas que causara la metralla

muy diezmado regresaba el regimiento.

Recordando aquel sargento sus
    quereres,
los soldados que volvían de la guerra

ofreciéndoles su amor a las mujeres
entonaban este himno de la guerra.

5. Y se oía, que decía,
    aquel que tanto la quería:
—Que si Adelita se fuera con otro
la seguiría por tierra y por mar,
si por mar, en un buque de guerra,
si por tierra, en un tren "melitar."

6. Y si acaso yo muero en campaña

And a young woman who valiantly
    followed
Madly in love with the sergeant.
Popular among the troops was Adelita
The woman the sergeant adored
Because she was not only valiant but
    beautiful
So that even the colonel respected her.

And one could hear the lover say:

"If Adelita would be my sweetheart
If Adelita would be my wife
I would buy her a silk dress
And take her dancing to the military
    ball."

One night when the troops came in

Among them was the sergeant
And one could hear the voice of a
    woman crying
Her prayer was heard across the camp.

Upon hearing her, the sergeant, much
    afraid
Of losing forever his beloved,
Hiding his voice under the night
To his beloved he sang thusly.

And after the cruel battle was over

And the troops returned to their camp
Because of the deaths caused by the
    machine gun
The regiment had incurred heavy
    casualties
And the sergeant remembering his
    loved one
And the soldiers returning from the
    battle
Offering their love to the women
Would sing this song of war.

And one could hear the lover say:
"If Adelita left me for another
I would follow her through land and sea
If by sea in a warship
If by land on a military train.

"And if I happen to die while fighting

y mi cadáver lo van a sepultar,	And my body is about to be buried,
Adelita, por Dios te lo ruego	Adelita, in the name of God I beg of you
que con tus ojos me vayas a llorar.	That you will shed tears for me."

This version comprises two parts: polished literary verses and verses taken from the older version. This second version evidences an educated poetic style, while in the first the lyrics share the popular vocabulary commonly found in folk songs. For example, the adjective *abrupta* (abrupt), the nouns *serranía* (sierra), *moza* (young woman), *amada* (beloved), *escolta* (guard), *plegaria* (prayer), *esbozo* (thicket), and the verbs *enamorada* (in love), *idolatraba* (idolized), *conduciendo* (conducting), *sollozaba* (cried), *escuchó* (heard), *ocultando* (hiding), all point to a more literary poetic style. The verses taken from the earlier "La Adelita" (strophes two, five and six) reflect a less sophisticated vocabulary.

This "La Adelita" is an example of the idealized, beautiful, and valiant soldadera type in its romanticized manifestation. The first strophe converts the love-sick person from a man to a woman. In the earlier version the voice of the soldier-lover introduced Adelita as the object of his unending love and affection. In the second version an omniscient narrator describes Adelita as "madly in love with the sergeant" and valiantly following him—as a camp follower, no doubt." The woman here is definitely on the battlefield in the high sierras, from which the soldiers carry out their military operations.

The strophe further concentrates on the Adelita persona, describing her popularity with the troops in general and highlighting her military attribute of bravery. This soldadera had won the respect and admiration of common soldiers as well as officers of the highest rank—"hasta el mismo coronel la respetaba."

The third strophe, however, has the brave and beautiful Woman Warrior uncharacteristically weeping. The sergeant, upon hearing her, begins to sing to her two verses taken from the earlier version (strophes four and six). These verses reiterate the theme of fear of separation: abandonment by the beloved and the possibility of dying in battle.

"La Adelita," like "La Cucaracha," became one of the most popular musical compositions among revolutionary soldiers. The name Adelita became synonymous with soldadera. Whether there was an actual Adelita is open to question. Romero Aceves (1982:279) suggests that Adelita was a nurse and not a fighting soldadera. Morales (1981) attributes one version of the song (he does not specify which one) to Sergeant Antonio del Río Armenta of the Carrancista troops, who is said to have written the ballad in honor of a nurse, Adela Velarde Pérez. In a private interview Velarde Pérez recounted her involvement in the Revolution as a nurse with the Carrancista troops and insisted that Armenta, a comrade in arms, had written "La Adelita" in her honor. She said that Armenta had died in battle in her arms after declaring his secret love for her.

An equally spirited debate surrounds "La Valentina" and the woman who inspired it. This popular revolutionary song appeared around 1909. The author is unknown. The plaintive lyrics tell of a love-sick suitor who is expressing his "passion" for Valentina. Oddly, although this corrido supposedly is based on a real-life guerrillera, the song never situates the lady-love on the battlefield. The poetic voice of the lover is concerned mainly with his love for Valentina and the prospects of death in war or at the hands of a rival.

La Valentina	Valentina
Una pasión me domina	A passion dominates me
es la que me hizo venir,	That's what brought me here,
Valentina, Valentina,	Valentina, Valentina,
yo te quisiera decir.	I wish to tell you so.
Dicen que por tus amores	They say because of your love
un mal me van a seguir,	A bad turn will be done to me.
no le hace que sean el diablo	I don't care if they're the devil
yo también me se morir.	I too know how to die.
Si porque tomo tequila	If I drink tequila today
mañana tomo jerez,	Tomorrow I'll drink sherry,
si porque me ves borracho	If you see me tipsy today
mañana ya no me ves.	Tomorrow you shall not see me.
Valentina, Valentina,	Valentina, Valentina,
rendido estoy a tus pies,	I surrender at your feet.
si me han de matar mañana,	If they're going to kill me tomorrow
que me maten de una vez.	Let them kill me now.

Although composed in 1909, "La Valentina" did not achieve great popularity until 1914, when the song was applied to Valentina Gatica, from the state of Sinaloa, who was a soldadera with the Obregón forces. Romero Aceves (1982:279) asserts that "the young woman was left an orphan when her father died in combat. She followed Obregón's troops becoming one more soldier among his troops. She was brave, daring, beautiful and attractive. She attracted attention with her military type clothing, her two cartridge belts slung across her chest, and her rifle hanging on her shoulder. . . ." Unfortunately for the real-life Valentina, as for many other soldaderas and Mexican women in general, she reaped few benefits from Mexico's social upheaval. After the Revolution, Valentina Gatica moved to Mexico City, "living in old age and forgotten in a shack around Peralvillo, where she was receiving a small pension that General Aaron Saenz acquired for her" (280).

The romanticized soldadera songs gloss over the guerrilleras' actual involvement in war and focus on the male soldiers' romantic liaisons with them. The woman is not taken seriously as a soldier and is denied the proper honor and respect she deserves. Paradoxically, however, the great popularity of the songs helped imprint the image of the soldadera in the public mind, thus validating and cementing in Mexican culture the soldadera archetype.

Archetypal

Finally we come to those songs in which the mythification of the soldadera is complete. That is to say, in these songs the character becomes an archetype representing the Mexican woman soldier in mythic proportions. The ballad no longer bases its narrative on actual verifiable events but on the deification and glorification of the soldadera as legend, as a human being larger than life. I have found only three such corridos: "Juana Gallo" (Vélez, 1982:44), "La Chamuscada" (ibid.: 52–53), and "La soldadita" (*Cancionero mexicano*, 1980:171). The first two are particularly significant (both have been translated into films), and I will analyze them here.

"Juana Gallo"

Entre ruidos de cañones y metrallas
surgió una historia popular,
de una joven que apodaban "Juana Gallo"
por ser valiente a no dudar.

Siempre al frente de la tropa se encontraba
peleando como cualquier "Juan"
en campaña ni pelón se le escapaba,
sin piedad se los tronaba con su enorme pistolón.
Era el "coco" de todos los federales
y los mismos generales tenían pavor.

¡Abranla, que ahí viene "Juana Gallo"!,
va gritando en su caballo: ¡Viva la Revolución!
Para los que son calumniadores,
para todos los traidores,
trae bien puesto el corazón.

Una noche que la guardía le tocaba,
un batallón se le acercó,
sin mentirles a la zanja no llegaba
cuando con ellos acabó.

Otra vez que se encontraban ya sitiados
teniendo un mes de no comer,
salió al frente con un puñado de soldados
que apodaban "Los Dorados", y salvó la situación.
Por vengar la muerte de su "Chón" amado
por su vida había jurado, conspiración.

¡Abranla, que ahí viene "Juana Gallo"!

"Juana Gallo"

Between the din of cannons and machine guns
There rose a popular legend,
Of a young maid nicknamed "Juana Gallo"
Because she was brave, no doubt at all.

At the front of the troops she would be found
Fighting like any "Juan,"
On the battlefield no "bald-head" [Federal soldier] escaped her,
Without mercy she shot them down with her enormous gun.

She was the bogeyman of all the Federal soldiers
And even the generals were scared of her.

Make way, here comes "Juana Gallo"!
She rides shouting on her horse: Long live the Revolution!
Beware all the liars,
Beware all the traitors,
Her heart is ready to fight.

One night when it was her turn as guard,
A battalion came close by,
I am not lying to you, they had not reached the trench
When she cut them all down.

Another time when they were all surrounded
Not having eaten for a month
She came right out with a handful of soldiers,
The soldiers known as "the Golden Ones," and saved the day.
Because she wanted to avenge the death of her beloved "Chón"
On her life she swore to join the insurgents.

I have not found this corrido in older ballad collections, such as Mendoza's, Campos's, or the Guerrero Collection. It appears, however, in most of the popular *cancionero* collections and in Gilberto Vélez's *Corridos mexicanos*. An author, Ernesto Juárez, is credited with the composition—which also tends to indicate a more recent vintage. In addition, the legend of "Juana Gallo" has been made into a movie. I am assuming, then, that the song is a result of the general mythification process which the soldier woman has undergone.

The title of the song, "Juana Gallo," underscores the archetypal nature of the soldadera presented. First, *Juana*—as well as *galleta* ("cookie") and *Adelita*—is a term applied to any soldarera (Soto, 1979:27). It is a derivative of *Juan*, which is the equivalent of *G.I. Joe*—the common soldier. Therefore *Juana* has its origin in its association with the male soldier: Juana, like her predecessor Eve, is an appendage to the male. Implicit is the assumption that she joined the Revolution not because she subscribed to its ideology but because she was in love with her "Juan," her man. *Juana*, however, in time came to mean soldadera, or "fighting woman."

The second name given to Juana is an appropriation from the male domain. *Gallo*, literally meaning "cock," is a metaphor for "fighter," someone who is brave and aggressive in the face of danger. This word—and not, as one might expect, *macho*—is the preferred designation for the valiant male corrido hero. Paredes (1967) asserts that it was not until the 1940s that the term *macho* began to be used in corridos. Examples of the use of *gallo* in corridos are abundant:

Año de mil ochocientos
noventa y uno al presente
murió don Demetrio Jáurgui
que era un gallo muy valiente.[8]

Year of 1800
Ninety-one current
Don Demetrio Jáugrui died
He was a very valiant cock.

Decía Benito Canales	Benito Canales would say
cuando se estaba muriendo	When he was dying,
—Mataron un gallo fino	"You've killed a fine cock
respetado del gobierno.[9]	Respected by the Government."

Le dio un balazo en la boca	He shot him in the mouth
y le dio otro en la cara	And another [shot] in the face
para que tenga recuerdos	So he would remember
del gallo de Santa Clara.[10]	The cock from Santa Clara.

Tiraba como ninguno	He was a marksman like no other
este Carlos Coronado,	This Carlos Coronado,
todo el Bajío lo quería	All in the lowlands loved him
porque era un gallo jugado.[11]	Because he was a skilled cock.

Transference of the term to Juana endows her with the superhuman qualities of the male. In addition, her linkage with the animal forces of nature is important in the mythification process, for by this anthropomorphism she is identified with the cosmos as a unified force of energy—Juana and nature are one and the same, a vital dynamic force. The cock, in addition, is a symbol of other cosmic phenomena: "As the bird of dawn, the cock is a sun-symbol, and an emblem of vigilance and activity. Immolated to Priapus and Aesculapiius, it was supposed to cure the sick" (Cirlot, 1962:51). It is furthermore a Christian image "regarded as an allegory of vigilance and resurrection." The female soldier through her name "Juana Gallo" has been transformed into a mythic entity, an archetypal representation of those numerous women who fought in armed conflicts.

The first strophe situates the female protagonist in the din of the battlefield and, more significantly, in the realm of legend, of mythic space and time: "surgió una historia popular." No specific time is stated as is traditionally done in corridos. The word *historia*, however, suggests "freezing" of an event in a temporal dimension. Its repetition in oral transmission will link it to ritual. By structuring the phenomenon in the framework of a story or narrative, the events can be repeated ad infinitum. "Juana Gallo" has passed from the realm of the specific to the realm of the archetype.

The female protagonist in the historia recounted in this ballad, furthermore, exhibits almost supernatural abilities—she is a superwoman, an Amazon. She is heartless with the enemy, whom she repeatedly vanquishes "en campaña ni pelón se le escapaba, / sin piedad se los tronaba con su enorme pistolón." Her weapon is a phallic symbol of gargantuan proportions. The "pistolón" parallels Juana's stature as a soldier—larger than life. The lines that follow ("Era el 'coco' de todos los federales / y los mismos generales tenían pavor") reiterate Juana's mythic proportions and power. The coco, or bogeyman, belongs to the supernatural realm. By attributing to Juana unlimited power, the song casts her as a female Hercules who is invincible and whose enemies, even the most stout of heart, tremble at her audacity. Juana, like the Amazons of old, fearlessly mounted on her horse, is the scourge of all that is evil—liars and traitors.

The final strophe reiterates Juana's immortality and mythic dimensions: although she has not eaten food for a month and in spite of this violation of physiological and biological laws, she confronts the enemy forces and defeats them, saving her battalion.

A touch of fairy-tale magic is provided by the soldiers who were chosen to accompany Juana to the fray, "the Golden Ones." These soldiers were Villa's elite troops, so denominated because of the bright goldlike cartridges and the khaki color of their uniforms (Braddy, 1970). They, too, achieved mythic stature in revolutionary lore because of their invincibility and bravery. Juana, surrounded by these golden, magical forces, can never be defeated. She is Diana accompanied by the rays of the sun.

The archetype of the Woman Warrior also appears in "La Chamuscada" ("The Burnt One"). Like "Juana Gallo," "La Chamuscada" has been made into a movie.

"La Chamuscada"

"La Chamuscada" le dicen 'onde quera,
porque sus manos la pólvora quemó,
entre las balas pasó le pelotera,
la "revolufia" sus huellas le dejó.

No hubo un hombre jamás a quien quisiera,
de entre la tropa ninguno le cuadró,
sólo a su padre le fue fiel soldadera
y al pobrecito una bala lo quebró.

Hoy, cuando escucha cantar esta tonada,
como que siente hartas ganas de llorar,
pero se aguanta, porque es "La Chamuscada,"
que por valiente llegó a ser general.

Yo vi a su padre morir entre sus brazos
y vi también al tradior que lo mató,
al muy canalla le dio cuatro balazos,
como cedazo dejó su corazón.

Desde aquel dí ya no fue soldadera,
con su canana repleta y su fusil
en las batallas fue siempre la primera,
las balaceras nomás la hacían reir.

Hoy, cuando escucha cantar esta tonada,
como que siente hartas ganas de llorar,
pero se aguanta, porque es "La Chamuscada,"
que por valiente llegó a ser general.

"The Burnt One"

"The Burnt One" they call her everywhere,
Because gunpowder burnt her hands,

Between the bullets she lived through the brawl
The Revolution left its mark on her.

There never was a man she could love.
From among the troops she liked none,
Only to her father was she a faithful soldier
And the poor man was killed by a bullet.

Today when she hears this song
She feels a great desire to cry,
But she does not give in, for she is "The Burnt One"
Who with her bravery achieved the rank of general.

I saw her father die in her arms.
And I also saw the traitor who killed him.
The scoundrel pumped four bullets in him
Like a sieve he left his heart.

From that day on she was no longer a common soldier
With her cartridge belt full and her rifle
In battles she was always the first,
The bullets only made her laugh.

As we see by the very title, this Woman Warrior is given from the inception of the song a tinge of the supernatural by association with the devil, for the devil in Hispanic popular tradition is referred to as "El Chamuco" or "El Chamuscado" because of his association with the fires of hell. The Chamuco is thought of as having the appearance of a horribly burnt semihuman monster completely covered with soot. The nickname "Chamuscada" therefore links this woman soldier with the supernatural powers of Satan. The ballad explains that she acquired her nickname from the explosion of gunpowder in her hands.

"La Chamuscada," like "Juana Gallo" in the previous ballad, is fearless and invincible. Bullets do not harm her, even though she is in the thick of battle. And like the Amazons of yore she is not interested in males. She has no use or liking for any of them except her father. When her father is shot to death, she joins the battle full time; she is no longer merely a camp follower but a dedicated participant in battle. Her skill and bravery prove so great that she is soon promoted to the rank of general.

Interestingly, "La Chamuscada" hears a corrido about herself and becomes emotionally distraught, wanting to break into tears; but, being the strong-willed Amazon that she is, she does not capitulate to her more sensitive nature and carries on.

CONCLUSION

As we have seen, representations of the soldadera in the Mexican corrido evolved from historical figure to romanticized love object to mythic archetype. A patriarchal perspective dominates all three representations of the fighting woman, however, and generally obfuscates the Mexicana's true role in armed conflicts. In spite of this inherent flaw, the corridos shed light on the soldaderas' participation in Mexico's Revolution and offer further proof of women's involvement in Mexico's search for democracy.

The soldadera corridos were the first artistic manifestations of women's participation in the Revolution. Repeatedly sung throughout the war years, they had a tremendous impact on the psyche of the Mexican people. Such widely popular songs as "La Adelita" and "La Valentina" reinforced the soldadera image, however romanticized and sanitized this representation may have been.

It was inevitable, therefore, that the archetypal image of the soldadera widely propagated by the corrido would show up in other artistic media, such as the novel and later on the movies. Women soldiers as fictional characters began to appear as early as 1915 with Mariano Azuela's *Los de abajo (The Underdogs)*. Later novels, such as Francisco Rojas Gonzales's *La Negra Angustias* (1948), Jesús Goytortúa Santos's *Pensativa* (1947), and Elena Poniatowska's *Hasta no verte Jesús mío* (1969), also treat the subject of soldadera involvement in wars.[12]

The film industry, although late in picking up the theme, nevertheless has produced a few movies in which the figure of the romanticized soldadera is the main protagonist (see part E, Works Cited and Consulted). The industry's interpretation of the saga of these heroic figures, however, generally does not provide a realistic historical perspective of women soldiers in the Revolution. Four Mexican films—*La Soldadera* (n.d.), *La Guerrillera de Villa* (1984), *La Generala* (1984), and *Juana Gallo* (1985)—are representative of the genre. In the first, the soldadera is a dumb, pathetic creature who is really uninvolved in the ideological struggle and is merely able to roll with the punches. The second film is a song-and-dance trivialization of the heroic figure of a female guerrilla fighter. The third, though it is an excellent movie and masterfully executed, is really a psychological study of a strong-willed *hacendada* more than an epic of the fighting woman. The fourth, *Juana Gallo*, is more attuned to the historical realities of the soldadera but suffers from the silver screen's penchant for adding a love interest and out-of-place humor.

Obviously, in examining the representations of the soldadera in the corrido—with all their faults—we can safely conclude that they are far better balanced than those in movies and novels. In fact, as we have seen, the soldadera representation in the corrido exhibits a well-defined process in which we can trace the evolution of the image of the guerrillera.

The psychiatrist Santiago Ramírez views the era of the Revolution as an important period in which Mexican women achieved maximum integration into the affairs of the nation:

> During the Revolution, an epoch which we can say from a sociocultural perspective is a confrontation with the Father, the Mexican male integrates women into the struggle, granting them the status of equals. For the first time in the history of Mexico, women are able to exercise their potential at the side of males in a struggle that takes them away from their babies' cribs. The songs of the Revolution, "La Adelita," "La Valentina," etc., are paeons to his female

comrade in arms. The possibility of contact between male and female acquired its maximum potential during the Revolution. (Ramírez, 1977:115-116, my translation)

In retrospect we see that an *acercamiento* (rapprochement) of equals failed to materialize after the Revolution. The soldadera was forced to fade into the woodwork by male leaders who, taking complete control, encouraged women to return to the home and become, once again, mothers and daughters. It was easier to glorify the soldadera and to mythify her than to grant her the vote.

Afterword

Starting from the premise that the archetype is a mental construct solidly grounded in reality and experience, I have endeavored to demonstrate how the archetypal representation of women in the Mexican corrido has been structured by four important vectors: historical forces, literary tradition, patriarchal ideology, and the social class of the troubador and his or her audience. Both the historical and the literary vectors vary in the influence they exert for each archetypal image. For the Great Mother archetypes and the Eve archetype, literary tradition is the determining factor; for the Protective Mother Goddess and the Soldier archetypes, history is the overriding factor in the structuring of the archetypal images.

All four archetypal images are equally influenced by patriarchal ideology and social class of bard and audience. Florid blotches of a patriarchal structure are evident in the conceptualization of a passive mater dolorosa whose powerlessness in the political and economic social order reduces the mother figure to a helpless entity who can only mourn for the death of her progeny instead of having the political power to change those conditions that led to the death of her son or daughter. We are cognizant of patriarchal influence in the overglorification of a female deity, the Virgin of Guadalupe, while males continue to oppress a large part of the female population. The patriarchal order shines through the violence directed at recalcitrant women who challenge male authority at a dance or in the privacy of the home. Women who are different from the "good" daughter, wife, or mother pay with their lives for their audacity in deviating from established patterns of feminine behavior.

The near silence on the heroic involvement of women at war in corrido lyrics or their representation as mere romantic objects reveals the structure of a patriarchal order that wishes to deny Mexicanas the right to vote, to hold office, and to exercise other rights for which millions of men and women gave their lives in the revolutionary struggles.

Even with all the weaknesses inherent in the genre, which cannot escape its patriarchal ideology, I find the corrido a valid social document that can provide a new perspective on Mexican women and their roles in Mexican society. As we have seen, the corrido does present an active, aggressive mother in opposition to a passive one; it does incorporate strong, audacious women who veer off the beaten path and assert their individuality. And the corrido's adherence to the reality factor provides us with additional viewpoints on the role of the soldaderas. We can see that the Virgin of Guadalupe is a respected and honored figure in the corrido. Her appearance as a powerful figure became acceptable because it helped reduce the tension between reality and the strong patriarchal perception that women are helpless entities to be taken care of. By granting power to Guadalupe, the tension was somewhat resolved. Men could acknowl-

117

edge the power of women from a safe distance; women could see themselves and their power reflected in Guadalupe.

In addition to the multiplicity of images gleaned from the Mexican ballad, a significant discovery in my analysis was the pinpointing of the process of archetypal formation in an artistic medium. Some feminists have posited that archetypes are not biologically inherited but are a result of historical forces that converge to shape a given archetypal image (see Green and Kahn, 1985). My aim in this analysis of corridos had as a primary objective to provide a step-by-step tracing of the various historical and cultural strands that have cohered to weave archetypal figures of women into these folk songs. I trust that these chapters have shed new light on the important but little understood process of archetype formation.

Notes

INTRODUCTION

1. See Campos (1962, vol. 1), Castañeda (1943), Menéndez Pidal (1968 and 1958), Mendoza (1939, 1954, 1964, and 1982), Paredes (1957), Prieto Posada (1944), and Simmons (1957 and 1963).

2. See Mendoza (1939, 1954, 1964, and 1982).

3. See Bonfil (1970), Campos (1962), Castañeda (1943), Dickey (1978), Mendoza (1939 and 1964), Paredes (1958), and Simmons (1957).

4. See definitions in Jung (1965:380, 1953c:par. 28, and 1960:380). See also the articles in Lauter and Rupprecht (1985). For an example of the application of the feminist archetypal method to literature, see Pratt (1981). For an older conceptualization of the archetype in literature, see Bodkin (1948).

5. See also Neumann (1973). For a discussion of the controversial aspects of the archetype vis-à-vis Neumann, consult Lauter and Rupprecht (1958:10–11).

6. Duvalier also identified eight secondary formulas: reiterated phrase or phrases admonishing the audience not to forget a particular event; an exclamation or reflection the corridista makes regarding the events narrated; biographical data pertaining to the protagonist; summary and synthesis of the main theme expressed in the corrido; an invitation from the corridista to buy the corrido (i.e., the broadside); the ending of the first corrido and an invitation to stay and listen to the second part of the song or to a new ballad; and the name of the author of the song (Castañeda, 1943:18). The meter, rhyme, and strophe structure of the corrido have been studied by Castañeda. Its most outstanding characteristic is its great flexibility in meter, rhyme, and strophe composition. This flexibility contributed in no small part to its popularity and survival. The most common meter in the Mexican ballad is octosyllabic, its rhyme scheme varying ABAB, ABBA, ABCB; it frequently exhibits a four-line strophe.

7. See Herrera-Sobek (1986, 1982).

1. THE GOOD MOTHER ARCHETYPE

1. Conceptualization of the oral-formulaic theory was possible as a result of Albert B. Lord's intensive studies on the Serbo-Croatian epic undertaken in Yugoslavia in the 1930s and the subsequent publication of these studies by his brilliant student Milman Parry (see Lord, 1960). The analysis of the collected Serbo-Croatian epics and the fieldwork done in Yugoslavia observing actual epic compositions and performances resulted in the discovery that the formulaic character of literature originated in oral tradition. Parry and Lord's work elicited an enormous scholarly response and opened a new field of endeavor, mainly applying the oral-formulaic method to a number of literatures. See John Miles Foley, *The Theory of Oral Composition: History and Methodology* (Bloomington: Indiana University Press, 1988).

2. Other studies include Baños (1973) and de Leñero (1969).

3. For a different perspective on this issue, see Ruiz (1985) and Fernández-Kelly (1983).

4. For other genres, see Hill and Browner (1982).

2. THE TERRIBLE MOTHER ARCHETYPE

1. For a thorough discussion of these ideas, see Guntrip (1969 and 1961), Winnicott (1965), and Klein and Riviere (1964). Schapiro (1983) has fruitfully applied these theories to the image of the mother appearing in the English Romantic poets.

2. Pearce (1950:295) states: "In New Mexico there lingers a folk belief that has its

roots in Mexico and Spain and is parallel in other European traditions. It is that of 'the bad son' whose rebellion against parental authority brings a curse and physical deformity in punishment." See also my study on "The Devil in the Discoteque: A Semiotic Analysis of a Mexican Legend," in *Monsters with Iron Teeth: Perspectives on Contemporary Legend,* ed. Gillian Bennett and Paul Smith (Sheffield, England: Sheffield Academic Press, 1988), 147–157.

3. See also Paredes (1959:88–92).

4. According to classical mythology, Cassandra had the gift of prophecy but the curse that no one would believe her prophecies. See Monaghan (1981:58).

5. Tucker (1981) cites several examples of the mother figure appearing in a mean, capricious, and even cannibalistic light. Tucker explains the popularity of these jokes and narratives among preadolescent girls as being related to the authoritarian roles of the mother and the need for independence in young girls:

> A girl on the brink of adolescence is apt to question, or at least closely examine, her mother's control over her daily life. Even if she is not yet beginning to go out on dates, she is keenly aware of her mother's power and her increasing need for independence. When this power seems excessive, the fear of its misuse can find an outlet through storytelling. (70)

Rich (1976:235) offers these comments regarding this particular mother-daughter relationship:

> Matrophobia . . . is the fear not of one's mother or of motherhood but of becoming one's mother. Thousands of daughters see their mothers as having taught a compromise and self-hatred they are struggling to win free of, the one whom the restrictions and degradations of a female existence were perforce transmitted. Easier by far to hate and reject a mother outright than to see beyond her to the forces acting upon her. But where a mother is hated to the point of matrophobia there may also be a deep underlying pull toward her, a dread that if one releases one's guard one will identify with her completely.

6. Little work has been done on the bola. But see Celedonio Serrano Martínez's note on "La Bola Suriana" in Mario Colín, *Corridos Populares del Estado de México* (México: 1952), 78–80.

7. Compare the ballad of "Belém Galindo" with an untitled ballad recorded in Alcalá del Río, Andalucía, Spain, and quoted in Machado y Alvarez (1981: 40–41), which details the death of Carmela, a pregnant young woman, at the hands of her jealous husband. Carmela's husband had been lied to by his mother about Carmela's faithfulness. The folk song states:

La suegra lo estaba oyendo,	Her mother-in-law was listening,
Que era digno de escucharse.	It's worth hearing her say,
"Toma, Carmela, tu ropa,	"Here Carmela, take your clothes,
Véte á parir con tu madre,	Go give birth at your mother's.
A la noche viene Pedro,	Pedro will come home tonight;
Yo le daré ropa limpia	I will give him clean clothes
Y le daré de cenar."	And I will give him dinner."
A la noche vino Pedro:	At night Pedro comes home:
"Mi Carmela ¿dónde está?"	"And my Carmela, where is she?"
"Se ha ido en casa de su madre,	"She went to her mother's house.
Que m'ha tratado muy mal,	She treated me badly,
Que m'ha puesto d'alcahueta	She has accused me of pimping
Hasta el último linaje."	To the last son."

3. THE MOTHER GODDESS ARCHETYPE

1. I learned this version from my grandmother Susana Escamilla de Tarango. For an official version, see Aguilera et al. (1981: 17–82). See also Lucero-White (1953) and the

studies by Lafaye (1976), Ricard (1947), Martí (1973), Piault (1975), and Wolf (1958). For views that challenge the veracity of the Virgin of Guadalupe apparitions, consult Maza (1984), Smith (1983), and Rodríguez (1980).

2. Rodríguez (1980:13).

3. Ibid.

4. See Smith (1983) regarding scientific studies conducted on the cloth where the image is imprinted. Infrared photography and computer enhancements were used in Smith's investigation.

5. As late as the 1950s, I saw Indians coming down from their villages in the mountains to pay homage to the Virgin of Guadalupe on December 12 in Reynosa, Tamaulipas.

6. Lafaye (1976:97).

7. See Bonfil (1970).

8. "De Demetrio Jáurgui," Eduardo Guerrero (1924).

9. "Corrido Patriótico," ibid.

10. "Muerte de Alberto Balderas," Mendoza (1961:269).

11. "De Madero," Mendoza (1954:25).

12. "Al Excmo. Sr. Capitán General Don José María Morelos," Campos (1962, vol. 1:25).

13. "Martirio y muerte del Señor Madero," Henestrosa (1977:123–125).

14. "De Valerio Trujano," Mendoza (1976:3).

15. "Los temblores de Veracruz," ibid. (345–349).

16. "Del General Joaquín Amaro," Henestrosa (1977:197).

17. "El Rebelde de Morelos," Campos (1961, vol. 1:239).

18. "La muerte de Pancho Villa," Guerrero Collection.

19. Mendoza (1964:198–200).

4. THE LOVER ARCHETYPE

1. John Keats, "La Belle Dame sans Merci," in Ferguson (1973:177–178).

2. There are many relevant studies on the *vagina dentata* motif. See, for example, Lederer (1968:44), Campbell (1977:73), and Eliade (1958:63). Karen Horney (1967:135) posits a psychological explanation for man's fascination and constant portrayal of the "evil woman" in art and literature.

3. For further insights on La Llorona, see Kearney (1969:200), Leddy (1948:272), and Glazer (1984:108–127). See also Rogers (1977:64–69).

4. See Lacan (1977:chaps. 5 and 8).

5. See Thompson (1977:125).

6. See also Girard (1984:211).

7. See Vasconcelos (1971:325–358) and corridos such as "La traición de Guajardo" in the Eduardo Guerrero Collection that narrate treachery and betrayal among Mexican fighting men of the Revolution.

8. See Mirandé and Enríquez (1979:24–31), Crow (1980:75, 81, 88, 99, 149, 399, and 864), and Del Castillo (1977:124–149).

9. See Vasconcelos (1971:407–422).

10. Reynaldo Martínez, "El regio traficante," *Pueblito* album sung by Los Cadetes de Linares, Ramex, L.P. 1010.

11. See Paredes (1957:23–32) and Samora et al. (1979).

12. Among revisionist works by Chicano sociologists, anthropologists, and historians we may include Mirandé and Enríquez (1979; see also Mirandé, 1985), Montiel (1970), Mora and Del Castillo (1980), Peñalosa (1968), Sena-Rivera (1979), and Senour (1977). Zinn (1975, 1980a, 1980b, 1982, 1984) has studied the Mexican-American family extensively. Del Castillo (1984) revises several stereotypical beliefs about the Chicano family, providing data from historical archives.

13. See Madsen (1964), Rubel (1966), Grebler et al. (1970), and Clark (1959).

14. See Clark (1959), Jones (1948), Madsen (1964), and Staples (1971).
15. See Leacock (1981), Stone (1976), and Sanday (1981).
16. See Mosher (1966:1–19).

5. THE SOLDIER ARCHETYPE

1. Several studies on mythology and on women mention the Amazons. See, for example, Hamilton (1969), Morford and Lenardon (1974), and Rose (1959). Two scholars discuss the controversial issue of the actual existence of the Amazon kingdom: Diner (1965) and Lefkowitz (1986). Diner takes a decidedly pro position, whereas Lefkowitz believes historical data do not support the existence of an Amazon principality. Monaghan (1981) leans toward accepting the existence of the Amazons.

2. For Pallas Athena's role in battle, see Lattimore (1951).
3. See Montalvo (1959).
4. See, for example, Randall (1981) and *Mujeres en Revolución* (1978).
5. See Arrom (1985:chap. 1).
6. See Soto (1979). See also Elena Poniatowska's novel *Hasta no verte Jesús mío* (1984), in which the protagonist, Jesusa, repeatedly uses the term *galletas* to refer to the soldaderas.
7. See General Felipe Angeles's personal account of the battle in Moreno (1978:85–103).
8. "De Demetrio Jáurgui," Guerrero Collection.
9. "Benito Canales," ibid.
10. "De Don Lucas Gutiérrez," Mendoza (1976:192).
11. "De Carlos Coronado," ibid. (193).
12. Examples of novels with soldadera content (albeit as minor characters) include Agustín Yañez, *Al filo del agua* (México: Editorial Porrúa, 1969); José Rubén Romero, *Rosenda* (México: Editorial Porrúa, 1962); José Vasconcelos, *Ulises Criollo* (México: Editorial Jus, 1978); Martín Luis Guzmán, *The Eagle and the Serpent* (New York: Doubleday Dolphin, 1965); and Josephina Niggli, "Soldadera," in *Mexican Folk Plays* (Chapel Hill: University of North Carolina Press, 1938).

Works Cited and Consulted

A. MAJOR CORRIDO COLLECTIONS

Arellano, Anselmo
  1976   *Los pobladores nuevo mexicanos y su poesía 1889–1950*. Albuquerque: Pajarito Publications.
Austin, Mary
  1919   "New Mexico Folk Poetry." *El Palacio* 7:146–154.
Bonfil, Alicia O.
  1970   *La literatura cristera*. México: Instituto Nacional de Antropología e Historia.
  1976   *Corridos de la Rebelión Cristera: La Cristiada*. Vol. 20. Linear Notes, Instituto Nacional de Antropología e Historia, LP MC-0780, INAH-20, México.
Calleja, Julián
  1956   *Método de Guitarra sin maestro*. México: El Libro Español. Various editions published. Nos. 1–9 published in 1951, 1956, 1963, and 1967.
Campa, Arthur León
  1946   *Spanish Folk-Poetry in New Mexico*. Albuquerque: University of New Mexico Press.
Campos, Armando de María y
  1962   *La revolución mexicana a través de los corridos populares*. 2 vols. México: Biblioteca de Instituto Nacional de Estudios Históricos de la Revolución Mexicana.
Campos, Rubén
  1929   *El folklore literario de México*. México.
  1974   *El folklore literario y musical de México*. México: Secretaría de Obras y Servicios. Colección Metropolitana.
Cancionero Mexicano. 2 vols. *Canciones mexicanas y canciones que han tenido gran popularidad en México*.
  1979–1980 México: Libro-Mex Editores.
Canciones de México: 200 joyas de la canción mexicana.
  N.D.   Guadalajara, Jalisco, México: Dibujos Musicales "Ambríz."
Castañeda, Daniel
  1943   *El corrido mexicano: Su técnica literaria y musical*. México: Editorial "Sucro."
Colín, Mario
  1948   *Corridos de Texcaltitlán*. Toluca: H. Ayuntamiento de Texcaltitlán.
  1952   *Corridos populares del estado de México*. México: n.p.
Corridos Mexicanos
  1965   México: Colección Adelita.
Corridos Mexicanos
  1984   México: Gómez, Gómez Hnos. Editores.
De Grial, Hugo
  1977   *Músicos mexicanos*. México: Editorial Diana.
Dickey, Dan Williams
  1978   *The Kennedy Corridos: A Study of the Ballads of a Mexican American Hero*. Austin: University of Texas, Center for Mexican American Studies.

Esparza Sánchez, Cuauhtémoc
  1976   *El Corrido Zacatecano*. México: Instituto Nacional de Antropología e
              Historia.
Espinosa, Aurelio Macedonio
  1953   *Romancero de Nuevo Méjico*. Madrid: Consejo Superior de Investiga-
              ciones Científicas.
Fuentes, Rumel
  1977   *14 corridos chicanos de Rumel*. Mimeograph copy.
Gamio, Manuel
  1971   *Mexican Immigration to the United States: A Study of Human Migration
              and Adjustment*. New York: Dover.
Gómez Maganda, Alejandro
  1970   *Corridos y cantares de la Revolución Mexicana*. México: Instituto Mex-
              icano de Cultura.
González, Jovita
  1930   "Tales and Songs of the Texas-Mexicans." In *Man, Bird and Beast,* ed.
              J. Frank Dobie. Austin: Publications of the Texas Folk-lore Society. Pp.
              86–116.
Guerrero, Eduardo
  N.D.   Collection of Corridos in the Biblioteca Nacional de México. Mexico
              City.
  1924a   *Canciones y corridos populares*. 2 vols. México: Publicados por Eduardo
              Guerrero. Collection of *Hojas Sueltas* in the Biblioteca Nacional de
              México.
  1924b   *Corridos Mexicanos*. Collection of *Hojas Sueltas* in the Biblioteca Na-
              cional de México, Mexico City.
  1931   *Corridos históricos de la Revolución Mexicana desde 1910 a 1930 y otros
              notables de varias épocas*. México: Eduardo Guerrero Collection at the
              Biblioteca Nacional de México.
Henestrosa, Andrés
  1977   *Espuma y flor de corridos mexicanos*. México: Editorial Porrúa.
Hernández, Guillermo
  1978   *Canciones de la Raza: Songs of the Chicano Experience*. Berkeley:
              Fuego de Aztlán, Chicano Studies Program, University of California.
Herrera Frimont, Celestino
  1934   *Los corridos de la Revolución*. Pachuca, Hidalgo: Ediciones del Instituto
              Científico y Literario.
Herrera-Sobek, María
  1979   *The Bracero Experience: Elitelore Versus Folklore*. Los Angeles: UCLA
              Latin American Center Publications.
Libro de Oro de la Canción: Canciones populares desde 1850 hasta 1953.
  1952   México: No. 2 edition published in 1953; no date for no. 3 edition.
Libro de Oro de la Poesía Mexicana. Vol. 2.
  1957   México: Libro Mex Editores.
Los Mejores Corridos Mexicanos
  1972   México: El Libro Español.
  N.D.   México: Album de Oro método de Guitarra Series. No. 9. Janibi Edi-
              tores, S. A.
Lucero-White, Aurora Lea
  1953   *Literary Folklore of the Hispanic Southwest*. San Antonio, Tex. Naylor.
Melgarejo Vivanco, José Luis
  N.D.   *"Juan Pirulero" y otros corridos*. Biblioteca Nacional de México.
Mendoza, Vicente T.
  1939   *El romance español y el eorrido mexicano*. México: Ediciones de la
              Universidad Nacional Autónoma de México.

1944   *50 corridos mexicanos*. México: Ediciones de la Secretaría Pública.
1954   *El corrido mexicano*. México: Fondo de Cultura Económica.
1956   *Panorama de la música tradicional de México*. México: Imprenta Universitaria.
1964   *Lírica narrativa de México*. México: Instituto de Investigaciones Estéticas, Universidad Nacional Autónoma de México.
1976   *El corrido mexicano*. México: Fondo de Cultura Económica.
1982   *La canción mexicana: Ensayo de clasificación y antología*. México: Fondo de Cultura Económica.

Menéndez Pidal, Ramón
1958   *Los romances de América y otros estudios*. Madrid: Editorial Espasa-Calpe.

Moreno, Daniel
1978   *Batallas de la Revolución y sus corridos*. México: Editorial Porrúa.

Paredes, Américo
1957   *"With His Pistol in His Hand": A Border Ballad and Its Hero*. Austin: University of Texas Press.
1976   *A Texas-Mexican Cancionero: Folksongs of the Lower Border*. Urbana: University of Illinois Press.

Poesías patrióticas y folklóricas y los corridos de la Revolución.
1976   México: Editores Mexicanos Unidos.

Posada, José Guadalupe
1977   *Las calaveras vivientes de Posada*. México: Editorial Cosmos-César Macazaga Ordoño.

Prieto Posada, Margarita
1944   "Del rabel a la guitarra: El corrido mexicano como un derivado del romance español." Master's thesis, Faculdad de Filosofía y Letras, Universidad de México.

Romero Flores, Jesús
1979   *Corridos de la revolución mexicana*. México: Costa-Amic, Editores.

Sánchez Juárez, Delfín
1977   *Poemas y corridos*. México: Manuel Porrúa.

Serrano Martínez, Celedonio
1973   *El corrido mexicano no deriva del romance español*. México: Centro Cultural Guerrerence.

Simmons, Merle E.
1957   *The Mexican Corrido as a Source of an Interpretive Study of Modern Mexico (1870–1950)*. Bloomington: Indiana University Press.

Stanford, Thomas E.
1974   *El villancico y el corrido mexicano*. México: Instituto Nacional de Antropología e Historia.

Taylor, Paul S.
1935   "Songs of the Mexican Migration." In *Puro Mexicano*, ed. J. Frank Dobie. Dallas: Southern Methodist University Press. Pp. 221–245.

Vázquez Santa Ana, Higinio
N.D.   *Canciones, Cantares y Corridos Mexicanos*. México: Ediciones León Sánchez.

Vélez, Gilberto
1982   *Corridos mexicanos*. México: Editores Mexicanos.

B. REFERENCES

Aguilera, Francisco M., Ernesto Corripio Ahumada, and Guillermo Schulenburg Prado
1981   *Album conmemorativo del 450 aniversario de las apariciones de Nuestra Señora de Guadalupe*. México: Ediciones Buena Nueva.

Alatorre, Angeles Mendieta
    1961   *La Mujer en la Revolución Mexcana*. México: Biblioteca del Instituto
            Nacional de Estudios Históricos de la Revolución Mexicana.

Amades, Juan
    1956   "Morfología del cuento folkórico hispánico." *Folklore Américas* 16
            (2):13–33.

Ankerson, Dudley
    1984   *Agrarian Warlord: Saturnino Cedillo and the Mexican Revolution in San
            Luis Potosí*. De Kalb, Ill.: Northern Illinois University Press.

Anton, Ferdinand
    1975   *La mujer en la América Antigua*. México: Editorial Extemporáneos.

Arrom, Silvia Marina
    1985   *The Women of Mexico City, 1790–1857*. Stanford: Stanford University
            Press.

Arróniz, Othón
    1979   *Teatro de evangelización en Nueva España*. México: Universidad Na-
            cional Autónoma de México.

Azuela, Mariano
    1962   *The Underdogs*. New York: New American Library.

Bachofen, J. J.
    1967   "Mother Right." *Myth, Religion, and Mother Right*. Princeton: Prince-
            ton University Press.

Bamberger, Joan
    1974   "The Myth of Matriarchy: Why Men Rule in Primitive Society." In
            Woman Culture and Society, ed. Michelle Zimbalist Rosaldo and Louise
            Lamphere. Stanford: Stanford University Press.

Bascom, William
    1957   "The Myth-Ritual Theory." *Journal of American Folklore* 70:103–114.

Begg, Ean
            The Cult of the Black Virgin. Boston: Arkana.

Berger, Peter L., and Thomas Luckmann
    1967   *The Social Construction of Reality: A Treatise in the Sociology of Knowl-
            edge*. New York: Doubleday.

Bodkin, Maud
    1948   *Archetypal Patterns in Poetry: Psychological Studies of Imagination*.
            New York: Oxford University Press, 1948.

Bracho, Diana
    1985   "El cine mexicano: ¿y en el papel de la mujer . . . quién?" *Mexican
            Studies/Estudios Mexicanos* 1(2):413–423.

Braddy, Haldeen
    1970   *Cock of the Walk: The Legend of Pancho Villa*. Port Washington, N.Y.:
            Kennikat Press.

Broyles, Yolanda Julia
    1986   "Women in El Teatro Campesino: '¿Apoco Estaba Molacha la Virgen de
            Guadalupe?'" In *Chicana Voices: Interactions of Class, Race, and Gen-
            der*. Austin: Center for Mexican American Studies Publications. Pp. 162–
            187.

Calderón de la Barca, Frances
    1982   *Life in Mexico*. Berkeley: University of California Press.

Campa, Arthur L.
    1979   *Hispanic Culture of the Southwest*. Norman: University of Oklahoma
            Press.

Campbell, Joseph

1973   *The Hero with a Thousand Faces*. Princeton: Princeton University Press.
1977   *The Masks of God: Primitive Mythology*. New York: Penguin Books.
Casasola Archive
1985   *Tierra y Libertad: Photographs of Mexico 1900–1935 from the Casasola Archive*. Oxford: Museum of Modern Art.
Casey, Edward S.
1974   "Toward an Archetypal Imagination." *Spring*, 1–32.
Caso, Alfonso
1964   "El águila y el nopal." *Memorias de la Academia Mexicana de la Historia*. 5(2):102–104.
Cassirer, Ernst
1955   *The Philosophy of Symbolic Forms: Mythical Thought*. Vol. 2. New Haven, Conn.: Yale University Press.
Catullus, G. V.
1964   *The Complete Poetry*. Ed. F. O. Copley. Ann Arbor: University of Michigan Press.
Chodorow, Nancy
1978   *The Reproduction of Mothering*. Berkeley: University of California Press.
Cirlot, J. E.
1962   *A Dictionary of Symbols*. New York: Philosophical Library.
Clark, Margaret
1959   *Health in the Mexican-American Culture*. Berkeley: University of California Press.
Coffin, Tristram Potter
1975   *The Female Hero in Folklore and Legend*. New York: Seabury Press.
Cromwell, Ronald E., and René A. Ruiz
1979   "The Myth of Macho Dominance in Decision Making within Mexican and Chicano Families." *Hispanic Journal of Behavioral Sciences* 1 (December):355–373.
Cromwell, Vicky L., and Ronald E. Cromwell
1978   "Perceived Dominance in Decision Making and Conflict Resolution among Anglo, Black and Chicano Couples." *Journal of Marriage and the Family* 40(November):749–759.
Crow, John A.
1980   *The Epic of Latin America*. Berkeley: University of California Press.
Cumberland, Charles
1974   *Mexican Revolution: The Constitutionalist Years*. Austin: University of Texas Press.
De Chasca, Edmund
1970   "Toward a Redefinition of Epic Formula in the Light of the Canto de Mío Cid." *Hispanic Review* 38:257–263.
De Hoyos Sainz, Luis, and Nieves De Hoyos Sainz Sancho
1985   *Manual de Folklore: La vida popular tradicional en España*. Madrid: Ediciones Istmo.
De Leñero, D. C. E.
1969   *¿Hacia dónde va la mujer mexicana?* Mexico City: Instituto de Estudios Sociales.
Del Castillo, Adelaida R.
1977   "Malintzin Tenépal: A Preliminary Look into a New Perspective." In *Essays on la Mujer*. Ed. Rosaura Sánchez and Rosa Martínez Cruz. Chicano Studies Center Publications, University of California, Los Angeles. Pp. 124–149.

Del Castillo, Richard Griswold
  1984   *La Familia: Chicano Families in the Urban Southwest 1848 to the
                Present.* Notre Dame, Ind.: University of Notre Dame Press.
Díaz del Castillo, Bernal
  1967   *Verdadera Historia de la conquista de la Nueva España.* México: Edi-
                torial Porrúa.
Díaz-Guerrero, Rogelio
  1955   "Neurosis and the Mexican Family Structure." *American Journal of
                Psychology* 112:411–417.
  1967   *Psychology of the Mexican.* Austin: University of Texas Press.
Diccionario Pequeño Larousse Ilustrado
  1968   Buenos Aires: Editorial Larousse.
Diner, Helen
  1965   *Mothers and Amazons: The First Feminine History of Culture.* New
                York: Julian Press.
Dorson, Richard M. (ed.)
  1983   *Handbook of American Folklore.* Bloomington: Indiana University Press.
Downing, Christine
  1981   *The Goddess.* New York: Crossroad.
Echanova Trujillo, C. A
  1945   *Leona Vicario: La mujer fuerte de la Independencia.* México: Ediciones
                Xochitl.
"El Día de San Juan"
  1980   *Cancionero Mexicano.* Vol. 1. México: Libro-Mex Editores, S. de R. L.
                Pp. 370–371.
Eliade, Mircea
  1958   *Rites and Symbols of Initiation: The Mysteries of Birth and Rebirth.* New
                York: Harper and Row.
  1960   *Myths, Dreams, and Mysteries.* New York: Harper and Row.
  1975   *Myth and Reality.* New York: Harper and Row.
  1974   *The Myth of the Eternal Return.* Princeton, N.J.: Princeton University
                Press.
Engels, Frederick
  1972   *The Origins of the Family, Private Property and the State.* New York:
                International Publishers.
Ercilla y Zúñiga, Alonso
  1977   *La Araucana.* México: Editorial Porrúa.
Fernández-Kelly, María Patricia
  1983   *For We Are Sold I and My People: Women and Industry in Mexico.*
                Albany: State University of New York Press.
Flaquer, Concepción Gimeno de
  1975   "Esposa y madre." In *La mujer y el movimiento obrero en el siglo XIX.*
                México: Centro de Estudios Históricos del Movimiento Obrero Mex-
                icano Año Internacional de la Mujer. Pp. 65–66.
Fontenrose, Joseph
  1971   *The Ritual Theory of Myth.* Berkeley: University of California Press.
Frazer, Sir James George
  1975   *The Golden Bough.* New York: Macmillan.
Frazier, Brenda
  1973   *La mujer en el teatro de Federico García Lorca.* Madrid: Playor.
Freud, Sigmund
  1950   *Totem and Taboo.* New York: Norton.
Frye, Northrop

1973   *Anatomy of Criticism: Four Essays*. Princeton, N.J.: Princeton University Press.
1976   *The Secular Scripture: A Study of the Structure of Romance*. Cambridge, Mass.: Harvard University Press.
Gallegos, Rómulo
1967   *Doña Barbara*. Buenos Aires: Espasa-Calpe.
García, Genaro
1979   *Leona Vicario: Heroina Insurgente*. México: Editorial Innovación.
García Márquez, Gabriel
1969   *Cien años de Soledad*. Buenos Aires: Editorial Sudamericana.
1970   *One Hundred Years of Solitude*. New York: Avon Books.
Gennep, Arnold van
1909   *Les Rites de passage*. Paris: E. Nourry.
Gilgamesh
1980   Ed. Federico Lara. Madrid: Editora Nacional.
Girard, René
1984   *Violence and the Sacred*. Baltimore: Johns Hopkins University Press.
Girón, Nicole
1976   *Heraclio Bernal: ¿Bandolero, cacique o precursor de la Revolución?* México: Instituto Nacional de Antropología e Historia.
Glazer, Mark
1980   "La Muerte: Continuity and Social Organization in a Chicano Legend." *Southwest Folklore* 4(1):1–13.
1984   "Continuity and Change in Legendry: Two Mexican-American Examples." In *Perspectives on Contemporary Legend: Proceedings of the Conference on Contemporary Legend*. Sheffield, England: Centre for English Cultural Tradition and Language. Pp. 108–127.
Goldenberg, Naomi
1975   "Archetypal Theory after Jung." *Spring*, 199–220.
1976   "A Feminist Critique of Jung." *Signs: Journal of Women in Culture and Society* 2(2):443–449.
1979   *Changing of the Gods: Feminism and the End of Traditional Religions*. Boston: Beacon Press.
Goodwyn, Frank
1947   "A North Mexican Ballad: José Lizorio." *Western Folklore* 6:240–248.
Gould, Eric
1982   *Mythic Intentions in Modern Literature*. Princeton, N.J.: Princeton University Press.
Goytortúa Santos, Jesús
1947   *Pensativa*. México: Editorial Porrúa.
Graham, Joe
1981   "The Caso: An Emic Genre of Folk Narrative." In *"And Other Neighborly Names": Social Process and Cultural Image in Texas Folklore*, ed. Richard Bauman and Roger D. Abrahams. Austin: University of Texas Press. Pp. 11–43.
Gray, Bennison
1971   "Repetition in Oral Literature." *Journal of American Folklore* 84:289–303.
Grebler, Leo, Joan W. Moore, and Ralph Guzmán
1970   *The Mexican-American People: The Nation's Second Largest Minority*. New York: Free Press.
Greene, Gayle, and Coppélia Kahn (eds.)
1985   *Making a Difference: Feminist Literary Criticism*. New York: Methuen.

Guthrie, W. K. C.
  1971   *The Greeks and Their Gods.* Boston: Beacon Press.
Guzmán, Martín Luis
  1965   *The Eagle and the Serpent.* New York: Doubleday Dolphin.
Hall, James
  1977   *Clinical Uses of Dreams: Jungian Interpretations and Enactments.* New
                York: Grune and Stratton.
Hall, Nor
  1980   *The Moon and the Virgin: Reflections on the Archetypal Feminine.* New
                York: Harper and Row.
Hamilton, Edith
  1969   *Mythology.* New York: New American Library.
Harkess, Shirley, and Cornelia B. Flora
  1974   "Women in the News: An Analysis of Media Images in Colombia."
                Revista Interamericana 4:220–238.
Hawkes, Glenn R., and Minna Taylor
  1975   "Power Structure in Mexican and Mexican-American Farm Labor Fam-
                ilies." *Journal of Marriage and the Family* 37:807–811.
Herrera-Sobek, María
  1979a   *The Bracero Experience: Elitelore versus Folklore.* Los Angeles: UCLA
                Latin American Studies Publications, University of California, Los An-
                geles.
  1979b   "The Theme of Drug-Smuggling in the Mexican Corrido." *Revista Chi-
                cano-Riqueña* 7(4):49–61.
  1979c   "Mothers, Lovers, and Soldiers: Images of Women in the Mexican
                Corrido." *Keystone Folklore Journal* 23(1–2):53–77.
  1980   "Imagen de la madre en la poesía chicana." In *Mujer y Sociedad en
                América Latina.* Santiago de Chile: Editorial del Pacífico. Pp. 253–261.
  1981   "La mujer traidora: Arquetipo estructurante en el corrido." *Cuadernos
                Americanos* 235 (March–April):230–242. English version in *Aztlán*
                (1982) 13:136–146.
  1982   "The Acculturation Process of the Chicana in the Corrido." *De Colores*
                6:7–16.
  1986   "'La Delgadina': Incest and Patriarchal Structure in a Spanish/Chicano
                Romance-Corrido." *Journal of Studies in Latin American Popular
                Culture,* 90–107.
Hill, Jane H., and Carole Browner
  1982   "Gender Ambiguity and Class Stereotyping in the Mexican Fotonovela."
                Studies in Latin American Popular Culture 1(1):43–64.
Hillman, James
  1970   "Why 'Archetypal' Psychology?" *Spring,* 217.
  1972   *The Myth of Analysis.* New York: Harper and Row.
  1975   *Re-Visioning Psychology.* New York: Harper and Row.
  1977   "An Inquiry into Image." *Spring,* 83.
Hobsbawm, Eric
  1981   *Bandits.* New York: Pantheon Books.
Hooke, S. H.
  1933   *Myth and Ritual.* London: Oxford University Press.
  1935   *The Labyrinth.* London: SPCK; New York: Macmillan.
  1958   *Myth, Ritual and Kingship.* Oxford University Press.
Horney, Karen
  1967   *Feminine Psychology.* New York: Norton.
Hubert, Henri, and Marcel Mauss

1964   *Sacrifice: Its Nature and Function.* Trans. W. Halls. Chicago: University of Chicago Press.

Hyman, Stanley E.
1958   "The Ritual View of Myth and the Mythic." In *Myth: A Symposium,* ed. Thomas Sebeok. Bloomington: Indiana University Press. Pp. 84–94.

Jacobi, Jolande
1959   *Complex/Archetype/Symbol in the Psychology of C. G. Jung.* Trans. Ralph Manheim. Princeton, N.J.: Princeton University Press.

James, E. O.
1959   *The Cult of the Mother-Goddess.* New York: Barnes and Noble.

Jeanmarie, Henri
1970   *Dionysos: Histoire du culture de Bacchus.* Paris: Payot.

Johnson, Allan Griswold
1972   "Modernization and Social Change: Attitudes toward Women's Roles in Mexico City." Ph.D. dissertation, University of Michigan.

Jones, Robert C.
1948   "Ethnic Family Patterns: The Mexican Family in the United States." *American Journal of Sociology* 53:450–452.

Jung, Carl G.
1928   "On the Relation of Analytical Psychology to Poetic Art." In *Contributions to Analytical Psychology,* trans. H. G. and C. F. Baynes. London: Kegan Paul.
1953a   *Collected Works of C. G. Jung.* Vol. 9, ii. New York: Pantheon Books.
1953b   *Collected Works.* Vol. 10. Princeton, N.J.: Princeton University Press.
1956a   *Symbols of Transformation.* Trans. R. F. C. Hull. New York: Pantheon Books.
1956b   *Collected Works.* Vol. 2. New York: Pantheon Books.
1959   "The Archetypes of the Collective Unconscious." In *Collected Works,* vol. 9, i. New York: Pantheon Books. Pp. 153–160.
1961   *Memories, Dreams, Reflections.* Ed. A. Jaffé. Trans. R. F. C. Hull. New York: Random House.
1964   *Man and His Symbols.* Garden City, N.Y.: Doubleday.
1965   *Civilization in Transition.* New York: Vintage.

Jung, Emma
1974   *Animus and Anima.* Zurich: Spring.

Keats, John
1973   "La Belle Dame sans Merci." In Mary Anne Ferguson, ed., *Images of Women in Literature.* Boston: Houghton Mifflin.

Kentner, Karen
1975   "The Socio-Political Role of Women in the Mexican Wars of Independence." Ph.D. dissertation, Loyola University, Chicago.

Kirk, G. S.
1975   *Myth: Its Meaning and Function in Ancient and Other Cultures.* Berkeley: University of California Press.

Kluckhohn, Clyde
1942   "Myths and Rituals: A General Theory." *Harvard Theological Review* 35:45–79.
1968   "Recurrent Themes in Myth and Mythmaking." *In Myth and Mythmaking,* ed. Henry A. Murray. Boston: Beacon Press.

Lacan, Jacques
1977   *Ecrits: A Selection.* New York: Norton

Lafaye, Jacques
1976   *Quetzalcoatl and Guadalupe: The Formation of Mexican National Consciousness, 1531–1813.* Chicago: University of Chicago Press.

Lanternari, Vittorio
   1963   *The Religions of the Oppressed: A Study of Modern Messianic Cults.*
                New York: New American Library.
Lattimore, Richmond (trans.)
   1951   *The Iliad of Homer.* Chicago: University of Chicago Press.
Lauter, Estella
   1985   "Visual Images of Women: A Test Case for the Theory of Archetypes." In
                *Feminist Archetypal Theory: Interdisciplinary Re-Visions of Jungian
                Thought,* Estella Lauter and Carol Schreier Rupprecht, eds. Knoxville:
                University of Tennessee Press. Pp. 46–92.
Lauter, Estella, and Carol Schreier Rupprecht (eds.)
   1985   *Feminist Archetypal Theory: Interdisciplinary Re-Visions of Jungian
                Thought.* Knoxville: University of Tennessee Press.
Leacock, Eleanor Burke (ed.)
   1981   *Myths of Male Dominance: Collected Articles on Women Cross-
                Culturally.* New York: Monthly Review Press.
Lederer, Wolfgang
   1968   *The Fear of Women.* New York: Harcourt Brace Jovanovich.
Lee, Rev. George
   1947   *Our Lady of Guadalupe: Patroness of the Americas.* New York: Catholic
                Book Publishing Co.
Leeming, David Adams
   1981   *Mythology: The Voyage of the Hero.* New York: Harper and Row.
Lefkowitz, Mary R.
   1986   *Women in Greek Myths.* Baltimore: Johns Hopkins University Press.
León-Portilla, Miguel
   1978   *Aztec Thought and Culture: A Study of the Ancient Nahautl Mind.*
                Norman: University of Oklahoma Press.
Limón, José E.
   1983   "Folklore, Social Conflict, and the United States–Mexico Border." In
                Handbook of American Folklore, ed. Richard M. Dorson. Bloomington:
                Indiana University Press. Pp. 216–226.
Lind, L. R.
   1957   *Ten Greek Plays in Contemporary Translations.* Boston: Houghton
                Mifflin.
Lizárraga, Sylvia S.
   1977   "From a Woman to a Woman." *Essays on la mujer.* Los Angeles: Chicano
                Studies Resource Center, University of California. Pp. 91–95.
Lord, Albert B.
   1981   *The Singer of Tales.* Cambridge, Mass.: Harvard University Press.
Lucero-White, Aurora Lea (ed.)
   1953   "Las cuatro apariciones de Nuestra Señora de Guadalupe." In *Literary
                Folklore of the Hispanic Southwest.* San Antonio, Tex.: Naylor. Pp. 86–
                106.
McDowell, John H.
   1972   "The Mexican Corrido: Formula and Theme in a Ballad Tradition."
                Journal of American Folklore 85:205–220.
   1981   "The Corrido of Greater Mexico as Discourse, Music, and Event." In
                *"And Other Neighborly Names": Social Process and Cultural Image in
                Texas Folklore,* ed. Richard Bauman and Roger D. Abrahams. Austin:
                University of Texas Press. Pp. 44–75.
Machado y Alvarez, Antonio
   1981   *El folk-lore andaluz.* Sevilla: Editorial Tres, Catorce, Diecisiete.

Macias, Anna
1973   "The Mexican Revolution Was No Revolution for Women." In *History of Latin American Civilization: Sources and Interpretations*, Lewis Hanke, ed. Boston: Little, Brown. Vol. 2, pp. 459–469.
MacLachlan, Colin
1974   "Modernization of Female Status in Mexico: The Image of Women's Magazines." *Revista/Review Interamericana* 4(Summer):246–257.
Madsen, William
1964   *The Mexican American of South Texas*. New York: Holt, Rinehart and Winston.
Malinowski, Bronislaw
1926   *Myth in Primitive Psychology*. London: Kegan Paul, Trench, Trubner.
Martí, Samuel
1973   *The Virgin of Guadalupe and Juan Diego: Historical Guide to Guadalupe*. México: Ediciones Euroamérica.
Mateos, Juan A.
1869   *Los Insurgentes*. México.
Maza, Francisco de la
1984   *El guadalupanismo mexicano*. México: Fondo de Cultura Económica.
Menéndez Pidal, Ramón
1959   *La epopeya castellana a través de la literatura castellana*. Madrid: Espasa-Calpe.
1968   *Romancero hispánico: Teoría e historia*. Vol. 2. Madrid: Espasa-Calpe.
Menton, Seymour
1953–54   "La Negra Angustias, Una Doña Barbara mexicana." Revista Iberoamericana 19:299–308.
Milá y Fontanals, Manuel
1959   *De la poesía heróico-popular castellana*. Barcelona: Instituto Miguel de Cervantes.
Mirandé, Alfredo
1982   "Machismo: Rucas, Chingasos, y Chingaderas." *De Colores, Journal of Chicano Expression and Thought* 6(1–2):17–31.
1985   *The Chicano Experience: An Alternative Perspective*. Notre Dame, Ind.: University of Notre Dame Press.
Mirandé, Alfredo and Evangelina Enríquez
1979   *La Chicana: The Mexican-American Woman*. Chicago: University of Chicago Press.
Monaghan, Patricia
1981   *The Book of Goddesses and Heroines*. New York: Dutton.
Monge, Chucho
1979   "Virgencita Ranchera." In *Cancionero Mexicano*, vol. 2. México: Libro-Mex Editores, S. de R. L. P. 556.
Montalvo, Garci Rodríguez de
1959   *Amadís de Gaula*. In *Libros de Caballería*, vol. 1. Madrid: Biblioteca de Autores Españoles.
Montiel, Miguel
1970   "The Social Science Myth of the Mexican American Family." *El Grito*, no. 3. Pp. 56–63.
Mora, Carl J.
1982   *Mexican Cinema: Reflections of a Society 1896–1980*. Berkeley: University of California Press.
Mora, Magdalena, and Adelaida R. del Castillo (eds.)
1980   *Mexican Women in the United States: Struggles Past and Present*. University of California, Chicano Studies Center Publications.

Morales, Salvador
   1981   *La música mexicana*. México: Editorial Universo.
Moreno, Daniel
   1978   *Batallas de la Revolución y sus corridos*. México: Editorial Porrúa.
Morford, Mark P. O., and Robert J. Lenardon
   1974   *Classical Mythology*. New York: David McKay.
Mosher, Joseph Albert
   1966   *The Exemplum in the Early Religious and Didactic Literature of England*. New York: AMS Press.
Mujeres en Revolución
   1978   La Habana: Editorial de Ciencias Sociales.
Nájera, Rafael
   1957   "La Corregidora." In *Libro de Oro de la Canción*. México: Libro Mex Editores. Pp. 47–53.
Neumann, Erich
   1973   *The Origin and History of Consciousness*. Princeton, N.J.: Princeton University Press.
   1974a   *Art and the Creative Unconscious*. Princeton, N.J.: Princeton University Press.
   1974b   *The Great Mother: An Analysis of the Archetype*. Princeton, N.J.: Princeton University Press.
Ortner, Sherry B.
   1974   "Is Female to Male as Nature to Culture?" In *Woman, Culture, and Society*, ed. M. Z. Rosaldo and L. Lamphere. Stanford, Calif.: Stanford University Press. Pp. 67–87.
O'Sullivan-Beare, Nancy
   1956   *Las mujeres de los conquistadores. La mujer española en los comienzos de la colonización americana. Aportaciones para el estudio de la transculturación*. Madrid: Compañía Bibliográfica Española.
Paredes, Américo
   1953   "The Love Tragedy in Texas-Mexican Balladry." *Folk Travelers*. Austin: Texas Folklore Society Publications. Pp. 110–114.
   1957   *"With His Pistol in His Hand": A Border Ballad and Its Hero*. Austin: University of Texas.
   1958   "The Mexican Corrido: Its Rise and Fall." In *Madstones and Twisters*, ed. Mody C. Boatright. Austin: Texas Folklore Society Publications. Pp. 91–105.
   1959   "The Bury-Me-Not Theme in the Southwest." In *And Horns on Their Toads*. Austin: Texas Folklore Society Publications 29.
   1967   "Estados Unidos, México y el Machismo." *Journal of Inter-American Studies* 9:65–84.
   1971–72 "El concepto de la 'medula emotiva' aplicado al corrido mexicano: Benjamín Argumedo." *Folklore Americano* 19–20:39–176.
   1979   "Mexican Legendry and the Rise of the Mestizo: A Survey." In *American Folk Legend: A Symposium*, ed. Wayland D. Hand. Berkeley: University of California Press. Pp. 97–108.
Parry, Milman
   1930   "Studies in the Epic Technique of Oral Verse-making I: Homer and Homeric Style." *Harvard Studies in Classical Philology* 41:80.
Paz, Octavio
   1961   *The Labyrinth of Solitude: Life and Thought in Mexico*. New York: Grove Press.
Pearce, T. M.
   1950   "The Bad Son (El Mal Hijo) in Southwest Spanish Folklore." *Western Folklore* 9:295–301.

Peña, Manuel
  1985   *The Texas-Mexican Conjunto: History of a Working-Class Music*. Austin:
              University of Texas Press.
Peñalosa, Fernando
  1968   "Mexican Family Roles." *Journal of Marriage and the Family* 30(November):680–689.
Pérez, Manuel Feans
  1976   *Santa María Nuestra Señora de las Américas*. Los Angeles: De
              Guadalupe Publications.
Pescatello, Ann
  1976   *Power and Pawn: The Female in Iberian Families, Societies and Cultures*.
              Westport, Conn.: Greenwood Press.
Phillips, Rachel
  1983   "Marina/Malinche: Masks and Shadows." In *Women in Hispanic Literature: Icons and Fallen Idols*. Los Angeles: University of California
              Press. Pp. 97–114.
Piault, Bernardo
  1975   *La Virgen de Guadalupe en México*. México: Editorial Jus.
Poniatowska, Elena
  1984   *Hasta no verte Jesús mío*. México: Ediciones Era.
Posada, José Guadalupe
  1972   *Posada's Popular Mexican Prints*. New York: Dover.
Pratt, Annis V.
  1981   *Archetypal Patterns in Women's Fiction*. Bloomington: Indiana University Press.
  1985   "Spinning among Fields: Jung, Frye, Lévi-Strauss and Feminist Archetypal Theory." In *Feminist Archetypal Theory: Interdisciplinary Re-Visions of Jungian Thought*, ed. Estella Lauter and Carol Schreier
              Rupprecht. Knoxville: University of Tennessee Press.
Prieto, Guillermo
  1940   *El romancero nacional—Musa Callejera*. México: Biblioteca del Estudiante Universitario.
Rambo, Ann Marie Rembley
  1985   "The Presence of Woman in the Poetry of Octavio Paz." In *Woman as
              Myth and Metaphor in Latin American Literature*, ed. Carmelo Virgilio
              and Naomi Lindstrom. Columbia: University of Missouri Press.
Ramírez, Santiago
  1977   *El mexicano, psicología de sus motivaciones*. México: Editorial Grijalbo.
Ramos, Samuel
  1975   *Profile of Man and Culture in Mexico*. Austin: University of Texas Press.
Randall, Margaret
  1981   *Sandino's Daughters: Testimonies of Nicaraguan Women in Struggle*. Ed.
              Lynda Yanz. Vancouver/Toronto: New Star Books.
Rank, Otto
  1941   *The Myth of the Birth of the Hero*. Trans. F. Robins and S. E. Jelliffe.
              New York: Johnson Reprint Corp.
Reed, John
  1969   *Insurgent Mexico*. New York: International Publishers.
Ricard, Robert
  1947   *La conquista espiritual de México*. México: Editorial Jus.
Rich, Adrienne
  1976   *Of Woman Born: Motherhood as Experience and Institution*. New York:
              Norton.

Robe, Stanley
    1977   "A Border Cancionero: A Regional View of Folksong." *New Scholar*
                  6:257–268.
Rodgers, H. L.
    1966   "The Crypto-Psychological Character of the Oral Formula." *English
                  Studies* 47:89–102.
Rodríguez Baños, Roberto, Patricia Trejo de Zepeda, and Edilberto Soto Angli
    1973   *Virginidad y machismo en México*. México: Editorial Posada.
Rodríguez, Mauro
    1980   *Guadalupe ¿Historia o símbolo?* México: Editorial Edicol.
Rogers, Jane
    1977   "The Function of the 'La Llorona' Motif in Rudolfo Anaya's Bless Me,
                  Ultima. *Latin American Literary Review* 5(Spring–Summer):64–69.
Rogers, Susan Carol
    1975   "Female Forms of Power and the Myth of Male Dominance: A Model of
                  Female/Male Interaction in Peasant Society." *American Ethnologist*
                  2:727–756.
Rojas González, Francisco
    1948   *La Negra Angustias*. México: EDIAPSA.
Romero Aceves, Ricardo
    1982   *La Mujer en la historia de México*. México: Costa-Amic Editores.
Romero, José Rubén
    1962   *Rosenda*. México: Editorial Porrúa.
Rose, H. J.
    1959   *A Handbook of Greek Mythology*. New York: Dutton.
Rubel, Arthur J.
    1966   *Across the Tracks: Mexican Americans in a Texas City*. Austin: University
                  of Texas Press.
Ruiz, Vicki
    1985   "Obreras y Madres: Labor Activism among Mexican Women and Its
                  Impact on the Family." In *Renato Rosaldo Lecture Series Monograph*,
                  vol. I, series 1983–1984, ed. Ignacio García. Tucson: University of
                  Arizona. Pp. 19–38.
Sahagún, Fray Bernardino de
    1950   *Florentine Codex: General History of the Things of New Spain*. Trans.
                  Arthur J. O. Anderson and Charles E. Dibble. Santa Fe, N.M.: School
                  of American Research.
    1956   *Historia general de las cosas de Nueva España*. Ed. Angel María
    (1568)   Garibay. México: Editorial Porrúa.
Salinas, Judy
    1979   "The Role of Women in Chicano Literature." In *The Identification and
                  Analysis of Chicano Literature*. New York: Bilingual Press/Editorial
                  Bilingüe. Pp. 190–240.
Samora, Julián, Joe Bernal, and Albert Peña
    1979   *Gunpowder Justice: A Reassessment of the Texas Rangers*. Notre Dame,
                  Ind.: University of Notre Dame Press.
Sánchez, Rosaura, and Rosa Martínez Cruz (eds.)
    1977   *Essays on la Mujer*. Los Angeles: Chicano Studies Center Publications,
                  University of California.
Sanday, Peggy Reeves
    1981   *Female Power and Male Dominance: On the Origins of Sexual Inequality*.
                  New York: Cambridge University Press.
Schapiro, Barbara
    1981   *The Romantic Mother: Narcissistic Patterns in Romantic Poetry*. Bal-
                  timore: Johns Hopkins University Press.

Segal, Robert A.
1984   "Joseph Campbell's Theory of Myth." In *Sacred Narrative: Readings in the Theory of Myth*. Ed. Alan Dundes. Berkeley: University of California Press. Pp. 256–269.

Sena-Rivera, Jaime
1979   "Competing Models and the Case of La Familia Chicana." *Journal of Marriage and the Family* 41(February):121–129.

Senour, María Nieto
1977   "Psychology of the Chicana." In *Chicano Psychology*, ed. Joe L. Martínez, Jr. New York: Academic Press.

Sigüenza y Góngora, Carlos de
1945   *Primavera Indiana*. México.

Simmons, Merle E.
1963   "The Ancestry of Mexico's Corridos." *Journal of American Folklore* 76:1–15.

Smart, Carol
1976   *Women, Crime and Criminology: A Feminist Critique*. Boston: Routledge.

Smith, Barbara Herrnstein
1968   *Poetic Closure: A Study of How Poems End*. Chicago: University of Chicago Press.

Smith, Colin
1978   *Spanish Ballads*. Oxford: Pergamon Press.

Smith, Jody Brant
1983   *The Image of Guadalupe: Myth or Miracle?* Garden City, N.Y.: Doubleday.

Sophocles
1958   *Antigone, Oedipus at Colonus*, and *Oedipus the King*. In *The Oedipus Plays of Sophocles*, trans. Paul Roche. New York: New American Library.

Soto, Shirlene Ann
1979   *The Mexican Woman: A Study of Her Participation in the Revolution 1910–1940*. Palo Alto, Calif.: R & E Research Associates.
1986   "Women in the Revolution." In *Twentieth-Century Mexico*, W. Dirk Raat and William H. Beezley, eds. Lincoln: University of Nebraska Press.

Soustelle, Jacques
1956   *La vida cotidiana de los Aztecas*. México: Fondo de Cultura Económica.
1964   *The Daily Life of the Aztecs on the Eve of the Spanish Conquest*. Middlesex, England: Penguin Books.

Sponsler, Lucy A.
1975   *Women in the Medieval Spanish Epic and Lyric Traditions*. Lexington: University Press of Kentucky.

Staples, Robert
1971   "The Mexican-American Family: Its Modification over Time." *Phylon* 32:179–192.

Sten, María
1982   *Vida y muerte del teatro náhuatl*. Xalapa, Veracruz: Universidad Veracruzana.

Stevens, Evelyn P.
1965   "Mexican Machismo: Politics and Value Orientations." *Western Political Quarterly* 18:848–857.
1977   "Marianismo: La otra cara del machismo en Latinoamérica." In Anne Pascatello, ed., *Hembra y Macho en Latinoamérica, Ensayos*. México: Editorial Diana. Pp. 121–234.

Stone, Merlin
   1976   *When God Was a Woman*. New York: Harcourt Brace Jovanovich.
Thompson, Stith
   1929   *Tales of the North American Indian*. Cambridge, Mass.: Harvard University Press.
   1977   *The Folktale*. Los Angeles: University of California Press.
Tinker, Edward Larocque
   1961   *Corridos & Calaveras*. With notes and translations by Américo Paredes. Austin: University of Texas Press.
Tucker, Elizabeth
   1981   "The Cruel Mother in Stories Told by Pre-Adolescent Girls." *International Folklore Review* 1:66–70.
Tuñón Pablos, Julia
   1987   *Mujeres en México: Una historia olvidada*. México: Fascículos Planets.
Turner, Frederick C.
   1967   "Los efectos de la participación feminina en la Revolución de 1910." *Historia Mexicana* 16(April–June):602–620.
Uroz, Antonio
   1972   *Hombres y mujeres de México*. México: Editorial Lic. Antonio Uroz.
Urquizo, Francisco
   1943   *Tropa vieja*. México.
Vanderwood, Paul J.
   1981   *Disorder and Progress: Bandits, Police, and Mexican Development*. Lincoln: University of Nebraska Press.
Vasconcelos, José
   1971   *Breve Historia de México*. México: Compañía Editorial Continental.
Villegas, Juan
   1978   *La estructura mítica del héroe*. Barcelona: Editorial Planeta.
Warner, Marina
   1976   *Alone of All Her Sex: The Myth and the Cult of the Virgin Mary*. New York: Knopf.
Wehr, Demaris S.
   1985   "Religious and Social Dimensions of Jung's Concept of the Archetype: A Feminist Perspective." In *Feminist Archetypal Theory: Interdisciplinary Re-Visions of Jungian Thought*, Estella Lauter and Carol Schreier Rupprecht, eds. Knoxville: University of Tennessee Press. Pp. 23–45.
Wolf, Eric
   1958   "The Virgin of Guadalupe: A Mexican National Symbol." *Journal of American Folklore* 71:34–39.
Wolff, Toni
   1956   *Structural Forms of the Feminine Psyche*. Zurich: C. G. Jung Institute.
Wolfgang, M. E.
   1958   *Patterns in Criminal Homicide*. Philadelphia: University of Pennsylvania Press.
Zamora, Oliverio M.
   N.D.   *Antología: Canciones folklóricas de México*. Guadalajara, Jalisco, México: Dibujos Musicales Ambríz.
Zinn, Maxine Baca
   1975   "Chicanas: Power and Control in the Domestic Sphere." *De Colores, Journal of Emerging Raza Philosophies* 2(3):19–31.
   1980a   "Employment and Education of Mexican-American Women: The Interplay of Modernity and Ethnicity in Eight Families." *Harvard Educational Review* 50(1):47–62.
   1980b   "Gender and Ethnic Identity among Chicanos." *Frontiers* 5(2):18–24.

1982a   "Chicano Men and Masculinity." *Journal of Ethnic Studies* 10(2):29–44.
1982b   "Mexican-American Women in the Social Sciences: Review Essay." *Signs: Journal of Women in Culture and Society* 8(Winter):259–272.

C. ADDITIONAL SOURCES

Bibliographies

Boggs, Ralph Steele. *Bibliografía del folklore mexicano*. México: Instituto Panamericano de Geografía e Historia, 1939.

Cabello-Argandona, Roberto, Juan Gómez-Quiñones, and Patricia Herrera-Durán. *The Chicana: A Comprehensive Bibliographic Study*. Los Angeles: Chicano Studies Center Publications, University of California, 1976.

Heisley, Michael. *An Annotated Bibliography of Chicano Folklore from the Southwestern United States*. Los Angeles: Center for the Study of Comparative Folklore and Mythology, University of California, 1977.

Simmons, Merle Edwin. *A Bibliography of the "Romance" and Related Forms in Spanish America*. Westport, Conn.: Greenwood Press, 1963.

Books

Abel, Elizabeth, and K. Emily Abel, eds. *The Signs Reader: Women, Gender and Scholarship*. Chicago: University of Chicago Press, 1983.

Alvar, Manuel. *Romancero viejo y tradicional*. México: Editorial Porrúa, 1979.

Alvarez Caballero, Angel. *Historia del canto flamenco*. Madrid: Alianza Editorial, 1981.

Anguita, Luis. *El Libro de Oro del Tango*. México: El Libro Español, 1975.

Arguelles, Miriam and José. *The Feminine: Spacious as the Sky*. Boulder, Colo.: Shambhala, 1977.

Barreiro, Javier. *El Tango*. Barcelona: Ediciones Júcar.

Barret, Michele. *Women's Oppression Today*. London: Verso Editions, 1980.

Baxer, C. R. *Women in Iberian Expansion Overseas 1415–1815: Some Facts, Fancies and Personalities*. New York: Oxford University Press, 1975.

Beauvoir, Simone de. *The Second Sex*. New York: Bantam, 1961.

Bénichou, Paul. *Creación poética en el romancero tradicional*. Madrid: Editorial Gredos, 1968.

Bonifaz de Novelo, María Eugenia. *Análisis histórico sobre la mujer mexicana*. México, 1975.

Bothmer, D. von. *Amazons in Greek Art*. Oxford: Clarendon Press, 1957.

Briffault, Robert. *The Mothers: A Study of the Origins of Sentiments and Institutions*. New York: Macmillan, 1927.

Brooks, Cleanth. *The Well-Wrought Urn*. New York: Harcourt, Brace and World, 1975.

Bullough, Vern L. *The Subordinate Sex: A History of Attitudes toward Women*. New York: Penguin Books, 1974.

Campbell, Joseph. *The Masks of God: Creative Mythology*. New York: Penguin Books, 1977.

——. *The Masks of God: Oriental Mythology*. New York: Penguin Books, 1977.

——. *The Masks of God: Occidental Mythology*. New York: Penguin Books, 1977.

Caro Baroja, Julio. *The World of the Witches*. Chicago: University of Chicago Press, 1965.

Castillo, Julia. *Cancionero de Garci Sánchez de Badajoz*. Madrid: Editora Nacional, 1980.

Ceja Reyes, Víctor. *El Catorce y la Guerra Cristera*. México: Editorial Universo, 1983.

Chase, Richard. *Quest for Myth*. New York: Greenwood Press, 1969.

Coffin, Tristram Potter. *The British Traditional Ballad in North America*. Austin: University of Texas Press, 1977.

Correa, Gustavo. *La poesía mítica de Federico García Lorca*. Madrid: Editorial Gredos, 1970.

Cotera, Marta. *Profile on the Mexican American Woman*. Austin, Tex.: National Educational Laboratory Publishers, 1976.

——. *The Chicana Feminist*. Austin, Tex.: Information Systems Development, 1977.

Coward, Rosalind. *Patriarchal Precedents: Sexuality and Social Relations*. Boston: Routledge, 1983.

Del Castillo, Adelaida, and Magdalena Mora, eds. *Mexican Women in the United States: Struggles Past and Present*. Los Angeles: Chicano Studies Research Center Publications, 1980.

De Vries, Jan. *Heroic Song and Heroic Legend*. New York: Oxford University Press, 1963.

Dodds, E. R. *The Greeks and the Irrational*. Berkeley: University of California Press, 1968.

Dronke, Peter. *The Medieval Lyric*. New York: Cambridge University Press, 1977.

Eagleton, Terry. *Criticism and Ideology*. Norfolk, England: Lowe and Brydone, 1978.

Eisenstein, Zillah R. *Capitalist Patriarchy and the Case for Socialist Feminism*. New York: Monthly Review Press, 1979.

Eliade, Mircea. *Patterns in Comparative Religion*. New York: World, 1958.

——. *Gods, Goddesses, and Myths of Creation*. New York: Harper and Row, 1974.

Elsasser, Nan, Kyle MacKenzie, and Yvonne Tixier Vigil. *Las Mujeres: Conversations from a Hispanic Community*. New York: McGraw-Hill, 1980.

Estrada, Jesús. *Música y músicos de la época virreinal*. México: SepSetentas Diana, 1980.

Falcón, Lidia. *Mujer y Sociedad: Análisis de un Fenómeno Reaccionario*. Barcelona: Editorial Fontanella, 1973.

Fetterley, Judith. *The Resisting Reader: A Feminist Approach to American Fiction*. Bloomington: Indiana University Press, 1981.

Franco-Lao, Méri. *¡Basta!: Canciones de testimonio y rebeldía de América Latina*. México: Biblioteca Era, 1967.

Frenk Alatorre, Margit. *Entre folklore y literatura*. México: El Colegio de México, 1971.

——. *Cancionero de romances viejos*. México: Universidad Antónoma de México, 1972.

Friday, Nancy. *My Mother/Myself: The Daughter's Search for Identity*. New York: Dell, 1977.

Freud, Sigmund. *On Creativity and the Unconscious*. New York: Harper and Row, 1958.

——. *Civilization and Its Discontents*. New York: Norton, 1961.

Friedan, Betty. *The Feminine Mystique*. New York: Dell, 1963.

Fussell, Paul. *Poetic Meter and Poetic Form*. New York: Random House, 1979.

Gallop, Jane. *The Daughter's Seduction: Feminism and Psychoanalysis*. New York: Cornell University Press, 1982.

Galván, Luz Elena. *La educación superior de la mujer en México 1876–1940*. México: Centro de Investigaciones y Estudios Superiores en Antropología, 1985.

Garner, Shirley Nelson, Claire Kahane, and Madelon Sprengnether. *The (M)other Tongue*. Ithaca, N.Y.: Cornell University Press, 1985.

Geertz, Clifford. *Myth, Symbol, and Culture*. New York: Norton, 1971.

Gelardo, José, and Francine Belade. *Sociedad y Cante Flamenco*. Murcia: Editora Regional de Murcia, 1985.

Geltman, Pedro. *Los Mitos*. Buenos Aires: Carlos Pérez, 1969.

Gil, Luis. *Transmisión mítica*. Barcelona: Editorial Planeta, 1975.

Greer, Germaine. *The Female Eunuch*. New York: McGraw-Hill, 1971.

Guerra-Cunningham, Lucía. *La narrativa de María Luisa Bombal: Una visión de la existencia femenina*. Madrid: Playor, 1981.

Hahner, June E., ed. *Women in Latin American History*. Los Angeles, Latin American Center Publications, University of California, 1976.

Hammer, Signe. *Daughters and Mothers: Mothers and Daughters*. New York: New American Library, 1975.

Henle, Paul, ed. *Language Thought and Culture*. Ann Arbor: University of Michigan Press, 1972.

Irigaray, Luce. *Speculum of the Other Woman*. Ithaca, N.Y.: Cornell University Press, 1985.

————. *This Sex Which Is Not One*. Ithaca, N.Y.: Cornell University Press, 1985.

Jackson, W. T. H. *The Interpretation of Medieval Lyric Poetry*. New York: Columbia University Press, 1980.

Jiménez de Baez, Ivette. *La décima popular en Puerto Rico*. Xalapa, Veracruz: Universidad Veracruzana, Cuadernos de la Facultad de Filosofía Letras y Ciencias, 1964.

Jiménez, Francisco. *The Identification and Analysis of Chicano Literature*. New York: Bilingual Press/Editorial Bilingüe, 1979.

Johnson, W. R. *The Idea of Lyric*. Los Angeles: University of California Press, 1982.

Kessler, Evelyn S. *Women: An Anthropological View*. New York: Holt, Rinehart and Winston, 1976.

Kramer, Samuel Noah. *Mythologies of the Ancient World*. New York: Doubleday, 1961.

Kuhn, Annette and Anne Marie Wolpe. *Feminism and Materialism: Women and Modes of Production*. London: Routledge, 1978.

Lacan, Jacques. *Feminine Sexuality*. New York: Pantheon Books, 1982.

La Cosecha: Literatura y la Mujer Chicana. Special issue of *De Colores*, vol. 3, no. 3. Albuquerque: Pajarito Publications, 1977.

Larvin, Asunción. *Latin American Women: Historical Perspectives*. Westport, Conn.: Greenwood Press, 1978,

Lévi-Strauss, Claude. *Myth and Meaning*. New York: Schocken Books, 1979.

MacCormack, Carol, and Marilyn Strathern. *Nature, Culture and Gender*. Cambridge University Press, 1980.

Medvedev, P. N./Bakhtin, M. M. *The Formal Method in Literary Scholarship: A Critical Introduction to Sociological Poetics*. Baltimore: Johns Hopkins University Press, 1978.

Melville, Margarita, ed. *Twice a Minority: Mexican American Women*. St. Louis, Mo.: C. V. Mosby, 1980.

Mill, John Stuart. *On the Subjection of Women* (1869). New York: Fawcett, 1971.

Miller, Beth. *Women in Hispanic Literature: Icons and Fallen Idols*. Los Angeles: University of California Press, 1983.

Mitchell, Juliet. *Woman's Estate*. New York: Random House, 1973.

Molina, Ricardo. *Cante Flamenco*. Madrid: Taurus Ediciones, 1981.

Murray, Gilbert. *The Classical Tradition in Poetry*. Oxford: Oxford University Press, 1927.

National Association for Chicano Studies. *Chicano Voices: Intersections of Class, Race, and Gender*. Austin, Tex.: Center for Mexican American Studies Publications, 1986.

Okin, Susan Moller. *Women in Western Political Thought*. Princeton, N.J.: Princeton University Press, 1979.

Olson, Alan M. *Myth, Symbol, and Reality*. Notre Dame, Ind.: University of Notre Dame Press, 1980.

Oñate, María del Pilar. *El feminismo en la Literatura Española*. Madrid: Espasa-Calpe, 1938.

Pagels, Elaine H. "What Became of God the Mother? Conflicting Images of God in Early Christianity." In *The Signs Reader: Women, Gender and Scholarship*, ed. Elizabeth Abel and K. Emily Abel. Chicago: University of Chicago Press, 1983.

Peradotto, John, and J. P. Sullivan, eds. *Women in the Ancient World: The "Arethusa" Papers*. 1984.

Pettit, Arthur G. *Images of the Mexican American in Fiction and Film*. College Station: Texas A&M University, 1980.

Pogolotti, Marcelo. *La clase media de México*. México: Editorial Diogenes, 1972.

Poster, Mark. *Critical Theory of the Family*. New York: Seabury Press, 1978.

Poesías a la Madre. México: El Libro Español, 1975.

Pomeroy, Sarah B. *Goddesses, Whores, Wives, and Slaves: Women in Classical Antiquity*. New York: Schocken Books, 1975.

Radius, Emilio, Augusta Grosso, et al. *La mujer en la nueva sociedad*. Bilbao: Editora Mensajero, 1971.

Reiter, Rayna R. *Toward an Anthropology of Women*. New York: Monthly Review Press, 1975.

Riencourt, Amauny de. *Sex and Power in History*. New York: Dell, 1974.

Robinson, Cecil. *México and the Hispanic Southwest in American Literature*. Tucson: University of Arizona Press, 1977.

Rocard, Marcienne. *La minorité mexicane à travers la littérature des Etats-Unis*. Paris: G.-P. Maisonneuve et Larose, 1980.

Rosaldo, Michelle Zimbalist, and Louise Lamphere. *Woman, Culture and Society*. Stanford, Calif.: Stanford University Press, 1974.

Rowbotham, Sheila. *Women, Resistance and Revolution: A History of Women and Revolution in the Modern World*. New York: Random House, 1974.

Rulfo, Juan. *Pedro Páramo*. México: Fondo de Cultura Económica, 1968.

Salazar, Adolfo. *La música de España: Desde las cuevas prehistóricas hasta el siglo XVI*. Madrid: Espasa-Calpe, 1953.

Sánchez, Marta Ester. *Contemporary Chicana Poetry: A Critical Approach to an Emerging Literature*. Los Angeles: University of California Press, 1985.

Schneir, Miriam. *Feminism: The Essential Historical Writings*. New York: Random House, 1972.

Seltman, Charles. *Women in Antiquity*. London: Thames and Hudson, 1956.

Stanford, Barbara. *Myths and Modern Man*. New York: Washington Square Press, 1972.

Stewart, Grace. *A New Mythos: The Novel of the Artist as Heroine 1877–1977*. Montreal: Eden Press Women's Publications, 1981.

Szertics, Joseph. *Tiempo y verbo en el romancero viejo*. Madrid: Editorial Gredos, 1974.

Tannenbaum, Frank. *Peace by Revolution*. New York: Columbia University Press, 1966.

Taylor, B. William. "The Virgin of Guadalupe in New Spain: An Inquiry into the Social History of Marian Devotion." *American Ethnologist* 1987; 14(1):9–33.

Van Hooft, Karen S., and Gabriela Mora, eds. *Theory and Practice of Feminist Literary Criticism*. Ypsilanti, Mich.: Bilingual Press/Editorial Bilingüe.

Villancicos y canciones religiosas de navidad. Sección de F. E. T. y de las J. O. N. S., 1958.

Virgilio, Carmelo, and Naomi Lindstrom. *Woman as Myth and Metaphor in Latin American Literature*. Columbia: University of Missouri Press, 1985.

Wimsatt, W. K. *The Verbal Icon: Studies in the Meaning of Poetry*. University of Kentucky Press, 1954.

Woll, Allen L. *The Latin Image in American Film*. Los Angeles: Latin American Center Publications, University of California, 1977.

Articles

Braddy, Haldeen. "Myths of Pershing's Mexican Campaign." *Southern Folklore Quarterly* 1963; 27(September):181–195.

Burkett, Elinor C. "In Dubious Sisterhood: Class and Sex in Spanish Colonial South America." In *Women in Latin America: An Anthology from Latin American Perspectives*. Riverside, Calif.: Latin American Perspectives 1979. Pp. 17–25.

Caraveli-Chaves, Anna. "Bridge Between Worlds: The Greek Women's Lament as Communicative Event." *Journal of American Folklore* 1980; 93:129–158.

Castellano, Olivia. "Of Clarity and the Moon—A Study of Two Women in Rebellion." *De Colores* 1977; 3(3):25–30.

Chodorow, Nancy. "Family Structure and Feminine Personality." In *Woman, Culture and Society,* ed. Michelle Zimbalist Rosaldo and Louise Lamphere. Stanford, Calif.: Stanford University Press, 1974. Pp. 43–66.

Fogelquist, Donald F. "The Figure of Pancho Villa in the Corridos of the Mexican Revolution." *Hispanic-American Studies* 1942; 3:11–22.

Hoberman, Louise S. "Hispanic American Women as Portrayed in the Historical Literature: Types or Archetypes?" *Revista-Review Interamericana* 1974; 4(Summer):136–147.

Jacquette, Jane S. "Women in Revolutionary Movements in Latin America." *Journal of Marriage and the Family* 1973; 35:334–354.

Lamphere, Louise. "Strategies, Cooperation, and Conflict among Women in Domestic Groups." In *Woman, Culture and Society,* ed. Michelle Zimbalist Rosaldo and Louise Lamphere. Stanford, Calif.: Stanford University Press, 1974. Pp. 97–112.

Larvin, Asunción. "In Search of the Colonial Woman in Mexico: The Seventeenth and Eighteenth Centuries." In *Latin American Women,* ed. Asunción Larvin. Westport, Conn.: Greenwood Press, 1978.

McGinn, Noel F. "Marriage and Family in Middle-Class Mexico." *Journal of Marriage and the Family* 1966; 28:305–313.

Miller, E. Joan Wilson. "The Rag-Bag World of Balladry." *Southern Folklore Quarterly* 1960; 24:217–225.

Ordóñez, Elizabeth. "Sexual Politics and the Theme of Sexuality in Chicana Poetry." In *Women in Hispanic Literature: Icons and Fallen Idols.* Los Angeles: University of California Press, 1983. Pp. 316–339.

Payne, L. W., Jr. "Recent Research in Balladry and Folk Songs." In *Man, Bird, and Beast,* ed. J. Frank Dobie. Austin: Publications of the Texas Folk-Lore Society, 1930. Pp. 161–169.

Rambo, Ann Marie Remley. "The Presence of Woman in the Poetry of Octavio Paz." *Hispania* 1968; 2(2):259–264.

Rosaldo, Michelle Zimbalist. "Woman, Culture and Society: A Theoretical Overview." In *Woman, Culture and Society,* ed. Michelle Zimbalist Rosaldo and Louise Lamphere. Stanford, Calif.: Stanford University Press, 1974. Pp. 17–42.

Rosenberg, Bruce. "The Formulaic Quality of Spontaneous Sermons." *Journal of American Folklore* 1970; 83:3–20.

Sifuentes, Roberto. "La mujer en 'Piedra de Sol' de Octavio Paz." *Aztlán, Chicano Journal of the Social Sciences and the Arts* 1973; 4(2):271–281.

D. DISCOGRAPHY

"Adiós Madre querida"
> Los Alegres de Terán *Fogata Norteña.* Caytronics CYS 1156.

"Amor de Madre"
> El Palomo y el Gorrión. D.L.V. USA 2003.

"Camelia la Tejana"
> Dueto Estrella. *Corridos.* Discos CRC LP-011.

"Canción a una madre"
> Los Cadetes de Linares. Ramex LP-1012.

Canciones a la Virgen de Guadalupe.
> Sunshine Records. ECO-23. Album includes "Plegaria Guadalupana," "Ofrenda Guadalupana," "Canto Guadalupano." "Navidad Guadalupana," "Reyna de América," "Mamá Lupita."

"Concha la mojada"
	La Jilguerillas. CBS 20686.
"Consejos de una madre"
	Dueto América. "De Alarido Canciones y Corridos." Colombia HL 8301.
"Corrido a Mariquita Beltrán"
	Toñito Solís "El Gilguerillo." Discos Landin 006.
"Corrido de Gregorio Cortez"
	Ramón Ayala y los Bravos del Norte. Tex-Mex. TMLP.7021. Includes "Contrabando y Traición."
Corridos de la Rebelión Cristera.
	Instituto Nacional de Antropología. No. 20. Includes nine corridos on the Cristero Rebellion.
"Corridos de Mujeres Famosas"
	Los Madrugadores del Bajío. Caliente CLT 7282.
"Dos Coronas a mi madre"
	Los Cadetes de Linares, *Cruzando el Puente de Ramones a los Algodones*. Ramex LP-1014.
"El adios de mi madre"
	Los Cadetes de Linares, *Cruzando el Puente de Ramones a los Algodones*. Ramex LP-1014.
"El amante de Camelia"
	Arnulfo el Coyote Blanco, Fogata Internacional Inc. FOG-110.
"Elena y el francés"
	Dueto América, "De Alarido Canciones y Corridos." Colombia HL 8301.
"El hijo de Camelia"
	Los Tigres del Norte. Fama-554.
"El regio traficante"
	Los Cadetes de Linares. Ramex LP 1010.
"El veinticuatro de junio"
	Los Gavilanes Juan y Salomón, *Corridos Norteños*. ECO No. 977.
Hombres que Hicieron Historia y se Volvieron Corridos.
	Felipe Arriaga. Includes "Lucío Vázquez," "Heraclio Bernal," "El hijo desobediente," "Benjamín Argumedo," "Benito Canales," and "Joaquín Murrieta." Caytronics CYS 1397.
"Jesús Cadenas (La Güera Chabela)"
	Hermanos Zaízar. "Cantando y Cantando Corridos y Corridos." Peerless 1840.
"Jesusita en Chihuahua"
	La Revolución. Gavi Records G-1019.
"Juana la traicionera"
	Los Tigres del Norte. Discos Fama 507.
"La Bracera"
	Los Paisanos del Norte. Anáhuac AN-1048.
"La Delgadina"
	Dueto América. Aguascalientes. Caliente CLT 7015. Includes "El Día de San Juan," "Valentín Mancera," "Los pavoreales" ("Lucío Vázquez").
"La emigrada"
	Los Rinches del Sur. Discos Arpeggio.
"La Martina"
	Ignacio López Tarso y sus corridos. Caytronics CYS 1292.
"La Pasadita"
	"Cancionero de la Intervención Francesa." Instituto Nacional de Antropología e Historia S.E.P. MC-403.
"La Patera (Juana la Patera)"
	Rosenda Bernal. Odeon MST-24312.

"Las pobres ilegales"
Yolanda del Río. RCA RKAO-9712.
"La Rielera"
Hnos. Zaízar, *Cantares de la Revolución*. Peerless 1014. Includes "La Cucaracha," "La Joaquinita," "La Adelita," "Marieta," "Valentín de la Sierra," and "La Valentina."
"La tumba de mi madre"
Los Tigres del Norte. *La Banda del Carro Rojo*. Fama 536.
Le cantan a las vírgenes más veneradas de México.
Las Palomas del Norte. Sonito Alva LP/AL-125. Album includes "Mi virgen ranchera," "Chaparrita de San Juan," "Virgen de los Remedios," "Virgencita del Roble," "Virgencita de Talpa," "Virgen de la Soledad," "Virgen de la Concepción," "Virgen de Zapopan," "Virgen María del Rosario," "Virgen de la Natividad."
"Los dos hermanos"
Dueto Castilla. *Corridos Norteños*. Audio-Mex 093.
Madrecita Querida
Includes "Ya no llores madrecita," "Perdón madrecita," "Consejos de una madre," "Limosna de un hijo," "La voz de mi madre," "Madre abandonada," and "Amor de madre." Caliente CLT 7039.
"Madre inmortal"
Hermanos Arellano. Anáhuac AN-1061.
"Mañanitas a mi madre"
El Palomo y el Gorrión. D.L.V. USA 2003.
"Me importa madre"
Los Hnos. Banda. *Corridos de siempre*. Audio-Mex ALD-2159. Includes "Juan Charrasqueado," "Benito Canales," "Lucío Vázquez."
"Nocturno a Rosario"
Los Alegres de Terán. Harmony HL 8463. Includes "Por el amor a mi madre."
"No sufras Madre"
Los Alegres de Terán, *Fogata Norteña*. Caytronics CYS 1156.
"Pancha la contrabandista"
Los Gavilanes Juan y Salomón. *Corridos Norteños*. Del Valle Records VLP Vol. 1040.
"Perdón Madrecita"
Vicente Fernández. Caytronics CY 105.
Por el Amor a mi Madre
Los Alegres de Terán. Includes "Mañanitas a mi Madre," "Amor de Madre," "Ni por mil puñadas de oro," "No sufras madre," "Pobre bohemio," "Por el amor a mi madre," "Cariño sin condición," "Con la tinta de mi sangre," "El hijo ingrato," and "Adios madre querida." Caliente CLT 7023.
"Rosita Alvírez"
Lalo González. *Lo mejor del Piporro*. Musart DC 787.
"Traiciones Políticas"
Los Tremendos Gavilanes Juan y Salomón. *Viva la Revolución*. Includes "Mi general Zapata," "México Febrero 23," "El Mayor de los Dorados," "Gral. Pascual Orozco," "Gral. Emiliano Zapata," "En Durango Comenzó," "Siete Leguas."
"Un encargo a mi madre"
Los Humildes, *A mis Amigos del Norte*. Fama-608.
"Ya encontraron a Camelia"
Los Tigres del Norte, *La Banda del Carro Rojo*. Fama 536.

E. MOVIES

La Generala. Madera Cinevideo. VHS, 1984. Madera, California.
La Guerrillera de Villa. Aztec Cinevideo. VHS AC-002, 1984.
La Soldadera. Video Latino. VHS DR-732, n.d.
Juana Gallo. Video Latino. VHS DR-770.

Index

"La Adelita": quoted and analyzed, 104–106; second version of, quoted and analyzed, 106–108; popularity of, 108, 115
Agripina, Doña, 94–96
Alaniz, Carmen Parra, Coronela, 91
Almanza, Arturo, "La Toma de Zacatecas," 98
Amazons, 84–85, 122n.1
Anton, Ferdinand: quoted on goddesses, 56
Araucanian Indians, 85–86
archetypal images of women, xviii–xix
archetypes: defined and explained, xiii–xvii; structured by four vectors, xiv, 117; and stereotypes, xviii; as valid social documents, 117; the process of formation of, 118
Armenta, Antonio del Río, supposed author of "Adelita," 108
atonement doctrine, 4
Aztec gooddesses, 3, 56
Aztec priests: quoted in defense of their gods, 39–40
Aztecs, 39–41

baptism, 31
battles: as treated in corridos, xiii, 43, 47–50, 68–70, 93–103, 110–114
"La belle dame sans merci" motif, 54–55, 57
"Benito Canales," 122n.9; quoted, 112
Berger, Peter L.: quoted on legitimation, 75, 76
Bernarda Espinosa, María, 88
bola (folk song), 32
brothers, rival, motif, 64

Calderón de la Barca, Frances: quoted on women in the Mexican army, 88–89
"Camelia La Tejana" (corrido), 67
Campbell, Joseph, 46–47; quoted on the protective goddess, 48, 49
campesino social class, xviii, 12, 13–14
canciones, xiii, 50–51, 104; mother themes in, 12–13
cannibalism, 63
Caso, Alfonso: quoted on special mission of the Aztecs, 40–41
casos, 20, 22
Cassandra, 120n.4
Cassandra mother figure, 24, 27
Cassirer, Ernst: quoted on mythic thought and astrology, 30–31
Castañeda, Daniel, 119n.6
castes, Mexican, 37
Cathedral of Guadalupe, 35, 36
Catullus: quoted, 44
cave motif, 22, 23

"El Chamuco" (the devil), 114
"La Chamuscada": quoted and analyzed, 113–114
chato (short-nosed person), 62
Chávez, César E., 43
Chicano scholars, 12, 68, 73, 74, 121n.12 (chap. 4)
childbirth: death of mother in, 85
Cirlot, J. E., 61, 66–67, 112
closure, poetic, 8, 9, 50
cock symbol, 111–112
"Combate de San Clemente": quoted, 100–101
contraband arms, 100
corridistas, 30, 44, 65; social class of, affects their use of archetypal images, xiv, 14, 61; skill of, in selecting motifs, 6–8; influence of literary traditions on, 9, 44; advice to listeners from, 25, 26, 27; farewell of, 27, 64
"Corrido de Benito Canales": quoted and analyzed, 70–71
"Corrido de Gabriel Leyva: Por Siete Caminos de Sangres": quoted, xi–xii
"Corrido de José Lizorio," 22, 30; quoted and analyzed, 17–24
"Corrido de la Muerte de Emiliano Zapata": quoted, 99, 101–102
"Corrido de la Toma de Torreón": quoted, 93, 94
"Corrido de las hazañas del General Lejero y la Roma de Torreón por el ejercito Liberador": quoted, 93
"Corrido de Lucío Pérez," 30; quoted and analyzed, 25–27
"Corrido de Martín Díaz": quoted and analyzed, 47–48, 49
"Corrido de Micaela (El 24 de Junio)": quoted and analyzed, 57–64
"Corrido de Valentín de la Sierra": quoted, 43, 50
"Corrido de Valentín Mancera": quoted and analyzed, 68–70
"Corrido del combate del 15 de mayo en Torreón": quoted, 93, 94
corrido, untitled, recorded in Alcalá del Río, Andalucía, Spain: quoted, 120n.7
corrido singers, xviii
corridos: explained, xiii; archetypal criticism of, xiii, xviii; authorship, xviii, 98, 108; patriarchal perspective in, xviii, 75–76; structure of, xix, 7, 44, 46, 48, 96, 119n.6; examples of mater doloroso motif in, 5–6; reflect mothers' position, 9, 12–14, 117; influence of social class on, xviii, 13–14; as exempla, 21, 24, 27, 75; influence of literary tradition on,

147